DUSK
on the
CAMPO

Sara Mansfield Taber

Henry Holt and Company

New York

DUSK
on the
CAMPO

A JOURNEY

IN PATAGONIA

In memory of Don Pepe

Copyright © 1991 by Sara Mansfield Taber
All rights reserved, including the right to reproduce
this book or portions thereof in any form.
Published by Henry Holt and Company, Inc.,
115 West 18th Street, New York, New York 10011.
Published in Canada by Fitzhenry & Whiteside Limited,
195 Allstate Parkway, Markham, Ontario L3R 4T8.

Library of Congress Cataloging-in-Publication Data
Taber, Sara Mansfield.
Dusk on the Campo: a journey in Patagonia / Sara Mansfield Taber.—1st ed.
p.   cm.
1. Patagonia (Argentina and Chile)—Description and travel. 2. Patagonia (Argentina and
Chile)—Social life and customs. 3. Taber, Sara Mansfield—Journeys—Patagonia (Argentina
and Chile) I. Title.
F2936.T3   1991
918.2'7—dc20   91-1978
ISBN 0-8050-1473-X (alk. paper)   CIP

Henry Holt books are available at special discounts
for bulk purchases for sales promotions, premiums,
fund-raising, or educational use. Special editions
or book excerpts can also be created to specification.
For details contact:
Special Sales Director, Henry Holt and Company, Inc.,
115 West 18th Street, New York, New York 10011.

First Edition—1991

DESIGNED BY KATY RIEGEL

MAP BY JACKIE AHER

Printed in the United States of America
Recognizing the importance of preserving
the written word, Henry Holt and Company, Inc.,
by policy, prints all of its first editions
on acid-free paper. ∞

10 9 8 7 6 5 4 3 2 1

For my parents

CONTENTS

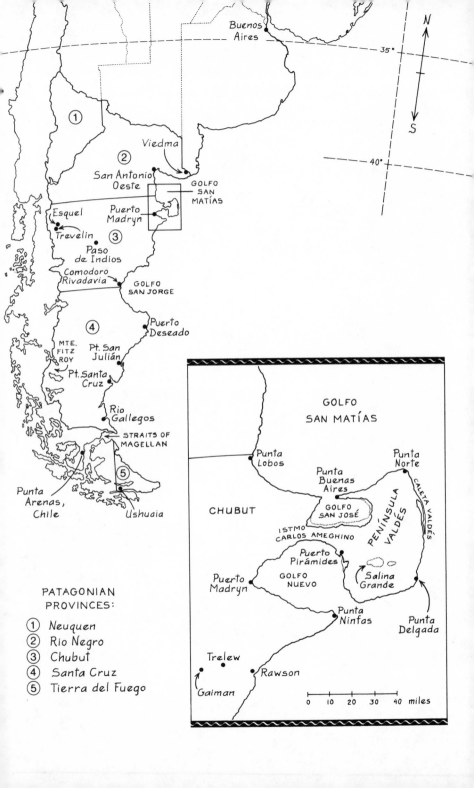

Buenos
Aires

35°

N

S

40°

①

Viedma

②

San Antonio
Oeste

GOLFO
SAN
MATÍAS

Esquel

Puerto
Madryn

Travelin

③

Paso
de Indios

Comodoro
Rivadavia

GOLFO
SAN JORGE

④

Puerto
Deseado

MTE.
FITZ
ROY

Pt. San
Julián

Pt. Santa
Cruz

Río
Gallegos

STRAITS OF
MAGELLAN

⑤

Punta
Arenas,
Chile

Ushuaia

PATAGONIAN
PROVINCES:

① Neuquen
② Rio Negro
③ Chubut
④ Santa Cruz
⑤ Tierra del Fuego

GOLFO
SAN MATÍAS

Punta
Lobos

Punta
Norte

Punta
Buenas
Aires

CALETA VALDÉS

CHUBUT

GOLFO
SAN JOSÉ

PENÍNSULA
VALDÉS

ISTMO
CARLOS AMEGHINO

Puerto
Pirámides

Salina
Grande

Puerto
Madryn

GOLFO
NUEVO

Punta
Ninfas

Punta
Delgada

Trelew

Gaiman

Rawson

0   10   20   30   40 miles

DUSK
on the
CAMPO

DUST

~~~~~~~

Minutes after we put down on Patagonian soil, we are hurtling along a dirt road, heading out into the barren wilderness that comprises this last 1,600-kilometer stretch of South America.

In the distance, a cloud of brownish dust is coming toward us. At first it appears ominous, like a dust storm, but we soon realize that it is simply an automobile coming from the opposite direction. The car nears.

The windshield of the dusty, ancient orange Ford is plastered with the flattened palms of at least ten human hands—children's hands and large adult ones placed every which way against the pane—they are so plentiful that I cannot see the driver or the inside of the car.

In a flash I see the hands, then the car hurtles by, our two dust plumes mixing so that, for a few moments, we are inside a swirling, murky brown cloud. Then we are on an empty road again.

Later I realize that the hands were protecting the windshield against the gravel flying up from our car, but the sight gives me my first shot of awe and fascination for the people who inhabit the desolation of Patagonia, a fascination that is to hold me in its grip for years to come.

~~~

We continue down the road. A wasteland of dry, gray, wind-flogged campo stretches out flat, to the north, south, east, and west. The land around us looks like an endless tan rug sprinkled with drops of dry manure and scribbled with low, black, thorny shrubs.

We spend hours riding through this blankness. The road seems to skim over the flat ground and to curve down ahead of the car in the distance, giving us the sensation that we will soon roll over the end of the earth.

A fox trots out among the knee-high pricker bushes. Barely distinguishable from the brush, with sticklike necks and drab feathers, two six-foot Darwin's rhea gallop away at the sound of the car engine. Their feathers billow behind them, loose, as they open their tiny vestigial wings, showing the white, downy petticoat under the top layer of tough brown-and-gray feathers. The down is white: the color of alarm.

Hares bounce out of the road as we make our passage.

We count eighteen golden-furred guanacos, including five gawky *chulengos*—the babies—more graceful than their llama cousins, some grazing, others strolling. Shreds of cloth whip across the road. Flimsy, unmended fence lines crisscross the plain, and huddles of sheep eye the car.

We hurtle and screech over the rough road, the driver nearly plunging into the ditch or flattening a sheep, over and over again. We don't pass any other cars.

There are only a few signs of women, men, or children. A wisp of black smoke rising out of nowhere, the driver tells us, is a herdsman cooking his afternoon meal of mutton. In a flash we see our first human being. A lone man, on horseback, herds sheep—moving dots among the spine bushes.

Once in a while we pass a small, weather-battered sign at the edge of the road that bears a woman's name—"La Isabelita," "La Julieta." At the sign, a track, or two barely visible wheel ruts, heads off at right angles across the empty turf, but we almost never see the sheep ranch that lies twenty-five kilometers down the trace.

In the middle of nowhere there is a dog, a dachshund, standing in the road. There is not a dwelling in sight, and we can see to infinity. The dog edges off to make way for the car, then stands in the road again.

The wind thrashes at the car and fills our eyes with grit, even with the windows closed. We huddle together to keep warm.

Not far from our destination, we pass an old coupe with its hood up and doors open; a middle-aged woman and a child stand beside it. The woman's dress slashes at her legs, her back to the bare thornland dotted with sheep. A couple of kilometers down the road we pass a man pushing, head down, against the wind.

On farther, I realize that the man could never have reached a house or a water source by dark, and I wish we had had the taxi driver stop. But the people had acted as though they hadn't seen us.

Just minutes before we reach the Whale Camp, where we are to live for at least a year, there is, to the side of a sheep gate, slung over a fence and straddling it, the skin of a large animal. It is the rump and tail, a strip of back, and the mane of a horse. The piece of horse is spread out, full length, over the wire. Later, I come to the chilly realization that it was a horse's scalp.

The Whale Camp, where Peter, my husband, and I would be doing research, lay 1,400 kilometers to the south, at Península Valdés, but we spent our first four days, immediately after arriving in Argentina, in Buenos Aires.

If Patagonia was dust, Buenos Aires was shimmer. The grandeur of the Argentine capital surprised us. With its broad avenues, noble monuments, and numerous parks, the city looked like a crumbling Paris.

We landed in Argentina, that June of 1978, with only a few

basic newspaper facts about the place. We brought with us the North American impression of a typical Latin American country with runaway inflation, widespread corruption, frequent military coups, and a penchant for torture. We had heard, though, from wildlife enthusiasts of another Argentina, a splendid country with provinces that ranged from rain forest in the north, to alpine meadows along the Andes, to the dry steppe of Patagonia, and finally, to subarctic tundra in Tierra del Fuego. This was the Argentina we were after.

After spending over two years in the outlands of Patagonia, I have been able to assemble an understanding of several of the historical forces at play in a nation characterized both by extraordinary, rich, beautiful, wild land and by extraordinary political chaos.

Argentina is a vast country—in area, the ninth largest nation on the globe—a state, at the southern tip of South America, the size of continental Europe. At 3,700 kilometers from tip to toe, Argentina is almost as long as the United States is wide. Onto this great stretch of land, however, are sprinkled fewer than thirty million people, making it one of the most sparsely populated countries on earth.

Although Argentina is an agricultural-pastoral country—its economy is based on the products of vast farms and ranches—the great majority of its people live in cities. Fully half of the Argentine population live in greater Buenos Aires, and over 25 percent of the remaining population live in urban zones, a proportion of urban to rural dwellers matched by few other nations.

The prime reason for the urbanization of Argentina is latifundismo, a land-division system whereby large land holdings are distributed among members of a small oligarchy. Most of the good land was early taken up by the conquistadors, their descendents, and the earliest European immigrants; latifundismo was well established by 1810. The big landowners used their great estates, or "estancias," for cattle and sheep raising—operations that required relatively few workers in a worker-short land. The few who monopolized the land were a greedy lot, and when public land, *tierra fiscal*, was offered for sale, they gobbled up most of it. In 1840 the average holding around Buenos Aires was 40,339 acres.

By the late nineteenth century, Argentina—which meant Buenos Aires and the concentric rings of small farms and pampas cattle ranches surrounding the capital—was the most prosperous and opulent country in Latin America. The provinces and territories to the north and south remained almost totally wild and undeveloped, while the nation lived off the rich soil surrounding the capital. Argentina's per capita income equaled that of Germany and the Low Countries and exceeded that of Spain, Italy, Switzerland, and Sweden. Argentina was the world's largest producer of corn, the second largest producer of wool, and the third largest producer of cattle and horses; it challenged the world leader, Canada, in wheat production. Most of Argentina's exports went to Europe, and Europe returned the favor by investing in Argentina.

Into this booming land poured European immigrants. Over three million came between 1880 and 1930—half of them Italians, a quarter of them Spaniards, and the rest French, Poles, Russians, Turks, Austrians, Hungarians, Germans, and British. They reset the ethnic makeup of the country and tripled its population.

Although Argentine immigration agents offered the prospect of land as an inducement to Europeans, in fact there was precious little land accessible to new settlers. The best public land had already been bought by the landed establishment, and it was difficult for immigrants to receive loans. Of the million who came in the 1880s, fewer than 10 percent were able to realize their dreams of buying land. The majority who did wind up on the farms and ranches worked as tenant farmers or as farmhand-*peones*. Most immigrants stayed in Buenos Aires or joined the work force in other cities. The population of Buenos Aires doubled between 1880 and 1890.

In spite of the onrush of immigrants, huge extensions of Argentina's territory remained sparsely peopled. The great estancias needed only a few of the workers to manage the immense herds of cattle and sheep. Patagonia—an arid sheep-raising area the size of Italy and Spain combined—remained almost vacant, with, to this day, a population density of fewer than one inhabitant per square kilometer. Argentina's rural population peaked in 1949; since then, people have left the countryside for the cities at a steady rate. In the decade of the 1960s, three-quarters of a million people migrated into Buenos Aires.

Peter and I were headed away from the concentration of people, money, and power that is Buenos Aires and into the vast, arid outback that is Patagonia. The contrast would be striking.

We passed our days in "La Capital," as everyone calls it, carrying out the endless shopping required for fieldwork. We combed the narrow shopping streets, searching out flashlight batteries in ill-stocked shops—ten at this shop, twenty-five at the next—and maps and boots.

There was a day spent at a laboratory in a beautiful, aging Spanish monastery, glass cases of poisonous snakes with darting tongues in its grand entry hall, where we obtained vials of antivenom for the Patagonian viper, and blurred hours spent in ornate offices, waiting for officials to supply us with the necessary research permission papers.

There were careening taxi rides through decaying but glittery and grand avenues, with screeching brakes and furious auto horns a constant din in our ears. There was fast, impassioned Spanish; haughty, chic women in leopard and guanaco skins on Avenida Florida; and hasty restaurant meals of tender beef and puffed *papas fritas*.

We had set ourselves down on the crowded streets of Buenos Aires in the center of a decade of record economic lows, widespread corruption, and unprecedented terrorism and political chaos. There had been five military coups in the country since, and set off by, Perón's ouster in 1955, and the country had had thirteen leaders, most of them generals, since the end of World War II. Two years prior to our arrival, with the installation of Lieutenant General Jorge Rafael Videla (following the house arrest of Isabel Perón), the "dirty war" against terrorism had been launched. The economy was steadily worsening, the country's debt was soaring, and unemployment and inflation were out of control.

The week in which we arrived, however, there was little sign of the low morale one might have expected in a country experiencing such bewildering tumult. Instead, nationalism rocketed through the streets—Argentina had won the World Cup. The Latin American country was, to put it mildly, beside itself.

Everywhere we went, people spewed to us streams of superlatives about their land. "Argentina is beautiful, no? Our country is *hermosísimo, fuertísimo, grandote!*" An uproar of honking cars and shrieks of pride did not stop all night long. After the victory, every ten minutes, the radio in every Fiat and Citroën blared replays of the last "Goooool!"

Jorge, however, a man we met in the house of an acquaintance, gave us a hint of the sentiments that simmered behind the honking horns—sentiments we were to hear throughout our stay. He went on a tirade—a rant that was an uneasy blend of depression and outrage—when we got to talking about his country.

"Argentina is the greatest country in the world. We are *un país riquísimo!* We have rich, rich land. We have beef, oil, wool, minerals, but something goes wrong every time. We have riches, but then why aren't we rich? One big matter is that we don't have enough people to develop Argentina. We need more people to move here.

"Another problem is, we Argentines could never rule ourselves. We could never function in a democracy. We don't think. We are incompetent.

"You are so lucky," he said. "You North Americans like to work. You accomplish things! We Argentines go to work all day and do nothing. We like to eat. We live for raviolis!"

He finished by standing and impressing his point with that uniquely Italian gesture of putting thumb and fingers together, as though gripping a piece of bread, and motioning back and forth to his mouth.

I was both saddened and alarmed by the mixture of humiliation and national arrogance in Jorge's words. Jorge's feeling of helplessness about the future of himself and his country were palpable. I had never heard anyone speak so fanatically and yet so self-deprecatingly about his country. The *porteños*, as the Buenos Aires residents are called, with whom we talked seemed desperate about the economic situation, but they also seemed to view their city as, literally, the hub of the world.

In Buenos Aires, whenever we mentioned to shopkeepers or government officials that we were headed south to Patagonia, their faces assumed a look of incredulity. They looked at us as though we were mad.

"Cold!" they immediately said.

"Wind!"

"Everyone wears feathers down there," said a shopkeeper, referring to Indian headwear.

"The people in La Patagonia are all *animalitos*," remarked an acquaintance.

"Why are you going there? You should stay here in Buenos Aires. Or you should go to Iguazú in the north, to see the waterfalls. Or you could go to Bariloche, if you like to ski. There is nothing down there in La Patagonia. Nothing! *¡No hay nada!*"

We had had prior warning about Patagonia's climate. In preparation for our trip, we had read reports by Patagonia's explorers. The brutal winds of the region had moved geologist George Gaylord Simpson to coin the proverbial saying that a person wishing to visit Patagonia didn't need to travel. He could just stand still, in one spot, and it would all blow by.

It was Simpson, too, who described, in his book, *Attending Marvels*, a plane that took off from Comodoro Rivadavia in the thirties and remained suspended, unable either to go forward or to land in the "savage" gale-force head winds, above the airstrip for four hours before it was able to descend into Comodoro again.

The *porteños'* disdainful comments about the Patagonians themselves, on the other hand, puzzled me. They reflected the immense and chronic gap between the capital and the interior of the country.

Buenos Aires, and its residents, ruled by the military dictator

Videla, who had his citizens terrorized into denying that their neighbors were disappearing, shimmered with sophistication and arrogance. But the dazzle seemed brittle, like an elegant lamp that would shatter the moment the last guest left the party.

Early on a crisp morning, we took off from Buenos Aires and headed south down the cone of South America. The plane transported us first over the green paradise of the pampas, then, quickly, over what appeared to be an endless, dead flat, yellow-brown sea. On our way we dropped into Mar del Plata, Bahía Blanca, and San Antonio, each town smaller and shabbier than the last, as we reached deeper into Patagonia.

The majority of the eight-hundred-thousand-square-kilometer area designated "Patagonia" is a vast tableland of extremely sparse vegetation, where only sheep can eke out a living. Historically, both Argentina and Chile have laid claims to the entire South American cone; however, at present Chile governs only the rainy, green strip from the western slopes of the Andes to the Pacific, while Argentina occupies a narrow band of alpine meadows and mountain forests on the eastern side of the mountains and the majority of the barren steppe that stretches east over the bulk of the continent to the Atlantic coast.

Patagonia first began to be settled by Europeans—southern Europeans in the north and British, Welsh, and Scotsmen in the south—in the 1860s. The immigrants were put to work transforming the vast, remote tracts of rangeland claimed, most often by earlier-arriving immigrants, into sheep estancias. The sere plain over which we were gliding was the breakfast of tens of millions of sheep.

Finally our plane neared our destination: Chubut, one of the five provinces of Argentine Patagonia, the others being Río Negro and Neuquén to the north and west and Santa Cruz and Tierra del Fuego farther south.

Chubut was only recently, in 1955, made a province of Argentina. Until then it was designated a national territory. (In the late 1800s it was still designated one of the Territorios Indios.) The province, located between parallels 42 and 46, a belt between the Andes and the sea, is the third largest in the country, after the provinces of Buenos Aires and Santa Cruz, and occupies 224,686 square kilometers. Its population in 1970 was 189,920, with the vast majority living in the five major towns of Trelew, Rawson, Puerto Madryn, Comodoro Rivadavia, and Esquel. Its population density in the same year was .85 inhabitants per square kilometer.

At Trelew airfield, where we disembarked, we were in another Argentina, a place utterly opposite to Buenos Aires. The bare, one-room terminal was packed with eighteen-year-old soldiers, dressed in olive drab, holding machine guns against their chests. Their lips quivered and their eyes narrowed with fear and contempt as they questioned us, holding us back, insisting on seeing our passports and research permits again and again. Only after an hour and a half were we allowed to leave the near empty building.

Using our blundering Spanish outside the terminal, we finally located a taxi driver who agreed to drive us the three hours to Península Valdés, and we set out north on Ruta 3, the long, straight cut of road that follows the bleak eastern edge of the Patagonian outback.

We proceeded for an hour through an endless scrubland, stopping briefly at the Prefectura, the Coast Guard station, in Puerto Madryn, the last town before the Península. It was only when we turned right off Ruta 3, at the sign for the town, and headed down an escarpment that I realized we had been on a plateau. As soon as we made the turn, we could see, for the first time, the South Atlantic and the town sprawled away from its edge.

Puerto Madryn appeared deserted. The town square consisted

of a few spindly, dust-coated trees, and the streets were lined
with low cement-block houses with closed shutters. It was Sunday, and the shop windows were chained and barred. We saw
a few quiet children, dressed in white, walking along the gravel
streets with the dust swirling around them, but no one else. The
Patagonian town had the dusty, sprawled, bedraggled look of
upstart factory towns in the Wyoming desert. But there were
also hints of an off-season beach town; a few faded colored
awnings whipped in the wind.

There was no one at the Prefectura to look at our permission
papers, but just outside the seaside whitewashed building there
was a bronze sign. We painstakingly made out its message.
"There is no water between here and Rawson. The distance is
seventy kilometers."

Shortly we were in the final two hours of our journey to
Península Valdés.

Península Valdés juts into the South Atlantic like an ax head,
cutting lopsidedly into the sea from the otherwise straight,
southwest-leaning coastline. The headland is South America's
analogy to Cape Cod, at nearly the same latitude, but south. It
is as though each continent felt compelled to make a foray into
the sea, drove an arm out into the winds, and then beat a
retreat, curling back toward the main body of land.

The surface of Península Valdés occupies 145 leagues, or 725
square kilometers, being 97 kilometers wide by 63 kilometers
long. An isthmus, 5 kilometers wide at its narrowest point, forms
an effective barrier between the headland and the rest of Patagonia, essentially making the Península an island. On a map, the
Península looks a little like a hummingbird sipping the shore,
with the northern gulf, Golfo San José, formed out of the opening between shoulder and bill and the southern, Golfo Nuevo,
a large opening under the bird's belly.

The Península's climate, we were to find, is at once more
moderate and more severe than its North Atlantic twin. In the
austral summer, from January to March, the temperature seldom

rises above eighty degrees Fahrenheit. The calmly sloshing sea is warm enough to beckon and cool enough to refresh. In the winter months, (June through August), though, the average temperature is about forty degrees Fahrenheit, and although there is almost never snow, the vicious Patagonian wind typically blows at a steady pace of thirty to fifty knots for days on end. Even in winter there are occasional balmy days when it is possible to take a dip in the ocean, and at any time during the summer a gale may take force out at sea and drive one inside to shiver, listen to the house quake, and watch gulls fly backward on the wind.

There is seldom rain on the Península. When it does come, though, it pours in torrents, and the Patagonian turf is obstinate when it comes to absorbing water. The dirt roads turn to lakes and oozing, sucking mud lanes. Even after the rain ceases, the ground refuses to yield, and for a month or more driving is treacherous. Patagonians spend hours each year in the road wallowing in mud, digging out their trucks. A telltale mark of a Patagonian truck is a pair of long wood boards, frayed and filthy, poking their ends out of its mud-covered bed. These possessions, prized in a treeless land, allow their owner to fashion temporary roads when their vehicles are lodged in especially determined patches of mud.

Península Valdés has little more to invite settlement today than it had when Europeans first explored the region a century ago. There are no telephone wires, no electricity, no plumbing, infrequent road grading, no mail service, and no schools. The Península has a total of about two hundred inhabitants, seventy of whom live in the tiny village of Puerto Pirámides, the remainder scattered over the campo on remote estancias.

In the past fifteen years the Península has come to be known, by *porteños*, as a place with wildlife. Foreign and Argentine naturalists make uncomfortable journeys onto the wind-flogged, barren Península to observe guanacos, penguin colonies, sea lions, elephant seals, killer and right whales, dolphins of three species, albatross, rhea, *gato montés*, fox, and cormorant colonies. I was among those bitten by the naturalists' descriptions.

~~~

It was late afternoon when we finally reached the Whale Camp.

We descended from the tableland down a rough washout that threw the car back and forth between gullies and ridges. Then, suddenly, like a world flung up before us, Golfo San José came into view: a great plate of blue-gray sea was whipping toward the land from as far into the distance as we could see and thundering onto the low, pebbled shore and scrub.

Following the track through the dunelands that interrupted two rows of cliffs leading north and south around the bay, we drove up to the Whale Camp.

A whitewashed cement house, a rude wooden A-frame, and a battered outhouse stood at the foot of the cliffs, facing the sea. The buildings stood not ten meters from the beach. This little sea-edge outpost, forty-five minutes from the last sign of another human habitation, was to be our home.

To our dismay, no one came out to greet us, and the house was locked tight as a vault. The researcher whom we were to replace was nowhere to be found. Having no other choice but to stay where we were, we sent the taxi driver back to La Bonita, the estancia indicated by the little roadside sign, where, we had been told, Don José and Doña Clara, the managers of the ranch on which the field station was situated, lived, to let them know we had arrived and to see if they knew anything about the key or the researcher's whereabouts.

Once the taxi disappeared around the bend, we hefted our two emperor-size duffel bags, five mammoth suitcases, boxes of batteries, tripods, and other assorted gear onto the concrete veranda that spanned the front of the house.

As we were assembling our gear, a baby guanaco rounded the corner from behind the house and came right up to us on the porch. The golden-furred animal with long legs, a proud head, and a supercilious eye nuzzled Peter lovingly. Then she got an ornery look on her face, chewed her cud, and spat a wad of green slime in my direction. We had forgotten that the researcher at the camp was raising a guanaco that had been injured while jumping a fence.

After Peter had given the beast a thorough massage, and she and I had sized each other up out of the corners of our eyes, Peter and I climbed the steep path up the washed-out, baked cliffs that rose directly behind the house to survey our surroundings. We walked along the top of the sixty-meter cliffs, trembling from the height, from the onslaught of the thirty-five-knot wind, and from awe.

The bay was a great madness of water. Ridge after ridge of gray water, rising and frothing, charged onto the beach in front of the house, which looked like an insignificant white die in a huge gray world of sea, land, and sky. Albatross and black giant petrels circled over the raging water, and gulls, with straggly feathers whipping off their flesh, rose up and down off the beach in a single, loosely woven sheet. Far off, against the towering clouds, we thought we could make out hundreds of petrels and albatross, swooping and flashing up and down from the water in a feeding frenzy.

As we squinted through binoculars, taking pains to hold them steady in the wind, we saw a giant black flipper and then the glistening black back of a right whale, just barely distinguishable in the darkness of the bay. Hearts tripping, we pushed our binoculars around the perimeters of the gulf; we sighted another whale, but we did not bring into focus one human dwelling.

Suddenly the bleak sky, the open sea, and the frigid wind were walls closing in. We pulled our hats close on our ears, breathed into our mittens to warm our noses, turned our backs to the sea and the onslaught of wind, and tramped inland.

Stopping once, we looked out again. Spread before us, from the toes of our shoes to the horizon, was another ocean: a drab, obdurate ground lay flat to the horizon. Miles and miles of low, wind-crippled bushes spread across the pallid land in a jagged, stabbing carpet over the round of the earth. The land was a fortress of emptiness.

As I stood in this gray, freezing, inhospitable frontier, a question formed between my chilled ears. What on earth was I doing here?

My father taught me, from the time I was very young, to suck stones. On the weekend hikes my family took, the four of us, my mother and father, my brother and I, carried canteens, but we were not supposed to drink from them. When we were thirsty my father picked stones from the streams we forded and gave them to us to suck.

Even though raised abroad, I grew up among North American myths. My father used to quiz my brother and me on U.S. history as we traveled through Europe. I gobbled library books on Daniel Boone and Abe Lincoln's cabin boyhood at the American schools I attended, and during my teens in Japan, I spent months steeped in Thoreau.

I knew my Indiana, country-bred mother had the grit to be a pioneer, and I grew up wanting to live in the woods as she had as a girl. I longed to be a member of a wagon train, and I imagined myself sauntering gallantly through a glorious, wide-sky country, my hand lightly touching my horse's flank, my head high and my heart buoyant. I wanted to taste that elusive North American elixir, pure independence.

It was these North American myths, this stone sucking, this "water discipline," that gave me a thirst for unknown lands, fueled my passion for testing my grit, and led me to live, twice, in 1978–1979 and again in 1984–1985, in the wilderness of Patagonia. The opportunity to study whales (on my first visit) and to collect the life stories of the Patagonians (on my second) was a chance to prove that I had the self-reliance and independence exalted in my culture.

Patagonia, however, and the people who inhabited her wastes were to give me lessons wholly unexpected. She would topple the little cairn of stones that had been my guidepost for twenty-four years, forcing me to fashion a new one out of unfamiliar materials: fox skulls, elephant seal teeth, South Atlantic beach pebbles, and ostrich dung.

~~~

About an hour after we mounted the bluffs, the light started to dim and the land to take on an even deeper bleakness. It was as if a gray shroud had been laid over the earth. Just as desolate feelings were beginning to take hold, we spotted, through our binoculars, a red truck parked beside the house at the camp and a wisp of smoke rising and speeding away on the wind. We made our way back along the cliff edge and down to the camp; there, by the smoke, were Clara and José, the old ranch couple. As we approached, the two small people rose from the fire to greet us.

They had built a fire in the camp's outdoor asado pit, a circular, four-foot-high windbreak of piled thornbush fagots about eight feet in diameter. It looked rather like a roofless igloo with a fire pit in its center. On a grate over the fire, a side of mutton was sizzling, and a pot of eggs was jiggling at a furious boil. A bottle of red Argentine table wine, hunks of dry bread, and knives were heaped on the ground. Beside them stood the guanaco.

The man's face was a delta of purple-and-red veins, the woman's was pale and furrowed; he looked about seventy, she about sixty. Both pairs of squinting eyes looked straight into ours above cheekbones sharpened and polished by years of wind.

José, in his jaunty British-style tweed cap, stood very still, feet planted wide apart. His face held a serene grin, and without wasting words on introductions, he said, "*Hola*, young ones. How was your trip?" He had a stick in his hand, with which he had been prodding the meat, and as he spoke, he patted it into his other palm. A thin windbreaker flapped around his chest, and the wind whipped his baggy pant legs. On his small bare feet he wore black, rope-soled alpargatas, which made him seem graceful, like a dancer. After greeting us he immediately turned shy and squatted down to poke at the mutton.

Clara hung back for a second or two. She was wearing a plain wool skirt that came to well below her knees and a tan Shetland sweater with the sleeves pulled right down over the

span of her hands for warmth. The wind must have been piercing
each stitch of her pullover. She was hunched, and though thickened
about the middle, she looked trim in her clothes. She wore no
stockings, and her smooth legs looked girlish. Her attire made it
appear as though she had listened to the taxi driver's account of
our plight, slipped into the closest pair of shoes, and rushed out of
the house in order to reach us as soon as possible.

The guanaco was tormenting Clara, chasing her in a circle,
intent on nursing. Using one hand to hold her skirt down as the
wind threatened to blow it above her knees, and waving the
other hand behind her to protect herself from the guanaco's
advances, she hurried up to us and kissed us each on both
cheeks.

She chattered to us, nonstop, in fast, animated Spanish. I
caught the simplest words and managed to translate a few
phrases, "*Pobres.* Poor things. Oh, it's too cold here. Life is hard.
You must keep warm. Are you warm enough, dearie? This camp
is too difficult for you! You are too far from your families! It's
lonely here. This weather is ugly. Life is too hard, poor things.
You must eat a lot tonight."

The tiny woman pushed us over toward the fire, and we
squatted inside the asado pit. Once we were inside the piled-
brush circle of the windbreak, the air ebbed to a constant pacing
cold, and I huddled down on my haunches like a chick, hugging
myself through my billowy orange down jacket. I watched the
eggs boiling on the tiny fire.

José stood, unaffected by the wind, and poked at the slab of
mutton laid over the flames with the branch of a thornbush.
Affable Peter gestured to José, and the two spoke haltingly, Peter
using his rudimentary Spanish. Clara sat beside me on a fruit
crate, chattering in soothing quavering clucks which I understood mostly through their cadences.

She coaxed me, again and again, to have more meat to fend
off the cold. "It's cold. *Come. Come,*" she said. "Eat. Eat." She
handed us ribs heavy with meat and fat, while she herself whit-
tled at a nearly bare bone. She ate filmy strips of pink meat as
she scraped them off and shivered.

Even inside the asado pit, the cold was harsh. Over and over, coatless Clara denied being cold while she quaked and shivered and hunched over so far that her bosom nearly rested on her thighs. Her pale face caught the firelight, and her short, dark hair, pinned above her ears, spun around in the wind. As she chattered and scraped with her dull knife, she darted glances at the guanaco and waved her hand ineffectually as it neared. "It's ugly. I don't like this animal," she said to me, scrunching her nose.

Now and then, as we sat, focused on the fire, the moan of a whale reached us on the wind. The sea crashed on the beach pebbles, only ten meters from us; the night grew progressively colder.

Clara's rapid, friendly words, though, bubbled on like a warm brook. She disregarded our simple Spanish and seemed to assume that we would understand everything she said. Now and then she would stop just long enough for me to nod and say, "Sí. Sí." Her eyes met mine for just instants, as though to rest them too long on mine would expose too much.

Hunched inside this odd thornbush windbreak, with the sea stampeding onto the shore only feet away, there was, in the bowl of my belly, both a disquiet I had never experienced before and a sense of being rocked.

After José and Clara assured themselves that we had eaten our fill, José held his cap on his head with one hand and stood up in the wind. Without ado, he and Clara motioned for us to come with them for the night, and feeling rescued, we squeezed into the middle of the bench seat of their truck. Clara let loose a last rush of admonishments at the guanaco and boarded beside me.

We rumbled the forty-five minutes to the couple's house over a dirt road that was indistinguishable from the surrounding ground and through a thick, starless darkness.

At the small house Clara sat us down and served us tea, then bustled us to a plain room with two single iron beds. The room had no light, and we climbed between the cold sheets in the dark. Clara left the door slightly ajar when she went out, as though we were children.

As I lay in the strange, cold Patagonian bed, feeling as far as I could be from any known world, an ominous image kept coming to me.

Just before we had driven from the camp, José had gone into the camp tool hut and brought out a ten-liter fuel canister. He poured some of the liquid on a clump of thorns and tossed a match on it; the bush exploded into flame. "Gasoline, not kerosene," he said, and then filled his tank.

We drove away with the bush still burning in the dark.

EGGS, MILK, AND TEA

~~~~~~

One still morning during our first months on Península Valdés, the cold was so keen that we were shivering even inside layers of sweaters, and in a bid for warmth we went walking. The wind was sobbing, like a child.

On a remote beach we found a whale calf, dead. It was a calf whose development we had been following from soon after its birth. It had had a habit of nudging its mother with its snout, so we had dubbed it "Nose."

The calf was an enormous black egg. The giant infant lay sprawled on its belly in the mud. Its flippers were two black table-size slabs of rubber at right angles to the humped body; its skin was like a perfectly tailored black rubber mitten, with two opposed thumbs for the flippers; and where the gulls had pecked away the thick skin, the exposed blubber was a fresh, pinkish white. The calf's tongue, swollen like a ball, stuck out of its mouth on the sand. The tongue had a notch in it, to fit on its mother's nipple.

We had arrived in Patagonia in the heart of winter, and during our first months there the winds were wild. The drone of the wind, accented with high-pitched whines and roaring gusts, accompanied us as we made toast over the stove in the morning and engulfed us and thrashed at us whenever we went outside.

It was bitter cold, and every day we would trudge up the cliffs and stand on the bluffs, facing into the incessant wind, looking out to sea for spouts and flippers.

Many days the wind was so forceful that it jittered our telescope and gave us headaches as we tried to find the mothers and calves we had come to study. It turned out that the hours spent scanning the gulf, just to locate some whales to observe, far outnumbered the hours of actual observation. Many days we went to the cliff hut, our observation post, and left after eight hours, having seen no whales at all. On our way back to the house at night, I would look out at the campo, fierce, the gritty wind stinging my cheeks and drying my tears instantly. At our dinners of lentils and rice, we would force on the room a grim optimism and try to squeeze some more juice out of our old, chewed conversations.

I was so determined to prove myself self-sufficient in every dimension, so enamored of bravery and lone survival, that I didn't recognize the signs of loneliness or even boredom. I wrote letters to my friends at home, describing the ponderous beauty of the whales and how lovely it was to have a pared-down life of eating mush and rising at dawn.

On days of high wind, when we couldn't see the whales for the whipped-up seas, I trudged along the necklace of debris at the high-tide line, looking for shells, sand dollars, and skate eggs, while the witchlike giant petrels—black albatross with six-foot wingspans—did sweeps overhead. Sometimes I counted the dead Magellanic penguins that had washed onto the beach, their white breasts blotched with oil from tankers passing far offshore.

Once, I was out among the tide pools, collecting the scallops that washed in after a storm, and on my way back up the beach I noticed a hump of brown rock. In the very instant that I was passing it, the rock moved. I streaked up the beach in terror

while the animal galumphed down to the sea edge. As I stood
panting, looking back, my hair in my face, the huge male elephant seal turned around and glared at me with a bloody eye.

About two months after our arrival, I stood on the tableland
at the top of the cliffs behind our house, gazing through binoculars toward the south. Far in the distance I saw a red truck
come to a stop. Two small figures and a sheep dog disembarked.
It was Clara and José. We hadn't seen them since they'd rescued
us our first day at camp. The pair of humans were barely distinguishable from the small, scrubby bushes that dotted the land
around them. They could have been bushes; the truck gave them
away.

The next day I went to see Clara.

I bathed—two pots of boiling water, two pots of cold—over
the drain in the room, and shivered dry sitting on a table in
front of the tiny gas heater.

Then I drove the truck off into the cave of gray wind. From
the house, a winding road took me from the sea up the eroded
cliffs to the wide dirt road that stretched flat and straight to the
western horizon. I hurtled over the fifteen kilometers of vacant
scrubland to Clara's. There wasn't a structure or a hill to mar
the blank, monotonous land.

After I had turned off the main road and proceeded a couple
of kilometers down the track that led to the estancia, a pair of
trees rising out of the cloud-darkened floodplain signaled a human presence. From a slight rise I could see the little settlement
in the center of the flat, unbounded expanse of campo. There,
in the low brush, was a collection of squat, whitewashed cement
buildings: the cubelike *peón*'s house, the asado shed, the barn, a
chicken coop, and corrals.

The two small pines, smartly upright and robust, stood like
guards over, and half hid, the rectangular, red-roofed, white
cement house. A wire fence enclosed the house and the trees
in a rectangle of yard. The fence was like a small girl's penciled
frame around a tiny scene she had drawn of tree, house, and
sun on an enormous, otherwise blank sheet of paper.

Clara had been scrubbing. When she met me at the white picket gate, which would have fit perfectly into the little girl's bright drawing, she was wiping her soapy hands on her apron. As she leaned to kiss me, a gritty crosswind whipped up the hem of her apron and it blew out from her waist.

"¡Tanto tiempo!" she said. "It's been too long, sweetie! How are you?"

Then the childless woman shooed me in the gate as though I were a little child. *"Pase. Pase."*

We crossed the small dirt rectangle of garden. It was bare, except for a pair of potted lilac bushes whose spindly, leafless branches were being harried by the sharp wind. Across the yard, scraggles of parsley clutched the ground on either side of the front door of the low, white rectangular house.

"José isn't here," Clara said as we entered the house. "He's out with the *peón*, checking fences. He won't be back until after dark." The day was dark as dusk already. It was eleven o'clock.

The kitchen floor glistened from its wash. Mop and bucket stood against a wall. Everything in the kitchen had a desperately clean appearance: the walls with their thin white paint; the rectangular kitchen table around which the room was ordered; the compact white stove and sink; the oversize, blunt-cornered refrigerator. All were faded and bore circular scrape marks, as though they had been subjected to decades of furious scrubbing by Clara's duo of bristle brush and cleanser.

Except for the few essential items of furniture, the room was entirely bare. The only evidence of kitchen work was a pair of leftover mutton chunks on a plate and three shining aluminum kettles, graduated in size, on the stove top. A small heater on the floor hummed; liquid in its purple bottle gurgled as the flame consumed the fuel, and there was a slight smell of kerosene. Wind roared outside and whistled through the stovepipe.

In the bare kitchen, Clara's wool sweater, biscuit white skin, and dark hair were a collage of color against scrubbed-out white. The skin of her face shone, accenting the deep-troughed crows'-feet and folds along her cheeks.

She pushed me onto one of the uncomfortable straight-backed chairs and hurried to the stove, a hand bracing her back. She put on the kettle for tea and disappeared into the pantry. When she came out she had a tan, plastic tablecloth. It was neatly folded, like a map, and embossed with white to look like lace. As she patted it smooth, her stiff hand knocked the table. There was that clean, plastic smell and the patting had a distinctly maternal sound. A pleasant kind of shiver trickled up my spine, as though she were patting my head.

"It's an ugly day. *Feo. Feo.*" Clara shook her head resignedly at the sky outside, as though it were a naughty child running far off on the plain. "You should have come to visit earlier."

She put a plate of cream crackers on the table; her hand shook as she opened a package of butter. She placed a plate in front of me, and I took a cracker. As she asked a string of questions, one tumbling over the next, her voice quavered.

"Don't you feel lonely here?" she asked. "This is a sad place. Very lonely.

"Life is hard here, don't you think? ... Do you like that camp? ... It must be hard for you without a woodstove. ... You must be cold.

"Don't you miss your family? ..."

Her expectation that I would miss home relieved me, while I denied it. "Oh, no, I love Argentina."

"But you're used to being near people ... where you're from." Clara added this last phrase as though certain that wherever that was, I must be surrounded by generous neighbors who visited every day without fail.

As she brought the teacups to the table, the old woman's voice chattered along with the calming clip of knitting needles. I didn't have to say much. She spoke for the two of us.

I sipped at the harsh tea.

"Have you had visitors?" Clara asked, and she listed for me

the visitors she had had in the last month, sucking on each precious minute spent in the company of another human being like a piece of candy.

"Roberta, from La Luna, over there, came by for just a minute. And Luis, my nephew, came by in his truck one day, on his way to his father's shearing."

She told me about the visit, three weeks before, from her niece, Elena, a teacher in Buenos Aires.

"On one day, Elena came in the morning. She stayed for tea at eleven, and then she stayed for lunch. We had fried eggs and mutton steaks and potatoes, and she had brought a rice pudding.

"And then . . ." A grin paused on Clara's face. The grin contained a touch of shame, as though what had happened were too good to be true. "Elena was still here talking at teatime and at dinner. So we had more eggs and a lettuce-and-potato salad, and the rest of the rice pudding. And coffee afterward." Clara stuck out her tongue with pleasure. Her faraway look cradled how precious and delicious the day had been. She had milked Elena's visit for the last drop.

Clara showed me the three pairs of stockings from the capital that Elena had given her. They crackled in their unopened wrappers, and she put them away in a drawer, piling them neatly in its dark recess. I wondered when she would wear them.

Clara held her spoon at the end of its handle and worked it in her teacup, almost sloshing the tea on the table with her awkward, arrhythmic stirring. Her face was wistful.

"The other day, after Elena left the Península to go back to the capital, José found a note wrapped in a plastic bag on the cattle gate at the main road. The note was from Elena. It said she would miss Tía Clara while she was gone.

"She said she couldn't come back to the south until summer. The flights have gotten very expensive. It's a shame.

"José doesn't like to visit," she said, gazing at the tablecloth. "I do. I like visits." She paused and then brightened.

"You will stay for lunch, Sarita?"

When I said I would, Clara got up from the table. The munching of my cracker eating joined the furious scraping of her potato peeling, and the smell of potatoes wafted in the air.

"Have you heard from your parents?" Clara asked for a second time.

Wind suddenly shrieked across the bare expanse outside the cell-size window, and Clara told me more of her news. Part of what she related was recent events, most of it consisting of the old stories and scraps of conversation that she had collected for decades.

Her brother, who had had a heart operation, she said, was staying at a *residencia* in town to recuperate. His wife, "*pobre*, poor one," had to stay in the campo to see that the new lambs got marked.

Angel, her sister Teresa's husband, had recently gone to his estancia in the interior and found eighty sheep, frozen hard as rock, up to their necks in snow. "It was hard for his heart. Hard for his love. He seems sad and thin."

She shook her head over Angel's losses, and then she told me about the car accident Angel had had years before.

"It's too much to ask of people, *pobres*."

She sawed off a large hunk of lemon from a saucer on the table and squeezed some of its juice into her tea. Silence fell, except for the heater's hum.

A few minutes later Clara bustled off to the bedroom and brought back a large wooden drawer full of photos. She showed me pictures of Elena and her two-year-old son, Pablito, a dark photo of her mustachioed father, and smudged, out-of-focus pictures of her younger self and her sisters, in long dresses, by a simple ranch house.

Clara lifted the teapot with an assertive plunk and poured me a third cup of tea. "Don't you want honey with your cracker?" She pushed the honey, jam, and butter across the table with her bent forefinger. They jostled each other along their passage, until they clinked my plate, and Clara grinned like a delighted child when I wound some honey onto my knife. She helped herself to a cracker, broke it into jagged pieces, and sopped them in her tea.

I asked Clara about her own days, without the companionship of a child or any other relative, in the campo.

"Oh, I'm very busy," Clara said. "In the morning, José and I get up at seven, unless there is herding to be done, like at shearing time, when José has to be out at five. José takes tea with milk in the morning and then he goes out to work. I clean the kitchen, do the washing, make the lunch, all those things. Until twelve, I don't see his face. He eats, then rests. He gets up at four and goes out to work until night falls, when he comes back. While I make dinner, in that interval, he reads. For dinner, I make fried mutton steak, a rice dish, or fried eggs, or mashed potatoes. We go to bed at twelve, after the news. José sometimes goes earlier.

"Sometimes I stay up late. A thing I like very much is to iron clothes late at night after José is sleeping."

Elena told me, in a later conversation, that her aunt was *maníaca*. She would stay up all night ironing napkins and table-cloths she never got to use.

Clara riffled through the loose photos in the drawer and handed me a picture of a little child in a cable-knit sweater. She told me that before she was married she used to make vests and little red leggings for her nephews and nieces.

Then she sat up straight and her eyes flickered to mine. She stirred her tea awkwardly, and it sloshed on the table as she formed the words of the question that owned her life. Once phrased in her mind, it slipped out of her as fast and inevitably as a whale calf being born. "Do you have children?"

"No, not yet."

Clara's shoulders relaxed, and she ate a bite of soggy cracker.

"We don't want children yet. I'm not sure about children," I fumbled. "I have a lot of work I want to get done first, and get my career going. I don't know how to fit children in with a career. I don't know, children seem like a big responsibility.

"In my country, we want everything," I added.

Clara cocked her head as she listened, puzzled, half-understanding but attentive, and in response to my conflicted tone, her eyes were soft. She moved a lock of her short hair out of her face, and her eyes, aimed down at the table, wandered unfocused.

"Me, yes. I always wanted children. I like them. Children are nice." Her voice lifted wistfully, and she lisped the last sentence as though she were talking to a small child.

Clara and I made lunch together—a salad out of boiled potatoes, the remains of a lettuce head, which Clara refreshed with a soak in a tub of water, and three boiled eggs. When I went to help with the eggs, they didn't peel right. Hunks of the white came off with the shell. "That's because they are too fresh," Clara told me. "I collected them this morning. The chickens only laid three." She clucked her cracked lips in disappointment. One of the eggs was half-size. "By tomorrow, they would have peeled better." With the salad, we ate the chunks of mutton vertebrae, which Clara had reheated in the oven.

We ate slowly. Tucked-away thoughts, rising from our separate orbs, swung back and forth between us like tides while we ate. I told her about my friend's divorce, and she told me about her friend's cancer. There was the washing to and fro of understanding and misinterpretation that sometimes came from not having the same bearings, the crowing eagerness that swelled when our sameness splashed between us, and the puzzlement and temporary receding that followed when our cultural or age difference prevented instant comprehension. We were like two girls swinging in opposite directions, eyes meeting as they came parallel.

In the middle of her mutton chop, Clara stood and went over to the window. "The wind is still high," she said, and then returned to her chair.

I looked at Clara. She was small, hunched, her back to the utterly blank square of wall. She sat with grace, her knees together, her feet side by side, flat on the floor, and she held her hands patiently in her lap.

"How do you live here, with this solitude?" I asked in a quiet voice.

Clara got up quickly, and as I finished the last bits of lettuce on my plate, she cleared the table. Her movements packed with purpose, she gestured hastily so I wouldn't get up.

I sat and she brought out a pile of glossy-covered magazines and pulled up her chair beside me. She pushed the pages of the top one, licking her fingers, pointing to pictures as she turned the pages. She paused at a photo of an elegant living room in a frozen-food ad and put her finger on the couch in the picture. "Look at that. What a thing!"

Then she told me about the dream house that Luis and Sara, her sister's son and daughter-in-law, were furnishing for themselves in Madryn. "They have a big kitchen, all organized, with a special closet for a washing machine! When the door is closed, you don't even know it's there. And then they have a dining room with a dining set, and a bedroom with a bedroom set Teresa and Angel got them, and a guest room, and a living room with a big couch, and two smaller easy chairs. And a clock on the wall. Teresa and Angel gave them a machine for making noodles. They have everything!"

Leafing through pictures of desserts, we clucked and grinned in rhythm. As we bent over the magazines, I realized Clara was giving me hints about how to wring pleasure from the dry cloth of campo life.

"Did Peter get back from town safely yesterday? How lucky," she said. "What a beautiful day it was, no?"

She then looked at me with a fragile brightness. "I like your hairpin," she said. It was a bobby pin with a butterfly on it, which a little girl on a ranch had given me in a burst of generosity. It was hideous, but I wore it to hold back my bangs when I was feeling low and my hair was dirty.

Then, her voice full of conviction, she offered me her secret, her key.

"Don't you take tea every day at four, my daughter? It is such a good time of day to sit down at the table for a few minutes before the dusk."

After we finished eating, Clara led me outside. It was already almost five, and the light was fading fast. The barren land lay prostrate before us.

As the wind tore at our hair, she fed little chunks of mutton, from the pocket of her apron, to the *calandria*-mockingbird chicks in the dirt square of yard, and then we went along to see her chickens. As Clara unwound the wire holding the coop gate shut, I spied an egg under a bush. The egg had been pricked by one of the bush's needlelike thorns, and its yellow and transparent fluids had dribbled out onto the ground.

Inside the pen there were scads of chickens, clucking and scratching around Clara's wool-stockinged, slippered feet. We stood and enjoyed their flutter for a while.

Back in the house, Clara was frisky. As I made motions to leave, she fluffed and bustled to the pantry. She called out to me, "It's very cold. The weather here is ugly, very ugly, in the winter. You're very thin. Have you always been so thin? Here on the coast, you must eat a lot. To keep warm. You have to eat a lot. Things like meat and eggs."

Then she emerged from the pantry with a package cradled in her arms like an infant. She pressed into my hands a large rusted can filled with brown eggs.

Outside, dusk had tinted the land gray and pink. As I turned the truck around, with the eggs touching my leg, braced between the seat back and my purse, Clara stood by the gate, holding up her knobbed hand in a wave.

The headlights of the truck fell across the old woman in a band of light. She was hunched almost double from back pain, and she waved vaguely toward the truck. Her eyes squinted from the assault of light, and I could see her mouth moving, as though she were still telling me things.

I could see Clara in the rearview mirror as I drove off, a smaller and smaller pencil figure against the vast, darkening sweep of shapeless earth.

In the following months there were days when the hours of watching mothers and calves rolling in the sea seemed a treasure and when our simple life provided a sense of deep sufficiency. But Patagonia rationed those days—there were far more when the gritty, raw weather, the drab campo, and the separation from family and friends made me feel trapped.

The remoteness and isolation began to grip me. I took to going to bed as soon as the light dulled. We had a bedroom like a cave—just big enough for a bed and with a single small window—and I would crawl in, as into a burrow, and pull the unmade, dirty, rumpled sheets and piles of old blankets and sleeping bags over my head. The twenty-knot wind would bang the tin roof. Whale moans would reach into the room and put me to sleep. I slept deep at night, and during the day, when I stole time away from the slow research.

Sixteen months after we arrived, it rained for three weeks straight, so we couldn't move an inch from camp. The land turned to mud, and the roads became long, impassable ponds. As the rain slanted toward the ground, gusts of wind attacked it, confused it, and forced it sideways, so that it drilled our faces. My hair frizzed. I spent the days trying to dedicate myself solely to the whale study, like a bootstraps stoic.

Then, for days on end, it blew thirty-five knots, and we couldn't see the whales in the angry seas.

The weeks of being cooped up in the damp house made both of us restless. We made a list of the things we ought to be doing with all this free time our Boston and Santa Cruz friends envied. The list began: Take photos of the storm, draw and paint, knit sweaters, press plants, read texts about animal behavior and take notes, read *The Brothers Karamazov*, take walks in the rain and write about what we have noticed, repair the mud holes in the road, keep very busy. At the end of the list, in a fit of giddiness, we added a new species of activities: Make a double batch of chocolate-chip cookies and eat them all, paint the windows of the cliff hut black, push the truck over the cliff.

I had taught myself to beat the washing with a brush, as I had seen Clara do, so one day during this period, when yellow streaks spread through the clouds, I allayed my wish for a movie and a hamburger by washing and beating the sheets. Within an hour of hanging them to dry, the wind had risen, with rain, and they were hanging, sodden, with their ends in the mud.

When the rains finally retreated—the giant waves rolled away reluctantly, sucking at the beach in long, greedy drafts for several days following—they left a weighted slate sky. Damp clung to the air, and the trousers and flannel shirts we had hung through the house stayed cold and wet. Finally the sea, all gumption lashed out of it, sloshed aimlessly in the gulf. After days of rain machine-gunning our tin roof, the silence rang. The occasional explosive exhalation of a whale was the only break in the quiet.

The heavy calm was, for me, grimmer than the active struggle with the storms. Even the whales lolled about in the shallows, barely moving, as though depressed or exhausted.

Peter walked up to the gate on the entrance road to the camp and tucked a note for José into the sheep gate there. The note said we were lonely, and our truck was stuck in the mud. The next day the old sheep rancher appeared. He helped us get our truck moving and insisted we come for tea that afternoon.

We drove over through the still, washed air, the campo damp and brown.

Around four, when we arrived, the yard around Clara's house looked like some kind of crazy man's laundry. There were buckets and pots scattered around the muddy yard and under the eaves, even a tin cracker box sunk in the mud. All the receptacles were overflowing with rainwater.

As we drew up to the house, we saw Clara peering timidly out of the kitchen window, like a fox from behind a bush. She had told us before that she was afraid of thieves, wandering horsemen, and gypsies. "Gypsies," she had told us, "will burn down the barn if you don't let them stay overnight."

Clara's hands, knobbed with arthritis, patted and knotted themselves together as she stood idle, for a moment, at the doorway of the house. But as she came across the yard, dodging the water tubs, there was a skip in her gait, a little lightness, like the stifled beginnings of a dance. She had curled her hair, and the little fluffs bounced in the breeze.

We followed her back across the obstacle course. I took off my oxfords at the door since they were caked with mud. Sitting there, the shoes looked like two bird's nests made of mud and thorns.

We sat at the kitchen table while Clara finished washing the mutton grease out of a roasting pan. She poured a kettle of what looked like boiling water right onto her scrubbing hands. She turned to us, keeping her hands in the sink. "What a beautiful storm, no? We got seventy millimeters in one day last week. José thinks the cistern might have enough water now to last the summer. He went out to check the sheep tanks. He'll be back in a little while."

She raised her lobster-red hands out of the sink and added, "I love using rainwater for cooking. It's delicious." To the desert-dwelling woman, the rain was like a shipment of gold coins.

Clara got down three teacups from the stand on the wall where they were kept. When she saw that one of them was chipped, she silently stabbed at it with her finger, scowled, returned it to the shelf, and picked up another.

She left the tea to steep in the boiled rainwater for a long time, and when she poured out the tea, it was so strong there were three black pools in the pale yellow cups.

Peter and I each downed two cups straight, as though we were simultaneously overtaken by a great thirst.

Clara brought to the table broad-bladed butter knives, a new stick of butter, a plate of crackers, and a can of condensed milk for the tea.

As she set things down on the table, Clara worked with the unthinking precision of one who had set a table for tea three times a day for scores of years. Her hands seemed to move of their own accord, like a pair of sheep moving down a path worn in the campo.

As her hands fixed and fetched, and we drank our tea, Clara chattered to us.

When we complained about the wind, she yelled from the pantry. "And so, why are we in La Patagonia?"

When she emerged again, she beamed and cocked her head

and sidled up to Peter. She became a frisky, quick coquette. "What time did *you* get up?" She poked him with a knobbed finger. "The rest of us have been up since dawn! You foreigners!

"How do you walk when you're that tall?" she went on. "Your legs don't even reach the floor!"

Peter was such a satisfying person to tease that Clara stuck out her tongue with delight.

Then, suddenly, she hurried to the pantry, as though she had forgotten something crucial, and returned with a small brown crock in her hand. Sliding it onto the table near me, she announced, her eyes twinkling, "*¡Y el dulce!*"

We each grabbed a cracker and slathered it with the thick, caramel-flavored jam that Clara had made from condensed milk.

Dulce de leche, most often taken as we were eating it, as a topping on bread or crackers, is as popular in Argentina as peanut butter is in the United States. We had seen devotees eat *dulce de leche* on top of ice cream or even straight from a bowl. Our friend Manuel, the park ranger, had told us *dulce de leche* was best *con dos chicas*, making the "curvy woman" gesture in the air.

We ate cracker after cracker. The smells of *dulce de leche* and black tea shifted on the drafts through the room.

Clara went to the window that was like a porthole in the blank wall and peered out over the gray sea of land. She turned to us: "José is coming."

Then she bustled off to fetch him something to drink.

As the slight, gray-haired sheep rancher with the wind-carved face stepped into the kitchen, Peter, who had been sitting in José's customary spot at the table, got up to offer José his chair.

As he was removing his tweed cap, José chuckled. "I was once in a house in Spain and I did the same thing to the head of the house. The man said, 'Stay there, *chico!* Wherever I sit, it's the head of the table!' You stay there, young one!" He stabbed with his finger.

Still chuckling as he seated himself, he teased Peter some more. "Seems to me I saw you down there on the beach with a net the other day." He had seen our truck up by the road, had worried that something was wrong, and had gone down to the edge of the cliffs to look over the camp.

"Looked to me like you were scaring fish, not catching them!"

Clara put a glass of wine in front of José, and the sheep man began to tell us the news. Leaning forward, he sucked his cigarette hard to gain momentum. The words that came were slow and penetrating.

"As for this latest claim on Patagonia by the *chilenos*," he began, "I don't understand it. But we Argentines are just as sure we are right."

José loved to talk politics. In this, he was rare among Península men.

"For me," he went on, "these boundary disputes are all about pride and jealousy. The Russians, the *norteamericanos*, the whites, the blacks, the yellows, the *chilenos*, they're all the same, but it seems like everyone wants to be superior to other people. Chile thinks it's better than Argentina. Argentina thinks it's better than Chile. Chile thinks it's better than Peru.

"I don't know anything . . . I have no family. I am my family. There's only me. . . . But as I see it, in all families—give me blacks, *chilenos*, whatever it might be, they're all the same—if you have, let's say, seven . . . nine children, if one of them is limited mentally, or deformed, the others will make fun of it. I think it is a thing of nature.

"Take some families: The children are fighting over candy. The father will come along and decide the one who wanted red gets yellow and the one who wanted green gets red, and so on. Isn't it always that one *chico* says, 'You love my brother more than me'?

"I know a little joke about this nationalism. Some men are at the races. They are strutting around saying the Argentine horses are the fastest in the world. Until, just at that moment, a *chileno*'s horse wins."

As José laughed his whole body jiggled, but he kept the laugh inside his mouth. His face went red and his eyes were wet with mirth.

He brought up the fact that in a couple of months it would be Columbus Day, a holiday I usually miss altogether and to which I never give much thought.

"What do I know," he said. "In a lot of places, people disagree about who discovered the New World. In Dominica, they are constructing an enormous cross to commemorate Columbus. They believe he landed there first. Then, those Scandinavians believe they found the New World first.

"As for me, I've heard it said that Columbus brought the first syphilis!"

José's chest bounced as he chuckled.

"They say that in América del Sur they conquered the Indians with pure blood. On the other hand, in Norteamérica, they were conquered with pure whiskey!"

I commented that I had heard that during the Indian massacres in Patagonia, the bounty hunters collected not only ears for their belts, but testicles.

"Oh, yes, but look, Sara, that's civilization!"

Clara broke in. "Whiskey, José?"

He waved his hand, dismissing the idea, and Clara turned to Peter. "And Peter?" she said, grinning. "Whiskey, Peter?"

Clara always offered Peter whiskey when we visited. Both of them knew he never drank it, and it had become a great joke between them. Clara always insisted, a gleam in her eye. And Peter always eventually replied, "Oh, all right. But please! Bring me five glasses, because one will not be enough for me!" Then he had to insist and insist that, really, he didn't want any.

"This tea and your *dulce de leche* will keep me fat enough," he said.

"Speaking of civilization," José went on, unfazed by the interruption, "what about this mass suicide in Guyana? This Jonestown. This man was a loco!"

He shook his head. "This is why mass is not for me."

A shot of annoyance at her differences with José ran through Clara's next comment. "José, no. He doesn't like church. As for me, *sí*. I like mass. I am Catholic."

Clara sat down and told us then about a Jehovah's Witness

in Madryn who was shot by the *militares* for refusing to salute the flag. His first allegiance, he said, was to God. *"Pobre familia,"* she said. "Poor family."

She spoke of the poor women in Madryn who had to work in a fish cannery for almost nothing: *"Pobre gente.* Poor people." She told us the story of a drunk driver who had hit a little boy: *"Pobre familia."*

And she told the story of the neighbor's child, Hugo, who was too intelligent and, therefore, disobedient. *"Pobre familia. Pobre chico."*

Then she summed it all up, shaking her head, *"Pobre gente. No se puede.* Poor people. One just can't." She repeated the two sayings in songlike alternation, ever more quietly, as they faded into silence, waiting until the conversation called for a new and identical rendition.

Clara described the barrios on the edge of Trelew—the *ranchos miseria.* "You see terrible houses of mud, with corrugated roofs, without doors, without bathrooms, but there's a television wire on top of every one. They all have televisions! From far away, all you see is a jungle of television aerials.

"I always look at those wires when we go to Gaimán," said Clara, the ranch woman who herself longed for a television.

José joked, "These *ranchitos*—probably built by UNESCO."

"Sí." The words popped out of Clara's mouth: "The whole world is going backward, like a crab."

Clara refilled José's wineglass, and as she set it down, she snatched his cigarettes from him. "You've had enough, José. You don't need any more!"

José turned to me. "And this book you gave me . . ." He had read a book by Jack London from cover to cover, three times, trying to understand the bad translation. I had given him the book as a gift, to help him understand my romance with wild places like Patagonia. Each time I had seen him since, he'd asked a few more fascinated questions.

"I read that most of the meat, when the Eskimos hunt, goes to the dogs. Is that right? . . . They eat mostly caribou. How do they prepare it for the winter?"

José took advantage of any thoughts we brought to him. When Dutch friends came to visit, he delivered a trenchant analysis of the Dutch role in World War II, thoughts he could have assembled only from scraps of news in the rare newspapers that reached Patagonia during the war.

"José reads every day," Clara explained. "He is like my mother. She used to read all the time—novels—and would take a candle to bed with her at night. José reads at four every day, after the siesta, while I fix dinner. He works in the morning, then has lunch, then naps, then reads. Mostly magazines, but also classics. He used to get magazines delivered to Pirámides by plane, but now that the plane no longer comes, we get magazines only when we go to town."

José and I commiserated about our lack of interest in the comic strips, while Clara and Peter exchanged news on their favorite characters.

We sat at the table, and at regular minute intervals, Clara asked if we wouldn't like more tea, assured herself we'd had sugar and lemon, pushed the cracker plate toward one of us, or retrieved the *dulce de leche* from the other end of the table, where one of us was hogging it. *"Come, come,"* she insisted every other minute.

It was dusk by this time, and the room had chilled. José shoved gnarled branches from the dried campo thornbushes into the woodstove. He lit the kerosene lamp, and there was a hissing roar as the mantle flared. Light played on José's rough, purple-veined cheeks.

I asked the question I had been wanting to ask for ages. Why had José emigrated to Argentina?

"Sure, I'll tell you," he said. "But mind you," he added with a chuckle, "I'm not like those *norteamericanos* who hid money under their mattresses for ten years as an investment and then found out they weren't ahead because of inflation. I didn't have any money to hide." He clucked his tongue.

"I emigrated to Argentina from Spain when I was nineteen, in the year 1930.

"I am from the town of Zamora, in León, near the border

with Portugal. It is an area of agriculture, no? Agriculture mixed with livestock and with a little of everything. But there, unlike here, people lived in villages, in tiny towns, and during the day they went out to the fields to work, and at night they returned to the village. Some people owned the land they worked, and others rented. And others didn't have anything. Those lived from work, like that, by day. My family had land—little, but they had some. In my village, compared to here in La Patagonia, there was more of a sense of property. Most everyone, rich or poor, had his own land. People didn't work for other people so much, like I work for Guerrero here, overseeing his sheep.

"In Spain, the families all lived in the village, and there you had everything. In the town were the farmers, the shopkeepers, and everyone from the town lived there. A big change from here. There were all the principal things right in the village—a school, a doctor, a church, police, everything."

Life in the 1930s for Spanish farmers, José said, was mean. A family's tiny plots of land might be scattered over twelve kilometers, one square of ground here and another several kilometers away, in the midst of hundreds of other little holdings.

"I don't know how the land reform worked after I left, but I doubt it worked well. Franco started collectives, to have people share land, but I have heard those are starting to close down. The *ricos* are used to the old ways, and it's hard to change tradition."

As a young man gazing over the tiny, dispersed plots that belonged to his family, José could see little future for himself in Spain. His wave *adiós* to his mother was a bid for betterment.

"I came here looking at the future, believing that I would have a better future. It's the dreams one has when one is young. It seemed that one came here and made money in shovelfuls, eh?

"In those years many came here. Every year people were leaving from my village. There, to speak of an Argentine was to talk of a friend, an intimate thing, to speak of something that belonged to one, of a brother."

The train that José took to the coast of Galicia, to board the ship, went through eighty tunnels. The consist was so long that when the train went around a curve, the amazed young boy with his heart in his throat could see the locomotive from his spot in a rear car. "It looked like a different train," José said, still astonished.

José told of his ocean voyage to Argentina. "Lots of people got sick, but as for me, no.

"When the ship put into port at Morocco, there were near naked men diving for coins and plates at the side of the ship. My brother and I went into town to buy cigarettes and have a look around. The markets were full of black faces. It was terribly crowded. I didn't like it, but it was interesting.

"I was in Buenos Aires for four days. In a special hotel that they had. This wasn't a luxury hotel, eh? It was a special immigrant hotel, and I was not the only one there. I calculate that there must have been three or four thousand there. And there we had a little of everything—all the races, eh? There were French, there were Poles, there were Italians, there were Portuguese, there were Spanish.

"Many people came here at that time. A lot came and then returned over to Europe. Don't believe that all those who came stayed here. Many, many returned. Lots—in that period, no?—stayed five or six years, returned for five or six years there, returned here, and went along like that. It was a matter of coming to see. And in their minds there was always the possibility of going back. Then there were some, like me, who came and stayed indefinitely.

"It wasn't a question of coming without anything. One could leave there and come here with secure work waiting for one, arranged ahead of time. If not that, one could come independently, on one's own account.

"Now, those who came just by their own account went to the Immigration Department in Buenos Aires and asked for work. In those years, it was easy to get. Anyone who wanted to could have work immediately.

"I didn't want government-arranged work. I told them that I already had work by my own account. My brother had arranged everything for me in Gaimán, on the farms settled by the Welsh just south of here. My brother had to do the paperwork for me. He had to demonstrate that he had work and we wouldn't go through a time of need or anything.

"Now, after just four days in Buenos Aires, I came down here. The Argentine government paid my passage from Buenos Aires down to Gaimán. The passage from Buenos Aires to Chubut didn't cost me a thing. The Argentine government paid for it because they wanted immigrants. I came by boat to Madryn. And in those years there was a train from Madryn to Gaimán, so I arrived by train.

"I had work in Gaimán, near my brother, more or less right away. I worked for six years on the farms there, and then I came to an estancia on the Península. Then I worked on an estancia outside the Península for a few years, and then I returned to the Península and I stayed here." He grinned.

"Here on the Península, I was immediately *puestero*. Right away. Me, I never worked as a *peón*, eh? I always worked on my own account, for myself.

"I have worked for Guerrero, here at La Bonita, for forty-one years," José said. "But I always worked for my own account."

José's pride in "working for himself"—in being a *puestero*, a percentage man, rather than a *peón*—reflects the fact that most immigrants, unable to own land and having to work for others who did own land, were not even able to rise to the level of sharecroppers, remaining *peones* their whole lives.

The agricultural ladder, for the vast majority of immigrant men, involved working as a *peón* on an estancia for a period of years and then, if a man was lucky, advancing to tenancy or sharecropper status. A *puestero* is a kind of tenant, a sharecropper who earns a percentage. Tenancy was the highest reachable rung on the agricultural ladder for the vast majority. Enterprising tenants could expand their scales of operation to enhance their incomes, but very few were able to own land, even though that remained the dream of most. In present circumstances, not only has the impossibility of owning land remained a constant, it has become increasingly difficult for *peones* to progress up the ladder, even so far as to become tenants.

Under the best of circumstances, being a tenant or share-cropper is a straightforward way to make a modest, and some-times decent, living. Since the owners furnish all the capital, the tenants can farm with little money. They supply the labor for the farm, receive all the mutton they can eat as well as shelter and sometimes transportation, and can, with the percentage they earn, save some money and, perhaps, buy a house in one of the Patagonian towns. *Peones*, in contrast with tenants, receive full room and board, a pickup, and only a tiny monthly salary.

José was *puestero* for Guerrero, a wealthy Buenos Aires poli-tician who was good to the couple, as *dueños* went. José received 25 percent of the take and, in return, performed all the tasks needed on the ranch. This meant repairing and maintaining the fencing, transferring sheep from one lot of grazeland to another, caring for newborn lambs, checking on the sheep in the rain, castrating and marking lambs once a year, maintaining the truck, grounds, and buildings, directing the shearing, clipping the wool around the sheeps' eyes several times a year, and bar-gaining for and obtaining a good price for the year's wool. For these services, Clara and José received about $200 a month. With their stipend, they had to furnish all their petrol, supple-mentary foods, clothing, heating and lighting fuels, medical care, and anything else they might need. Until just six years before I met them, they had lived in the *peón*'s quarters—two rooms, no plumbing.

"It is a life," Clara stated.

The lantern whirred—the light a bright white fireball—and we all sat quiet. The rising wind gave an occasional howl.

"And so, José, how do you like La Patagonia?" I asked at last. "How does it compare with where you came from?"

José drew deep on his cigarette. His eyes shied down to the table. Then he spoke.

"Just recently, I received the first news that I have had in over fifteen years from one of my six siblings left in Spain.

"This brother of mine now has three hundred animals, cows and sheep and horses," José said, his eyes grave. "And more, he says he now owns a lot of land, all contiguous. I haven't seen it, so I don't know whether it is true or not. When I lived there, it was not possible to own a large piece of land."

The rancher took a drink from his wineglass. "I don't have any animals. I have a tiny farm in Gaimán, but no real campo. I left because I thought it would be impossible to succeed in Spain. Now I don't know whether it was better for me to come here or not."

José had come to Argentina at the tail end of the surge of immigrants from Europe. Like most others in the flood, he had arrived in Argentina half a century too late. The vast tracts of open land advertised by Argentine immigration agents in Europe were not actually available to new immigrants. By the time José and the thousands of other poor immigrants arrived in Argentina, their only options were to settle in the city or to work as sharecroppers or work hands for the earlier-arriving immigrants who had amassed huge tracts of land and hoarded them. José and the other ill-informed young men could not fulfill their dreams of owning land. They may be seen, in sad light, as the immigrants who went to the wrong place.

"Only the people who were already rich got land on the Península. There were laws, in claiming land, that said a man had to work and live on a place for so many years before he could get the title, but many people ignored the laws and lived in the city and ran the land from there. Of those who made claims, and lived there, very few ended up with the land on which they had spilt their sweat. By the time the land finally went up for sale, they didn't have the cash. During my time, there has never been any land auction, or free claim opportunity, that I knew of. A poor man couldn't get land. Our only choice was to be a *peón* or a *puestero* for some other man.

"Now look at my brother. He has everything, under the new government. It could be that I never should have left."

"*Vamos*, let's go to Spain!" piped up Clara.

"*Soy argentino*," José said. "I couldn't go back now. I am Argentine," he said, but his words were threaded with doubt.

José's sense of having two *patrias*, and his unresolved question about whether it was beneficial to emigrate and leave his family behind, seemed to be with him, like a rock hanging from his belt, every day.

When her husband spoke in company, Clara often said, "José is a Spaniard," in order to explain his accent. José's speech, sprinkled with soft, Castilian "th" sounds, contrasted with the harsher, more emphatic Italianate Argentine speech; his speaking attitude, as well, was unusual in its calm and economy. And José himself, fifty-five years a Patagonian, always jabbed at his breastbone when he first met someone. "*Soy español*," he said.

Once, a Swiss friend of mine, visiting José with me, offered him a pack of cigarettes that she had bought on her way through the Madrid airport. José drew in the smoke slowly, savoring it, and twisted the cigarette to get a look at it. He couldn't contain a grin. "Smoke from Spain, eh?" His Castilian heritage seemed both a source of pride and a kind of protection. The loss of Spain, of his mother and his siblings, was as indelible in José's mind as the eye-straining campo had become.

When I asked whether he heard from his family in Spain, José said, "No, no. I never write to my family. No, no. And I almost never see my brother in Gaimán. I am not one for much family," he said, cautioning with his finger.

Clara took over. "You asked why José came to Argentina. . . . It was me! He came for me!"

At our urging, Clara told the story of how she and José had met. "We met in the hospital in Madryn, when Elena was receiving treatments for her burns."

Clara's niece had been badly burned on her torso and arms when, as a child of four, she'd climbed into the cab of her father's truck, where there was a heater on the floor. Her father was at the back of the truck, loading the bed, when Elena's dress caught fire. The spirited little girl spent months in the hospital, first in Madryn and later in Buenos Aires. Clara sat at Elena's bedside during most of her recuperation. The whole Península had rallied around the little girl, and José, at the time a bachelor *puestero* at La Bonita, was one of Elena's most frequent visitors.

José was already forty-one, and Clara ten years younger, when they married. For their honeymoon, the couple went to Bariloche for the one extravagance of their lives. Bariloche is a pristine ski resort settled by Germans and Swiss that has all the features of an Alpine village, with charming chalets, specialty chocolates, and snow-blanketed mountains. The couple from Península Valdés stayed in one of the chaletlike hotels. There, one evening, Clara said, she saw the guests dancing. Every night thereafter, she went down and peered into the hall.

"I would have danced," she said. "As for me, yes! But José didn't want to. He wouldn't come down with me."

José told us that one time he and Clara were returning to the campo at three A.M. and Clara saw a house with a dance in progress. She made him stop the car. They turned out the lights of the car and watched the people waltzing.

"The whole house shook, the doors trembled, and dust was flying," José said, and then pointed to Clara. "And this one wanted to see all that in the middle of the night." He laughed across to his wife, and their eyes met.

At last José rose, gestured to Peter, and took him outside, patting him on the back as they went. "Come on, young one. Let me see about sharpening that dull knife of yours."

As they went out Clara leaned close to me and said, "Look! We two talk and they two talk."

When I went to fetch the cheese from the pantry, Clara's sanctuary, she followed and whispered to me among the plates and tinned jam that José's stomach pained him. Her hands clutched at her apron as she said it.

One winter day a few months before, when we were in town searching for a store called La Zanahoria Feliz, the "Happy Carrot," we pulled up beside Clara sitting in the red Chevy truck in front of a small red-brick medical clinic. She sat in the middle of the bench seat, diminutive and ladylike, twisting her hand-kerchief. José had an appointment with the doctor and had re-fused to let her accompany him.

She kept saying, "I keep telling him to stop smoking. It's bad. It's bad for his health. It's ugly."

Three hours later, the back of the truck now filled with veg-etables and gas canisters, we drove by the same spot. Clara was still sitting in the middle of the seat, her concerned, bright eyes following the passersby on the sidewalk.

Worry had flicked through my mind at the time, but I dis-missed it. I couldn't believe someone I loved would ever have a serious illness.

"The first thing is health," Clara said.

I nodded. "I'm sure the doctor will take care of José," I said.

Back at the table, nibbling cheese, Clara and I discussed the flavors of ice cream we liked best. She liked them all—chocolate, vanilla, lemon. When they were in town last time, she'd said to José as they were driving along, " 'José, I'm in the mood for ice cream.' He stopped and got me two little cones.

"But I had eaten them up by the time we got to the next rise. He had to get me another kilo at the grocery store!"

Chocolates, like cheese, were Clara's bane. She and I, we had discovered, could talk about our common weakness for hours. "In town, I bought a box of special chocolates from Bariloche for my sister for her birthday. When we got back, I put them in the pantry, to save them until I saw her. Well, I couldn't stand it. So I had one. I ate it. Later in the morning, I thought it wouldn't hurt to have another, so I ate a few more. By noon, only half the chocolates were left. I thought, Well, that's a good amount to give her. But in the afternoon, I decided that since there were only half left, I would have to change boxes anyway, so I had a couple more. Finally, when there was only one left, I thought, Oh, it's not polite to give just one piece. I ate it. I am a danger. I'm warning you!" She pointed to her chest and cocked her head merrily.

Just before Peter and I left that day, Clara put her arm around me and took me into the pantry. There, on the wall, was a red-

and-gold religious calendar—the only hanging in the house—and beside the calendar a can of condensed milk. She took it off the shelf and handed it to me.

She told to me how to make *dulce de leche*, using gestures to explain. "Just take the label off and put the can in a pot of boiling water. Boil it for either two or three hours, depending on how dark you like it. Follow your taste. Then just take it out of the water, open the can, and *listo!*"

Well fed with *dulce de leche* and news, replete in all respects, Peter and I made our good-byes to José and Clara and drove home across the juiceless, prickled campo.

With time in the campo, boredom, lack of stimulation, and the monotony of the land eroded my sense of perspective. I felt as though I were slipping, adrift, losing track. Patagonia seemed an unyielding place, a motherland with a scrawny breast, a harborless ocean. Instead of endowing me with a sense of self-sufficiency, Patagonia had taught me the desperation of isolation.

Finally, after eighteen months, at the conclusion of the second whale season when the last mother-calf pair had migrated toward the Antarctic, it was time for us to go.

Just before we left, we visited Clara and José one last time. Clara gave me one of those tea-straining spoons: "*Un regalo,*" she said. "A gift."

That day all four of us, Clara, José, Peter, and I, went outside into the dirt yard where the two spindly lilac bushes stood and took photos. Peter set the camera on the truck and had to run back to get in the picture. None of us said much. José looked down as we climbed into the truck and didn't say good-bye.

I left Patagonia, stripped, unsure of how to live. I knew my answer, my culture's creed of self-reliance, was somehow insufficient, but I still clung to it. I continued to hang on to the notion that one could attain an ultimate independence, and I departed that barren country certain that I had failed to attain the North American ideal. I had a sense that I was in the wrong church, but I didn't know of any other.

On the other hand, I had never felt so understood or so calmed as I had with two people in that desolate, gray, wind-parched land. Clara and José had a deep strength, one I didn't understand.

Back in the United States, Patagonia was in my belly. From time to time I went to the bowl of stones I had collected from the beach in front of camp and fingered them, piled them up, as I looked out the window. I took tea religiously, every day at four.

Five years later I returned to Patagonia. I went back to the Península in the guise of a doctoral student, ostensibly to trace the history of the Patagonians and to find out how a Patagonian survived in a milkless land. Finding answers to this question seemed crucial to my ability to live with myself.

For the years following my first exposure to Patagonia, I had known I would have to live there another time. I had to see Clara and José again, and I sensed that that ill-fitting land possessed something my own culture couldn't give me.

Patagonia is an odd place to go for cradling.

RETURN TO THE CAMPO

In December 1979, when we left Patagonia, we stopped briefly in Buenos Aires. In the capital, as on the Península, no one even mentioned the *desaparecidos* ("missing persons"), and it was only when we got to the transit lounge at Kennedy Airport and bought a magazine that we glimpsed the atrocities that had been going on in Argentina all through the time we were there.

In 1984, when we returned to Argentina, the Malvinas war had recently come to its humiliating conclusion, the dirty war had been exposed, and Alfonsín, the first democratically elected leader in over fifteen years, had been installed in the Casa Rosada. It was as though we had returned to a totally different country from that in which we had lived five years before. In place of the grim shoppers in long dark woolen coats that we had encountered on the Buenos Aires streets in the late seventies, there were street musicians, long-haired college students, and kiosks crammed with magazines sporting glossy covers that shouted the joys of *libertad*. The country was as jubilant about democracy as it had been those few years before, when, under the pall of terrorism, it had won the World Cup.

When I left New Hampshire in August, the overripe blackberries, plump and dripping, were slopping from the bushes in my mother-in-law's yard. Five days later, when I joined Peter in Patagonia, the spikes of the thornbushes had been so brittled and sharpened by the winter cold that walking in the campo was like receiving a series of injections in one's calves and feet.

The Patagonians with whom I spoke during my first few days back had the same response to the happenings in Buenos Aires that they had had during our previous visit. To the people of the Península, the capital seems a vague, faraway world. Protected from disaster by a ready source of mutton and by assured housing, the sheep ranchers felt the political and economic fluctuations in Buenos Aires in only the dimmest sense.

"I don't understand what is going on in Buenos Aires," Península dwellers would say. "Those *porteños* are all crazy."

"I just want to be left alone to live. I want life to be *tranquila*."

We went to see Clara and José immediately on my return to the Península. We got ourselves settled into the newly built Quonset hut at the Whale Camp, and then we raced to La Bonita.

When Clara met us at the gate she was so surprised and delighted that she almost tripped as she led us back into the house. Moments later José greeted me with a warm kiss on both cheeks. I was so happy I couldn't stop looking at him.

His gray eyes held the same gentleness, but his large, lumpy nose was even grander than I remembered. He looked elegant. He had put on a little girth, so that he seemed more robust than before.

I told José it made me very happy to see him again.

"It makes me happy, too," he said. His eyes were even and smiling, and in spite of my tendency toward self-deprecation, I believed he was actually glad to see this skinny, outspoken, foreign woman.

"We have fresh meat," he said, "so you young ones have to stay for an asado!"

Clara had made a flan and carried it, her arthritic hands shaking, across the campo to the asado room. She said over and over that the flan wasn't cool enough and put it in a basin of water drawn from the tap outside.

In the bare room we ate a quarter of a sheep, lettuce from the neighbors' luxuriant garden—the *peón* there had brought it over—and Clara's lovely flan.

While eating, we talked about traveling. Clara said, a twinkle in her eye, that she had been planning to visit us while we were in Norteamérica. "But this one," she said, pointing to José, "wouldn't go with me."

Then she said, "This time, when you go back, I am going to visit you for sure."

"We'll meet you at the airport in Boston," Peter told her, "on February twenty-fifth."

"*Bueno*, I'll be there. You had better be there because I will be getting off the airplane. At Boston airport!" Clara giggled with delight at the unlikely prospect.

José then quipped, "People always want to travel. Some go to Spain. Some go to France. Some to Germany. Me, I could go to the Rural, the big cattle fair in Buenos Aires, and see bulls from Spain, Germany, and France. What need have I to travel?"

Later, back at the house, where Clara served us after-dinner tea, we talked about the news. Cachorro, José's *peón*, sat with the four of us.

In a few weeks there was to be a vote about a referendum to divide the islands of Tierra del Fuego between Argentina and Chile. The referendum was on everyone's lips. This vote was the Argentines' first real test of the democratic regime and their first taste of voting and democracy in years.

When José began to speak, I settled with my feet curled under me, comfortable and purring like a cat. Political talk was the meat of my family's dinner table.

Clara didn't want to vote, so she joked, "I'm a *chilena*. I don't have to vote."

"Look," José said, "as I see it, a vote for *sí* is to lose land, but a vote for no is a vote for war. This is a problem from the past. In this case, the *chilenos* are in the right. They have been living on the islands for years. Besides, war never solves anything. If we go to war, and even if we win, they will still want the islands, and when the time comes they will grab."

Clara said, "There are *chilenos* next door. We are compatriots."

Peter said to her, half-teasing, "It's democracy now. You have to vote."

Clara didn't see the sense of it. The politicos would do what they wanted anyway. "I'm *chilena*," she went on with the joke, "so I don't have to vote. Besides, the radio says it's not obligatory to vote, so I don't have to vote. With the *militares*, we all voted because it was obligatory. Now it's democracy, so I don't have to vote!"

"I'll take Cachorro to vote in Pirámides," José said. He continued, "In the Malvinas war, three people, the generals, told the people we had to go to war. This time it's the people telling the president we don't want war. Who knows if a time will come again when there are three people who want to send the people to war. This vote is really a test to see if the government will listen to the people."

Then he reiterated, "As I see it, the vote has to be *sí*, or there will be war."

"*Ojalá*, José. . . ." Cachorro's voice rose from his chair off to the side of the room. He intended to vote "no."

"And as for this Alfonsín," Cachorro went on, "it seems to me you either have freedom of speech and no money or a dictator and money."

I commented that at least Argentina was a good place to grow old because of the universal retirement system.

"*Mira*, look, Sara," José said. His gentle, explaining tone made me feel like his granddaughter. "It is not so simple. The other day in town, I met a retired postal employee and he told me his income as a retired person. It shocked me. It was only eighty-five hundred pesos a month. This man said he could only afford meat twice a week. They didn't have money to repair their house. And worse, he couldn't afford to visit his new grandchild in Mar del Plata. That is a shame."

The talk wandered on to the weather and sheep—José allowed that it had been a pretty good year so far, and the lambs were fat—and then Clara asked us about our families.

I asked José what he had heard from his family in Spain.

He said, "I found out from my nephews in Gaimán that two of my brothers are dead. There were seven of us. Now we are just five brothers and sisters." There was sadness in his voice.

Clara piped up, "José would go to Spain if his parents were still alive. We even go to see his brother in Gaimán now, sometimes."

"Speaking of brothers," José said. "My brother in Gaimán had a picture of one of my brothers in Spain. When I saw it, I thought it was me!"

José had seemed to dismiss the importance of family bonds when I had spoken with him five years before. I heard a new thread of pleasure running through his comments about his family now.

"Two of my nephews in Gaimán," he said, "married Welsh women—"

"I'm a Welshman, you know," Peter interrupted.

José continued, "One married an Owens and the other an Evans."

Peter joked, "Well, that means you're one of my relatives, José! Owen is my middle name, and Evans is my brother's middle name."

"That makes us cousins," José concluded, laughing. His nose turned redder than ever as he laughed, and he poked Peter.

Thinking of the discussions we'd had in years past about the relative benefits of being Argentine or Spanish, I asked José if he felt like a Patagonian now and whether he thought there was a Patagonian identity.

He said, "Cachorro and I argue about this a lot. He can have his opinions. He thinks he is more of a Patagonian than I because he was born in Pirámides. As I see it, I am as Patagonian as most, even though I wasn't raised here. No one in La Patagonia is of pure blood. Everyone comes from outside. All the governors come from outside. The mayor of Madryn has only lived here about twelve years.

"It doesn't seem to me that there is a strong Patagonian identity. If there were, they wouldn't be trying to create it—with advertisements on the radio to get people to come settle, to bring in industries. *'Poblar La Patagonia,'* they keep saying, but very few come, eh? These *porteños,* sitting in these confiterías talking all day, they think coming here would be like going to prison."

I asked the old rancher whether he was glad he had emigrated to Patagonia, to the campo.

"Really, I am not displeased by this place," he said, "because I am very happy. I think that if I had stayed in Spain, I would not have lived as I have lived here. I don't know how this can be represented, but I don't think so."

José seemed to be at peace with himself. He had renewed contact with his family and seemed to take pleasure in visiting them. And he had proclaimed his identity as a Patagonian. Clara was the same frisky, playful person she had always been.

As we were leaving, José told me that he had decided I was the same, only a little thinner. He told us to come back as often as we could.

Spurred by the knowledge that returning to see Clara and José had been the right thing to do, I put myself to the task of trying to discover the Patagonians' secret.

DIGGING

~~~~~~~~~~

Early in my second stay in Patagonia, I watched an armadillo consume a seawater-logged cormorant, pink sinew by pink sinew. The prehistoric beast then dug straight down into the earth. Dirt flew, and in an instant the animal was gone. At the time I didn't know that I was witnessing something key to survival in Patagonia—the story of the settling of Patagonia has much to do with digging.

In the beginning there was the wind. For aeons the notorious gusting force stampeded, unhindered, down the 1,600-kilometer north-south monotony of Patagonia, South America's southern cone, and shrieked and swirled around the salty wastes of Península Valdés, one of the continent's initiatives into the South Atlantic. During this long period before written history, the wind did not chill the cheek of a single human being. Dun-colored mammals and white birds were the only living creatures that held sovereignty over the dry and open terrain. Maras—the odd Patagonian rodents that look like a cross between a dog and a rabbit—foxes, hares, weasels, wild cats, and armadillos scurried between Patagonia's scrub bushes and slipped into holes in the

ground to escape her punishing blasts. For thousands of years
Patagonia was alone with herself, Península Valdés a vacant,
prickled hump sticking out into the sea.

Much later the Tehuelche—Indian hunters of the Darwin's
rhea, the three-toed ostrich, and the swift, wild, llamalike guanaco—and other tribal bands ventured into the open scrubland,
and Patagonia's wind, for the first time, stung the eyes of Homo
sapiens. The Tehuelche regularly migrated from the main body
of the continent out onto Península Valdés to hunt guanaco, as
arrowhead middens in the dune areas even now reveal. With
the Tehuelche began a tenuous association between human beings and the gray, lonely outreach of Península Valdés.

In 1774 a small group of Spanish friars, led by Juan de la
Piedra, settled on the shore of Golfo San José, the northern bay
of Península Valdés, not far from the dunes where the Indians
camped. There, for thirty years, the men lived miserable lives.
They were beaten by the wind, suffered shortages of both food
and water, and endured a killing loneliness until August 8, 1810,
when they received a strange mercy. That day, while the friars
were in church, Indians massacred all but one man. The wind
danced over and disintegrated the gaunt dead bodies and thrashed
the lone survivor, who fled to Viedma on foot to tell the tale.

Thereafter, for a time, few Europeans ventured onto the the
Península. Winds from off the Península, though, blew into the
faces of a few souls clinging to railings of explorers' ships as
they gazed toward the land from the frigid seas and wondered
at the sight of the Península's tawny wastes.

Finally, in 1852, Justo José de Urquiza, revolutionary president of Argentina, looked outward from the capital toward the
vast, unexploited lands to the south and put into practice the
philosophy of liberal thinker Juan Bautista Alberdi: *"Gobernar Es
Poblar."* "To govern is to populate." Following this dictum, he
set into motion a program for peopling the vacant hinterlands
of his country.

An Immigration Bureau established in the capital sent agents
to various parts of Europe to recruit settlers, and in 1862 the
Congress authorized the contracting of groups of immigrants for

colonization ventures in the national territories—regions outside the provinces ruled from Buenos Aires. The southern territories included what were to become the Patagonian provinces of Neuquén, Río Negro, Chubut, Santa Cruz, and Tierra del Fuego. The 1862 law promoted colonization by offering contracts to immigrant families in which each family would be granted 104 acres free after two years of occupancy.

Drawn to Argentina by the 1862 legislation, 153 Welsh colonists disembarked from their ship, the *Mimosa*, on the western edge of Golfo Nuevo, the southern gulf of Península Valdés, at the site of present-day Puerto Madryn and made the first permanent European settlement in the territory of Chubut. Each of the original colonists received 62 acres on arrival and, in 1875, were given 247 additional acres free, as well as the right to purchase 741 acres more at two pesos per acre.

These devout and rigorous people, determined to found a New Wales at whatever sacrifice, pushed doggedly against the wind and planted and irrigated a section of the desert one hundred kilometers south of Península Valdés into an oasis of fruit orchards and vegetables that thrived for several decades.

The "Colonia Galesa" opened northern Patagonia to European settlers, and today the northwest gales that cascade down from the Andean peaks onto Patagonia's flanks are called *Viento del 28*—"Wind of the 28th"—for it was on July 28, 1865, that the Welsh pioneers put ashore.

Between 1868 and 1876, under various laws, colonization companies bought huge chunks of land in Patagonia, but often they did not subdivide them, as they were supposed to do. In a short time eighty-eight men came to hold over 5 million acres, an average of 147,325 acres per landowner.

In 1879, General Julio A. Roca led a military expedition to Patagonia, and in one murderous drive he and his men expelled and exterminated the resident Araucanians and Tehuelches. The "Conquest of the Desert" was heralded in Buenos Aires as a grand feat. In practical terms it cleared away the last obstacle to the establishment of estancias on the wild, open campo.

Shortly thereafter, in 1885, 541 of the officers and soldiers who had participated in the Conquest of the Desert were awarded over 11 million acres of land in the southern territories. Each person received 20,908 acres, and many of the soldiers bought additional land, at the low price of twenty centavos per hectare, and amassed giant hunks of the desolate campo. Few of them took up residence, however. Despite this initiative on the part of the Buenos Aires government to encourage the settlement of Patagonia, the flat, thornbush-dotted campo remained virtually uninhabited.

An 1884 colonization law authorized the award of 625 hectares (1,544.37 acres) to settlers who had two hundred pesos in their possession and did not own land elsewhere. Under this legislation, the settlers would receive title to the land in two years by paying five hundred pesos. The first settlements in Patagonia, excluding the Welsh colony but including several outposts in Chubut, were founded under this law. Between 1892 and 1898 more pieces of the southern territories were offered for colonization, the last of the large grants.

Around the turn of this century, in response to the colonization laws, handfuls of Europeans, either fresh from Spain and France or from settlements like Patagones and Viedma to the north, picked their way south on horseback to settle and dig wells in the beyonds of inhospitable Patagonia. They obtained land by hook or by crook, buying it blind at an auction, making claims to land for later purchase under constantly changing homesteading laws, or simply squatting. Some of these valiant families, Basques in particular, began to sprinkle themselves and their flocks and herds around the salt plain of Península Valdés.

In the year 1882, a man named Gumersindo Paz left Viedma, a fort and farming town of about 1,500 Basques and other Europeans at the northern limit of Patagonia. Paz, a cigar-smoking Basque with black hair, a thick beard, and heavy brows, traveled alone on horseback southward down the dusty sweep of Patagonia, to explore the infinity of open country and perhaps claim a piece of it for his family. Recent legislation in Buenos Aires encouraged homesteading in the southern territories; a man could claim a couple of thousand acres of *tierra fiscal*—government land—and, if he worked it and resided on it, he could buy it after a set number of years.

As Paz rode, an atom in a vast no-man's-land, the only sounds he heard were the raucous whinnies of the male guanacos, the merciless whining of the wind, and the litany in his head, "Where will I next find water? Should I turn back now? Am I crazy?" Every day the heavyset rider passed deeper into the oblivion of monotonous desert. Gray scrub trampled out, flat, in every direction—there was not a dwelling or a human soul. As he went, this hulk of a man hugged himself against the wind and rolled cigars and smoked them.

About five hundred kilometers south of Viedma, Paz's horse swerved east, left the north-south continental mass, and stepped along a seven-kilometer-wide isthmus onto Península Valdés. As he wandered, clutched by a fear of vanishing into oblivion, every few kilometers Paz wrote his name on a cigar paper and dropped it. If he died, anyone who came after him would know he had been there.

Paz and his family became the first non-Indian settlers of Península Valdés. On his exploration Paz had liked the look of the dunes on the southern edge of the hatchet-shaped peninsula. Two years later he returned with his family to the barren headland, bringing with him thirty-six mares and some cows and sheep, and settled near Salina Grande, a great salt pan. The family slept in a lean-to made of *chapa*—a kind of corrugated sheet metal—and collected their water from one of the only springs on the 97-by-63 kilometer peninsula.

Over the next forty years the track Paz and his family blazed, from Puerto Madryn to the Península, was beaten hard as other settlers, following the family's example, drove their herds out onto the barren reach of land.

In 1889 Carlitos Zabaleta left Azqueta in the Spanish Basque province of Navarra and walked north toward the sea. The tiny village where he had spent his boyhood was a jumble of white-washed children's blocks on the dome of a hill in a vast rolling terrain of neatly planted fields. At the doorstep of one of the square, three-story houses, the young teacher kissed his wife and his many children and assured them that he would send for them. Then he set off for Argentina.

As he walked down the track through soft, rolling fields of wheat, oats, maize, and beans, every seven or fifteen kilometers he came to a cluster of houses similar to that of his home village. The world in which he strode was a wide quilted land with a wheat-colored background appliquéd with green fields and salted with the pinks and purples and yellows of the native weeds. Heather pink herbs laced the intermittent white-splotched stone walls, and, not far from home, he picked a pear from the orchard behind the monastery wall. It was hot and humid; there were drops of rain; a cuckoo sounded.

At the end of his sea passage, Carlitos quickly acquired a post as a teacher in Mar del Plata, a sea coast town south of Buenos Aires. As soon as he was settled in his lodgings, he sent for his wife and children in Navarra.

After teaching school in Mar del Plata for eight years, hoping to further improve his and his family's lot, Carlitos took a job managing a sheep estancia to the south, in Patagonia. He took the post without ever having laid eyes on the Patagonian campo, having no notion of the contrast between that parched, isolated terrain and the bonny fields of Azqueta. Like many immigrants, he took the job in Patagonia hoping, eventually, to buy land of his own—all this while lacking even a day of experience with sheep ranch work.

By the year 1914 the Navarran teacher's dreams came true. At year's end he had three thousand animals of his own, and he had bought an estancia near a roadside tavern at Puerto Lobos, just eighty-six kilometers north of Península Valdés. On the rough spread of unfenced hinterland, Carlitos and his wife raised a flock of children who, like the family's sheep and goats, grew fat and made a home of the parched, wind-flogged Patagonian sheeplands.

~~~

Félix Irazazabal and his family cooked, ate, and pulled up their blankets in a seaside cave at the foot of a four-hundred-foot cliff when they first arrived at the Península from Tandil. The year was 1897, and the family had brought with them eight hundred sheep.

While the boys in their woolen knee pants and the girls with floppy bows on their heads played on the beach, Félix scouted for land, using the cave as his base. His heart swelled when he came to the dunes overlooking Golfo Nuevo, the southern gulf of the Península, and it was there that he decided to settle his family. It was on that overlook that he might have sensed not only the beauty, but the power of the dune.

From the Golfo Nuevo sands, Félix spun his visions into reality. He ignored the raw wind that tore at his clothes; he just squinted into the grit storms and went about his business. He drove the cold and the daily hardship and the bleakness from his mind, and he took on the dune. A man of ambition, a workhorse, and a lover of trees, Félix planted apple and peach orchards, vineyards with numerous varieties of grapes, and olive groves. But he did not stop there. He transformed four whole hectares of the sloping, sandy ground into a garden so luxuriant that everyone still marvels over it.

Rafael, a man raised by one of Félix's sons, told about the garden. "But this garden was stupendous! The land had slope, so this man leveled it with crates. He shoveled dirt into these crates, fastened the crates to horses, and the horses pulled them to where he needed them in the garden. In that fashion, he totally evened out the loose, sandy land. All with crates, and pulled by horses. We're talking about four whole hectares of land, and every bit of it worked. Everything well done. A well-ordered garden. A beauty."

Perhaps part of the reason that Félix could transform a dune into an arboretum was that he possessed magical powers.

"This man, Irazazabal," Rafael one day whispered in a reverential tone, "he has a special sensitivity. He can find water with a divining rod. People say that if there are water currents, as we call them, passing under Félix's bedroom, he can tell. He senses them in his body. They don't do much bother, but he can tell they are there.

"Now I have seen him make studies of the land and say, 'Here's water at, more or less, this many meters.' And, sure enough."

Over the following years. Félix amassed more than fifteen leagues of land—enough to establish sheep stations for each of his eight children—and he eventually owned twenty thousand sheep, spread over various properties on the Península. Windmills spun and wells went into his grounds and wire fences crisscrossed his acreages. Félix planted pines and eucalyptus all along the kilometers-long entry roads to some of his sheep stations. He called the main estancia Bella Vista—"Beautiful View."

The enterprising young rancher crowned his accomplishments with a beautiful "mansion." The house, constructed of *chapa* and fresh-painted white, had a gingerbread courtyard and gingerbread trimmings on all its eaves. Slowly but surely, over the years, the sands that Félix loved and claimed when he first laid eyes on the Península built up against the walls of the Irazazabal mansion. They leaned and sloped against the sweetly framed windows.

In the end, Félix's mansion was covered by the dune.

When in 1908 Angel Irabi turned his back on Berastegui, his boyhood home in the Basque country, and set out for someplace across the ocean called Argentina, he checked that his *boina*, his floppy Basque-style beret, was properly on his crown. Then he loped down the slope toward the village plaza to join the clutch of other boys and men, among them one of his brothers, who were also leaving.

Scattered below Angel as he walked were the monolithic stone *caseríos*, the barn houses of the village families, and the ancient church that rose in a giant rock outcrop, like the Lord Himself, above everything. The village dwellings were like lumps of oatmeal cookie dough dropped in the bottom of a bowl, with the sides of the bowl formed by mountains. Bright green daisy-littered hay fields and stands of corn and wheat rose up the lower sections of the slopes. There were fern tangles farther up where Angel and his brothers collected vegetation for cow beds. At the top ridge of the circle of mountains, there were stands of maples, oaks, and chestnuts good for making heavy, carved furniture, and on the common land meadows of the uppermost slopes, there were sheep and cows.

As Angel descended toward the center of the hamlet, he crossed clover fields and plodded along the edges of meticulous vegetable gardens. Behind him on the hill was the house in which he had lived for all of his fourteen years. It was one of the humbler *caseríos* in the village but built like the others: a stone structure with six or eight cows, some pigs, goats, and chickens kept in a manger in the lowest level, a hayloft in the peak of the house, and low-ceilinged living quarters sandwiched between. In all the *caseríos* it was as though the people were living in the barns, rather than the cows living in the bottom of a building dominated by humans.

Angel's home was nestled right into the hillside at the edge of Berastegui. In the manger of that dwelling, Angel's mother had cooked the family meals over an open fire on the floor. There, gathered around the iron pot, Angel and his numerous brothers and sisters had taken their daily three meals: corn tortillas or chestnuts and a glass of milk for breakfast and lunch, and spoonfuls of stewed beans from the communal pot for dinner.

One of Angel's nephews, who remained in the village, said, "Berastegui in those years was a place where if the hen laid an egg the family dispatched a child to run it to the market, to sell the egg for some bread. Then they waited for another egg."

In young Angel's family, the children had no underwear. They held up their pants with hanks of rope, and when Sunday came, because the family owned only one pair of rope-soled alpargatas, the boys took part in a relay race. One boy would race down the hill, with the shoes in his hands so as not to wear them out, put the cloth shoes on his dusty feet when he got to the cold stone foyer of the church, and enter to pray. Afterward he would race back up the hill and hand the alpargatas to the next brother in line. It was as though the brothers were passing the torch.

In every *caserío*, even the immense, wealthier-looking ones closer to the church, the younger boys were leaving Berastegui. There was not enough to eat; there were too many children. The oldest sons received the *caserío* and the land and paid a sum to their brothers to help them make their way elsewhere.

Mothers wept as their slender-hipped sons crossed the valley and disappeared down the mountain path toward the sea.

Angel was no different from the other boys who were leaving. When he joined his brother and the others going to Argentina, he had butterflies in his belly, but his confidence was bolstered by the news sent back from an older brother from a place called Península Valdés. Apparently Alfredo had come to own a huge portion of land. He even had another family, also Basques, working for him. He owned a concession to a sealing business and was making a fortune from oil and skins. He was a big man, an *hombre*. To Angel, that sounded all right.

"You know how it is. When you're young you want to try something new. My father heard there was open land, so he decided to come here," said Angel's Patagonian-bred son, a boy given his father's name, in explaining his father's motives for leaving the Basque Provinces.

The group from Berastegui disembarked from their ship in Buenos Aires and stayed there long enough to buy land at an auction. Angel grabbed a parcel in the interior of Península Valdés about thirty kilometers from that of his older brother. To that unseen spot he proceeded, and there, in the unprotecting scrub, he went about breaking in his land. Needing water, he dug a well; he built corrals for his animals and ultimately fenced his property.

During the first years on the Península, Angel, like many newcomers, populated his thorny lands with cows. It seems that the campo was much greener when the settlers first came. Angel had fifty cows and got seven liters of milk a day. With time the rains dried up, Angel junior reported. "Where we used to get three hundred millimeters, now we get only seventy."

After a couple of disastrous years, Angel the settler learned that the Península grasses were not sufficiently nutritious nor the rainfall reliable enough to support cattle, and he decided to replace the cattle with hardy merino sheep. So, in 1928, he, along with twenty other settlers and accompanying cooks and crew, drove thousands of sheep south from Tandil, a town just 360 kilometers south of Buenos Aires. As a first step, they drove the animals east from Tandil, 230 kilometers to the coastal town of San Antonio. There they loaded the animals onto a train that carried them the 1,250 kilometers to Puerto Madryn. In Madryn the horsemen met the sheep again and drove them onto the Península. Angel made the same trip twice more while the sheep already on his lands grew plump bellies and heavy fleeces.

"In those times, everyone on the Península was a foreigner," the younger Angel said. "There were Italians and Spaniards and Germans and an Englishman, and there were lots of Basques.

"Papá met my mamá—she was a Spanish Basque, too—and they were married in the church in Pirámides." Pirámides, now a tiny beachside village of seventy on Golfo Nuevo, was then a small but bustling port out of whose cold waters wool transport ships headed toward Buenos Aires.

Angel lived in a hole in the ground covered with two pieces of sheet metal awning until he had finished building, for his wife, a strong three-room house of mud blocks that he made from his own ground.

The couple was fertile, and they produced six children: five daughters and the son named for his father.

The children thrived on the Península until the son was just five years out of his mother's womb. Then, one day during young Angel's fifth year, his mother went berserk.

As the tale goes, and the seventy-one-year-old son repeats it again and again to anyone who listens, young Angel and his sisters and parents had stopped at home between two long wagon trips to change the horses. All the children save Angel had climbed down from the wagon, and their mother, who hadn't much experience with horses, took the blinders off the horse. At that point the animal started—seeing young Angel behind him

on the wagon bed—and lunged off. He ran away with the beloved boy. The woman was knocked to the ground by one of
the wagon wheels. As she fell she shrieked, "My son! My son!"

The children's mother then collapsed and did not speak a
clear word again for over twenty years.

"No one knows what happened except she herself," says the
son.

Within days of his wife's fall, the senior Angel left a caretaker
to look after the estancia and transported his children and dis-
traught young wife north to Tandil, where he had relatives. For
years he traveled from doctor to doctor in search of a cure for
his wife, but none was ever found. From the moment of her
fall, Angel's wife was a tree twisted beyond recognition.

In 1925, after a boyhood spent on a fruit farm in Viedma, Clara
Olazar's father, Sebastián, a burly Basque from the French side,
followed in the hoofprints of his uncle's horse. Like Gumersindo
Paz he rode south, where he settled a piece of campo next to
that of Angel Irabi. Beside him rode his new Parisian wife. The
couple lived with a cousin while they built a house, and children
came.

Clara, one of those children, said, "My father was tall and
blond with clear eyes and white skin. He was best called fat.
Mama had black hair and white skin. She was tall, beautiful,
elegant.

"My mother," she further explained, "had to adapt to life
here, because she was from Paris and Buenos Aires." Sofía, Clara's mother, was a small girl, still holding her mother's hand,
when she, her mother, and her maternal grandmother emigrated
to Argentina. The three-generation trio of long-skirted females
left Paris and voyaged down the North Atlantic across the equa-
tor and into the South Atlantic in order to make a fortune.

Another of Sofía and Sebastián's daughters said, "They were
already well off, but everyone in France at that time was talking
about how Argentina was a gold mine. *Una mina de oro!* They
did well in Buenos Aires, and put the money in a French bank.

Then, when the 1900 crash came, the bank shut down, and they lost it all."

With her, into the desert, on packhorses and wagons, elegant Sofía brought memories from France: deep, hefty silver spoons with shovellike bowls and squared-off heavy knives came in one trunk, along with fruit plates, dessert forks, soup tureens, and serving platters large enough to feed forty. Into another package, Sofía tucked a couple of dolls, both from her girlhood in France. One was a tiny doll that Clara recently handed down to her niece, Elena; another, a doll standing about two and a half feet high, a plaything Clara had coveted from her sister for all of her sixty-five years, had real human hair.

There had been a long and amicable association between the Irabis and the Olazars, since they held adjacent campos, and finally the knot was tied. One year the youngest Olazar daughter, Teresa, and the only Irabi son, Angel, who were exactly the same age, took charge as newlyweds of the wind-shattered Irabi estancia.

Clara, the second of Sofía's three daughters, and her husband, José, have lived on an estancia twenty kilometers from that settled by Sofía and Sebastián, and ten kilometers from that of Teresa and Angel, for forty years. There, in the tiny house set in a rough and vast emptiness, the childless woman drinks tea from her mother's teacups.

Margarita and Antonio Lasarte, from the Basque Provinces via Buenos Aires, claimed Península Valdés lots 71 and 51 in 1900. They just kept driving their sheep farther out onto the Península until they reached a spot that had not yet been claimed: two leagues of land near Punta Delgada. The couple traveled by horse, and with them they brought two tiny daughters; three more daughters were born rapid-fire on the Península in 1901, 1902, and 1903.

The land on which the Lasartes built their house was only a few kilometers from the sea, and all through their days the little girls could hear sea lions bawling, whales roaring and crashing their flippers on the waves, and magellanic penguins braying like jackasses. The wind shrieked, too, as though to drown out the competing mammalian sounds.

Margarita's granddaughter, Liliana, a cheery gray-haired woman in her fifties who wears hand-sewn floral-print dresses, told stories about her grandmother's life. "At my family's estancia, La Margarita, which my brother now looks after, where my mother and then all of us were born and raised, there is a big photo of my grandmother at her wedding. She wore a black dress. I have always thought that so strange—a black dress for your wedding!

"My grandmother gave birth to my mother and her sisters totally alone. She, alone in the house, was the midwife! She didn't have a single comfort. Nothing.

"My grandmother had five girls. She never had one boy, so these girls had to go out on horses and look after the sheep. They did all the herding between the sisters, my mother included. My mother always said that it was very tiring work because in those years there were no fences and they had to get up with the sheep at night. During the day they herded the sheep into one part of the land, and the next day to another. At dusk they brought them back near the house. At night, though, while the sisters were sleeping, the wind often changed, and the girls had to get up and follow the sheep bells to round up the sheep again, because the animals always go into the wind. If you don't go after them, without fences, they just go and go. It's not like that now. With fences, it's much easier.

"In those times there weren't windmills or pumps, either. They had to dig wells and use *tinas*, as they call them. These *tinas* were barrels that they cut in half. They attached handles to them, and horses drew the water to the livestock. That was the only way to get water."

The other sisters sold their shares of La Margarita to Liliana's mother, so she and her husband took over the stewardship of the land settled by Margarita and Antonio. Liliana's father was a Basque who left home at sixteen and, once on the Península, never saw his mother or any other member of his family again.

The next generation, nine children including Liliana, was born in the house in which their mother was born, and the grand-mother who had given birth to the mother without any assis-tance stood by at her grandchildren's births.

Like their mother before them, when they weren't collecting wood on the campo or following sheep, Liliana and her siblings struggled down from La Margarita to the sea to imitate the penguins, gaze at the whales rolling in the surf, and dig in the beach stones.

"Why did all these people come to La Península, anyway? They must have been desperate in the places they were from to go to all the trouble to come here. Things must have been really bad in Spain, in the Basque country."

Rafael, a strong-framed, silver-haired Península Valdés sheep ranch manager, son of Basque pioneers of Península Valdés, mused into the air as he sat at his kitchen table fingering a wineglass.

"What a sacrifice these men made. I can't imagine their rea-sons for coming. Because they didn't have any other resources? I don't know. People who were committed to working, they were."

He turned to Liliana, his wife, also a descendent of Basques. "My old man and your old man must have been real adventurers.

"And I tell you," he went on, "the first settlers here were this Félix Irazazabal, this Paz, this Olazar, this Irabi, these people who came down from Patagones and from I don't know what other places.

"These very first people on the Península came on a whim, they say. They just came, on horseback, to see what was here. They rode farther and farther away from the places they had come from, and they didn't even know if they would return. They didn't know whether they would find water or whether they would meet up with Indians, or what crossroads they would come to. They might make a passage of seven or eight days and not find a thing to eat or drink. These people accomplished nothing less than a miracle. Nowadays we have all kinds of things to help us in a wilderness, but these people didn't bring anything with them—not an idea, nothing.

"They came, looked around. Then they went home and rounded up their livestock and came back. They just took possession of the lands. Back then this was all just open campo. There wasn't a single fence. Nothing. That's why people came. They came, found this place, and settled in this desert. Because it was a desert. We call it a desert of solitude. A total desert, no? It seems they liked it for some reason. They saw a future."

The sixty-one-year-old sheep rancher spoke low and seriously in his kerosene-lit kitchen. "A lot of those who came here were Basques. You can still see it in the names. Irazazabal was Basque. Arbeletche was Basque; Lasarte was Basque; Gavilondo was Basque; Eche, yes, he was of Basque descent. Later, this Telechea was Uruguayan, but of Basque descent. Then there was this Ariztemunio, he was Uruguayan of Basque descent. Erosarena— Basques, too. The majority of the people who came were Basque. I think each man came on his own account and they got together here. Lasarte, Sayzar, Mendara, other Basques, were coming little by little.

"A lot of these Basques came and didn't settle here. They left. They did well work, fencing, and then they left and settled other places. The Verrasas, Basques, too, went around here on the Península digging wells."

Rafael's voice thickened with respect, and the large, lean man shifted on his chair. "Now, what healthy people, what strong people, these Basques were! What brutes for work. Mules! Do you know that there were some Basques that lifted *bordalezas*? A *bordaleza* was a barrel—a cask—of wine. One *bordaleza* must have contained one hundred eighty to two hundred liters.

"As I said, there were Basques who would grab a cask of wine, lift it, and load it onto the top of a wagonette. Two hundred or more kilos! Incredible." Rafael bear-hugged an imaginary barrel, staggered around the room, and sat down again at the table.

"And these Basques were regular-size people. Regular. They were . . ." Rafael held out his own large, callused hands to indicate huskiness. "But what strength!"

Another day Rafael, continually puzzling about his forebears on the Península, commented wryly, "It is hard to believe these people wanted to settle here because there's no water.

"It is a rare lagoon or pond on the Península that doesn't show signs of these first people who came here. Like maybe you find a big hole. You see that they had a little hut—they stayed in that hole with a piece of corrugated metal over it, for an awning. You find bottoms of bottles, a few pieces of wood, you see that there are some shearing scissors. It's a rare lagoon that doesn't have signs.

"Most of these early people had to dig wells. Imagine, they had to dig wells as deep as one hundred eighteen, one hundred twenty meters. With a pick and shovel. Take that in. Incredible. What work! You still find these holes that are seventy, eighty years old, and they are like the day they were made. It's an art.

"They lowered buckets in with a rope and pulled the dirt up by horse. They made a kind of pulley system. They put a branched pole on each side of the opening. These they called the *catres*. Then they put another one lying across the top. Then they attached the rope on a pulley and put a bucket on the end of the rope. They filled this with dirt, and the horse pulled it up and out. They had one person in the mouth of the well, and another received the dirt and took the bucket and emptied it.

"Back then they made wells abundantly wide. They made them, maybe, inside a hundred and fifty centimeters in diameter. Nowadays the shafts are much reduced. And they cut the wells with a pick. But what sacrifice, eh? In those days, people worked.

"These people must have had a lot of will to have something of their own. I have never figured out how they knew, who gave them the idea that digging deep down there might be water. I ask you, who could have given them the notion that at forty, fifty meters down there could be water?"

None of the ranchers' stories brought home to me what it meant to be a pioneer in Patagonia quite so vividly as did Rodolfo Zabaleta's tale of settling an estancia just north of Península Valdés.

The eighty-five-year-old sheep man's daughter, Nora, introduced me to him, and as we drove to his Puerto Madryn retirement home, she told me a story about her father in his youth. Her eyes shone like sunlit Navarran daisies as she spoke.

"Until recently my papá had been to the doctor only two times in his whole life, both a long time ago.

"Once, he was working on a windmill and the blade cut two fingers off at the nail. Another time, he had just finished lunch and he took a swig from a bottle. It turned out to be *aquarina*, a horse medicine. He took a liter of milk on top of it and vomited it up half an hour later. He was bad off. They rushed him to San Antonio. He joked to the doctor that he had taken the stuff for worms. The doctor told him that you only give a horse one tablespoon, and that's it for the horse. He asked my father why he wasn't dead. My father spent the whole night with ice, but he made it through. He never went to the doctor again.

" 'What a brute this Basque is!' the doctor said."

The middle-aged schoolteacher then parked her compact Renault beside a stucco house on a broad Puerto Madryn street and led me into a formal, dark, cool living room.

"We children are his sunshine," she explained. "Since he has retired from the campo, he waits all day for our visits. He is nearly deaf, and he's so bored now, poor old thing, sitting in front of that TV."

Spanish-style, olive brocade, heavy-cushioned chairs were positioned around a low coffee table. Beyond this formal room was a lighted dining room with a kitchen at one end and a television at the other. Occupying the midsection of the room was a three-meter-wide Formica eating table. Beside it, and facing away from it, several chairs were clustered and aimed at a large TV set, which was flashing red, yellow, and purple shapes. We walked into the modern kitchen.

An old man sat beside the television, deep in a worn, overstuffed chair. He was dressed in estancia clothes—a faded khaki shirt and loose trousers. His squat face was tanned and unshaven, and the skin of his cheeks fell in folds. The eyes set in the grizzled face were cataract-clouded and bluish, yet they looked directly into mine when we were introduced. Nora sat at the kitchen table with her elegantly dressed mother, and I took a chair near Rodolfo, who had to strain to hear me, a strange young woman. I shouted my question.

"I would like to hear about how your father came to Patagonia."

He cupped his ear, as though trying to hear above a gale, and shouted back to me.

"Eh?"

"How did your father happen to come to Patagonia?"

Another husky, loud, "Eh?"

"Why did your father come to La Patagonia?"

Finally Nora, who was chatting at the table with her mother, yelled to her father.

"How did Grandfather happen to come to La Patagonia?"

"Oh!" said Rodolfo, delighted, and the old campesino was off, in a rumbling voice, the raconteur. He chuckled at his old father, Carlitos, the naive schoolteacher who had left the poppy-flecked fields of Navarra to take up life in the Patagonian sheep-lands.

"My father came because they said that here a person filled himself with money. He came to fill himself with money and go back to Azqueta!" Then he told me the saga of his father's move to Patagonia.

I asked him, then, to tell me about his own childhood.

"When we first moved to the campo," he said, "we never saw anyone because the whole thing was desert. The zone was completely unpopulated. There was no one there. We didn't see a single person from outside the family until we had been there two months and a man came by on a horse. It had been two months since we had seen anyone, but there were twelve of us, so we had company!

"And then, after a while, it all got settled. People began to settle all the land around.

"In those days all the families were huge. Now they're all tiny ones. In only a few years after we settled over there, there were ten families nearby, and not one had under ten *chicos*.

They were all families of ten, twelve, thirteen. One couple on the hill had twenty-two children."

Rodolfo cupped his hands around the childhood memories in his mind. "Ah, no!" he said. "You lived badly in that time. Me, when I was seven years old, every morning I had to walk a whole league to find the horse troop. We didn't have the silage or the means to keep horses in a shed. Every single day I went off to find the horses.

"We *chicos* spent every day of the year outside. A boy in those days worked the whole day long. He went around the campo with the sheep. He lived in the campo and only came home to sleep. Because there were no fences then, and it was all open range, each day my brother and I had to go out with the sheep onto the campo. We pastured them in open campo. We would take *churrascos* [thin-sliced steaks] with us, and while one of us did a few rounds with the sheep, the other made the *churrascos*. We ate there at the side of the sheep, and at dusk we returned home with the sheep.

"Then, at night, we entertained ourselves by playing games among the twelve of us. Then we ate dinner, and in the morning, when the day had just dawned, we had to leave again for the campo.

"And out there where we wandered with the sheep, there were wild cows and mares. We had to go out on foot very carefully because of the cows. Bad cows. Those cows didn't even know people. They didn't have a brand on them. One time they had my father surrounded. He climbed some bushes. The cows had him surrounded!" A hearty laugh burst from the old man's lips.

The hoarse voice went on again. "There was nothing out there. *Nada.* There was no school. My father was a teacher, though, so he taught us. He taught the older ones for short times in the night, and the older brothers and sisters taught the younger ones. Once we lived on the campo, not one of us went to school.

"I first came to know Madryn in 1907. I came here to the pueblo, for the first time, when I was seven. I came with my father, by cart. We left from there where we lived, and we kept going the whole day in the cart. At night we slept in the open campo. We traveled all the next day, and then, in the afternoon, we arrived here.

"There were already businesses in Madryn by then, even though it was a tiny pueblo. We spent two days here and did the shopping, and we returned again in the cart. We took back supplies to last us for three months. We bought sugar, *yerba* [the herbs for making mate], flour. My father had built a mud oven and we made bread at home."

The old man turned to describe one of the harrowing adventures of his boyhood.

"In the year 1918 there was a drought, and the campo didn't yield anything, and all the livestock were about to die. That year my brother and I were looking after the sheep over there where I grew up, because my father had gone to live in the pueblo. Our sheep were all dying. Far out there in the campo, though, we knew there was a lagoon, with water and with grasses around it, that they called Media Luna, so my brother and I went out there with the livestock to save them. We spent the year out there in the campo.

"While we were out there, the drought broke, but then it rained every day the rest of that year, or snowed. It snowed the whole winter. That was the year it even snowed in Buenos Aires. The only time it snowed in Buenos Aires.

"We were at the side of a bush day and night. We didn't have a tent even if we had wanted one. There, by the bush, we cooked, and there we slept, in *recados*—bedrolls made out of our saddles. We went to bed wet, and we got up at dawn wet.

"One had to get through rough spots back then. People say that you can't survive in those conditions. They say a person would get sick, or even die. But we didn't get a bit sick. One can get used to anything. One adjusts oneself to the bad life. When one is brought up, from the time one is young, with changes of fortune, one gets accustomed to it. We passed the whole winter out there at the side of a thornbush to save the sheep. In the end we did save them, and we chopped a lot of lamb tails that year."

In his teens, Rodolfo left his father's land to seek his fortune. He spent five years helping out at his sister's Península Valdés estancia, then devoted fifteen more to caring for the sheep on his father's estancia when the old Basque died. Then, at last, Rodolfo had a chance to attain the dream he'd inherited from his father. Following Carlitos's example of hard work, he was able to claim, break, and fence his own spread of the dry Patagonian hinterland. His resources were few and the process was slow, but perseverance was in Rodolfo's blood.

"I went off to settle my own piece of campo. In those years any person could take possession of campo. You just went and made a claim. You hoped to get a place with a natural watering hole. That was the most important. Then, when you found the land you wanted, you went to the town and paid a rent to the government. Then you just went out there and settled. Later on, you could buy the land.

"Mind you, by that time you could hardly settle campo because there was no money. You had to have money to be able to settle a piece of campo. So out there, near my father's campo, I put myself to work as a tavern keeper in Lobo, and I also had a hotel and restaurant. From that base in Lobo, I built an estancia. Little by little, over the four years I was in Lobo, I fenced the property. With a little Lobo and a little campo, I was able to settle a sizable piece. I began with two leagues, and I went along settling it little by little, then I got four, then six, and I had eight by the time I finished.

"You could have your campo, but you had to make the sacrifice of going out to live in the desert and fence the land. And you had to dig a well."

After building a three-room house out of mud blocks made from his own earth, and fencing his piece of dry, flat monotony, Rodolfo did what all Patagonian settlers were compelled to do. He hunted his property for a pond or a stream. Finding no water, he began to dig.

With the first spadeful of earth, Rodolfo began the maddest task of his life.

"Out there, in that dry soil, I dug a well ninety-five meters deep. With pick and shovel. For seven months I was down in the well with two *peones.* Every single day, in the morning and at night, I was down in the well. And in the end I brought out saltwater. Seven months and saltwater!"

To a wandering shipwrecked mariner, or an albatross flying over Patagonia at the turn of the century, the dry and treeless campo would have appeared uninhabited, but within burrows and holes in the cracked, wind-paddled earth there were creatures breathing. Armadillos, foxes, weasels, and the guinea pig–like cuis were scurrying and procreating within the epidermis of the earth. And beside them, in larger shafts, lived and toiled settler men and women and children.

The pioneers in Patagonia did not seek to live in graceful harmony with the elements, to saunter off alone into the wilds, as I, armed with the North American mythology of Thoreau and Daniel Boone, had imagined. Their objective was to get the better of a wasteland. Necessity dictated that the Península Valdés settlers crack open the broad, dry ground that spread before them and discover a water vein that would allow them and their sheep to survive among the tough and bitter thornbushes. Digging was the answer to Patagonia: the answer to shelter, to nourishment, to hope.

WIND AND FRUIT

~~~~~~~~~~~~~~~~~~~~~~~~~~~~~~~~~~

Trelew is a sprawling, dust-blanketed town with one of the few airstrips in Chubut Province. On the road from there to Península Valdés, there is a single marker in an otherwise flat continent of thorn scrub: about an hour into the four-hour drive, a 150-foot cone juts from the desert floor. On the vast circumference of land that surrounds the cone, there is not a single tree. The land is dotted with low spine bushes and littered with broken rock. The cone looks like a breast hatched from the ocean floor.

The taxi driver, who transported us to Península Valdés on our first visit there, stopped the old Ford Falcon when we came opposite the landmark and got out. The short, swarthy man spat and kicked the tires, bent toward our window, and motioned with his cigarette.

"Over there, they call that Loma María," he said. "In about 1865, a Welsh woman brought her child to light right there."

The cone was named for the woman who was one of the group of Welsh pioneers who first settled Chubut Province. The straggle of men, women, and children who had voyaged to Patagonia to create a New Wales was trekking southward from Puerto Madryn, where they had made landfall, in search of a skinny freshwater stream over sixty kilometers away, when the woman's knees buckled. The immigrants had had no water for two days.

The tale about the Welsh woman caught my attention that first day in Patagonia, but I didn't fully understand the import of what the taxi man was telling me until many months later.

As we sped on I stared out the window at the dusk-dimmed monotonous desert and tried to imagine settling, much less giving birth in, such an inhospitable place.

Grit and cold gusted up through the seams of the car all through the journey, and by the time we arrived at the isolated camp where we were going to be living, our thick jackets and duffel bags were coated with a layer of blondish ash.

A few days after we arrived at the little camp, tucked at the edge of the desolate bay, I panted up the eroded cliff that rose at the back of the house to begin to explore in more detail the land that would be my tramping ground and my keep for the next year and a half.

At the top of the cliffs, there she was: Patagonia, a dry hide stretched over an immense flatness; a thin woman's body, flayed. Calf-high spine bushes clutched the earth's skin like intermittent groups of whiskers. The black-green clumps, crystal clear at my feet, each pricker defined as if I'd put on magnifying glasses, spread and spread maniacally over the land into a shapeless blur.

As I stood stiff in my insulated boots and my orange down parka, Patagonia's chill wind screeched into my ears, burned my cheeks. Squinting far off, north, south, east, west, I could not detect a single human dwelling. I could not see even one tiny pond flash to relieve the rambling, tan-gray monotony. There was not one bright orb of fruit. Not one tree.

Loneliness washed over me in a shriek of wind.

Like every woman new to Patagonia, I was a sapling to be lashed and bent by her winds. I was a pear ripe to be peeled and left white and exposed for easy disintegration. It was my task to take in Patagonia's grim vistas, stand tall to her winds, and fashion a life on her skinny flank.

Throughout my stay in Patagonia, my thoughts turned time and again to María, the Patagonian settler writhing on the sand, trying to give birth. As her body contracted on the hard ground, the wind must have whipped at her. Thorns pierced her clutching hands and tense buttocks. Her groans, and the whispers of those attending her, were the only sounds aside from the roars of the wind.

A set of questions materialized in my mind that first week and became a refrain in my head. How can a woman thrive in a void? How can she put out buds? How does a woman breast these waves of emptiness?

During my second stay on the Península, I went from estancia to estancia, to the older women who had settled Patagonia, to find out what it was like for them and to obtain the key to living in a vast emptiness.

One day I drove to Emilia's to record some of her eighty-two-year-old mother's life story. As I drove up, the salt flats to the north side of the Goikoa *puesto* were still soft from the recent rain. Little blades of grass trickled in the wind on the drying mud. A muddy track led from the pond, where a vehicle had been stuck, back to the main track. The view across the pan to the collection of buildings was dreary—a giant, dead, flat plain. I drove up beside a little barn and caught sight of Julia, Emilia's mother, her thick, swollen legs visible behind the skimpy trees in front of Emilia's house. She had heard the sound of the engine and had come out to see whose motor was grinding across the campo.

The old woman bustled up to me and gave up her soft cheeks for a double kiss.

I followed her round shoulders inside and sat at the table, which was clean except for a pile of neatly folded ironing. The iron stood, end up, on a layer of towels where the old campo woman had been working.

Julia hurried to the kitchen counter to make tea. Busy with her preparations, she came over now and then to talk. When she stood beside the table, it came to above her waist.

Julia is very stout. She wears simple, button-front widow's dresses, and whenever she raises her arms to my shoulders for a kiss, the loose, dimpled skin of her upper arms hangs out of the short sleeves of the frocks and flaps. She wears a gold ring on one pudgy finger and large, round gypsy hoops through her ears. These, with her dark hair and dress, give her a stark elegance. Bright eyes, blurred behind glasses, are part of a steady, eager face. With her smooth skin and jet-black hair, she appears sixty rather than eighty-two.

On this day her black hair was done in curls that flopped over her forehead. She shuffled heavily on her slippered feet, yet she moved steadily, surely. As she fixed tea she warned me, "I don't have cakes, just crackers," but when she brought the basket of crackers, she pointed to some slices of homemade fried bread and told me I should eat that. Soon she delivered to the table two cups of milky tea, with the grains of powdered milk still visible, and then sat down opposite me to tell her story.

The old woman was earthiness itself and delightful. When she told a joke, she opened her toothless mouth very wide and cackled until she had to bend over double and put her head on her arms on the table. She yawned frequently—big, lusty yawns—smothering her mouth sometimes with her loose-fleshed hand. She spoke in a witch's voice, a long monologue punctuated with lusty sighs.

Julia was raised for her first fifteen years by two sets of guardians—first by her godparents, both of whom died while she was under their care, and then by "a nice Italian couple" in Patagones, to the north, while her parents worked on the Península. When the second set of guardians died, Julia's parents fetched their daughter and brought her back with them to the Península.

Julia spent the next six years working hard on her father's land. "Where my papa was, it was all open land—there weren't any fences then. So, when it came time to dip the sheep, we had to be on top of a horse at five in the morning, to herd them all in. The women, too. It was different then.

"Then you had to dip the sheep by hand. So, with a lot of animals, you had to spend whole days, morning to night, treating them."

Not only did teenaged Julia ride, but she drove the truck out into the campo to collect wood, was an expert with a rifle, and captured ostrich for meat with *boleadoras*, a primitive lasso that when hurled catches animals by entangling their legs.

After a two-year courtship with a handsome young estancia manager she met in the village of Pirámides on the Península, Julia married at the age of twenty-one and moved with her new husband to a stretch of the Península not far from her father's land.

The estancia on which Julia raised her six boys and five girls is so remote that even local people would seldom stray there. To this day the road to the ranch is almost impassable, and still it is a place where the only sound one hears above the wind is the far-off din of sea lions barking.

At Estancia La Siberia, Julia's husband had a dual occupation. He was caretaker for an estancia owned by the Irabis, and he was also concessionaire for a seal harvesting business.

Through the winter months Roberto lived on a cliff overlooking the seal colony and only returned home every fifteen days or once a month. During those months that her husband oversaw the clubbing of sea lions and elephant seals, the rendering of the seal fat, and the salting of the skins, and broke up fights between the workers, Julia carried out the sheep work back at the estancia with the children that heaved out of her year after year. The work never ceased.

"When he went to the seal colony in the winter, I stayed home with the *chicos*. It was hard work, but what could you do? One had to do it. He always left a *peón* on the estancia, and that man herded the sheep, and the *chicos* and I threw them in the dip. We had big baths then. The first few years, too, we had to shear the sheep by hand. Everyone in the family with shears in their hands. It's not like with a machine, which is fast. The neighbors all helped each other. It was very different then.

"The *chicos* and I often ate *churrascos* and nothing else. We would run out of potatoes and we couldn't go to town to get them in the winter. We only went to town two or three times a year, when we could. But we were all healthy. I used to make bread, and we had lots of cows. We milked them and had huge urns of milk, and made little cheeses for the house."

As Julia spoke, it was hard for her to sit still, and she squirmed around on the chair. She told me it was "the rheumatism" that made it hard for her to sit. She was without any self-consciousness, often rubbing her shoulders, shifting her legs, and feeling her knees. "Oh, it pains me. But when God gives you something, you must *aguantar*. You must tolerate it. Life is like that, dear.

"I can do anything, the only thing is the rheumatism. There are days when I can't move an arm, with the pains. I feel it in my shoulders and my knees. They say there's no cure; it's like cancer. I have suffered a lot. And when there are storms like that, when it's about to rain, ai! Mother of God! Crazy with pain. The shoulders, the knees, the spine! It seems that they have set you on a barbecue grill. One has to *aguantar*—what are you going to do?

"Some people say there is no God, but for me there's a God. I don't know how, but I know. I have always believed in God, and for me, there is God. When I am in the pueblo, I go to mass. I always offer masses for the relatives I have. I have a lot of family."

The conversation turned away from Julia's current concerns back to her life on the campo, back to my question. How was it for her living in such an isolated place?

Julia shrugged, as if that had never been a great concern to her. "I never felt lonely there. In those years, people didn't.

"Sometimes people from outside came to eat with us, but not very often. People who work on the campo don't leave home much. Very little, very little.

"I have had a good life," she stated, as though the reason

ought to be obvious. "I have eleven children—six boys and five girls. I raised all my children in the campo. Eight of them were born there, and all my children have come out well. Not one child has problems. Thanks be to God, all the boys have good work and all my daughters have married well. They all have good companions.

"We had big families then. I have forty grandchildren and thirty and some great-grandchildren—many of my grandchildren are grown."

For Julia, settling into the campo was no task at all. It was something native to her. Like a mother seal, she bore tender babies, year after year, on the pebbly Patagonian shore. Her young ones' needs kept her running, and their boisterous, yelping play animated the desolate neck of land. It was all she could do to keep their stomachs full and prevent them from drowning in the sea near the seal colony. She never even heard the shrieking of the seals or of the wind.

"Love is blind. Once you are married, there is no other solution."

This is how Gracia sums up her early married years in the campo.

Mornings, in the mid-1930s, Gracia, a young woman raised in Buenos Aires, now the wife of a Patagonian settler, would look out her door, allow the parching wind to dry her eyes, and then pick up a bucket. Rodolfo Zabaleta, her chosen husband, an eager and earnest man who possessed a dream of settling his own piece of wild campo, had failed to unearth water on the hunk of cracked land to which he had staked claim. Thus, his pretty wife picked up the pieces of their hope and took on the job of finding the water needed to nourish not only her five children, but a handful of cows, some chickens, and several hundred sheep.

Rain—collected in buckets placed under the eaves or fetched from the lagoon—was the only good water to be found. Very often the clouds gave little. The shallow lagoon on the family's land was an oblong of drying mud, and Gracia's buckets were often empty. Nearly every day the new mother had to drive a truck over a hummocky trace to another pond fifteen kilometers away. There she loaded a day's worth of water into barrels and drove the vital substance home.

Back in her two-room house, the strong young woman poured buckets of the water into tubs and washed the children's clothes. The same pair of arms and hands poured, into a special pot, all the water that was ready to throw out, for washing potatoes.

Years later, when I talked to her, Gracia was wearing a rich purple-and-red dress. Her face was smooth, her gray hair neat and coiffed. She looked younger than sixty-nine. Seated in the big eat-in kitchen of her retirement home in Puerto Madryn, she bore the confidence of a woman who lives how she wants to live. In clipped, bright, formal phrases she told me of her difficult adjustment to married life in the campo.

"It was hard for me in the campo because I was raised in Buenos Aires. I was born on the Península, my family has land there, but I lived in Buenos Aires until I was sixteen. My family moved to the capital so we children could go to school. I was raised very well, with servants and everything. I was educated in the city until I was sixteen or seventeen, and then the family came to the campo.

"I came here because Papá was an entrepreneur. He did lots of business. Sometimes he was high, and sometimes he was low. In one of the lows, he had to come here to work. Papá had a hotel in Lobo. That was when I got to know my husband, and then I didn't go back to Buenos Aires again. I stayed here."

She looked across the room at her farmer husband, almost twenty years her senior, in his faded work clothes, and stated matter-of-factly, "Love is blind."

A practical young woman, Gracia turned her face into Patagonia's wind and did what had to be done. She fetched water for her children, but she would be damned if she was going to let Patagonia deprive her children of the education she valued as a city-bred person.

"We didn't want to raise our children without schooling, and in the campo there is nothing."

Gracia sent her oldest son to be schooled in Buenos Aires, with his grandparents. Then, when the other children had grown a little bit, Gracia took them to Madryn so they could go to school there. Rodolfo stayed in the campo to look after the sheep.

"If we didn't give the *chicos* some schooling," Gracia's husband said, "they were going to be a bunch of brutes, like me. They were going to have to herd my sheep!" The old man chuckled, and his wife did not contradict him.

Through her children, Gracia defied Patagonia. She stood proud as a tree.

Vitoria's stories about her early married life in the campo come out in sentences that wax and wane, ebb and flow, with pain rushing and flowing.

"I suffered a lot living in the campo. Yes. We lost out on a lot. Because, even though Pirámides, where I spent my girl-hood, was a tiny town, it was a town. And there we had girl-friends. We had everything. No, it cost me. I missed town a lot. In the campo the twilight would arrive and leave you with sad-ness."

During the early part of the century, Puerto Pirámides, a tiny seaside village, was the principal port for the Península. It was from Pirámides that wool from the Península estancias was shipped, and goods from Buenos Aires arrived at the dock, around which twenty or so sheet metal houses and warehouses were scattered. Pirámides was an important gathering point for all Península Valdés inhabitants; for most campo people, the seventy-person village was as novel, glamorous, and inaccessible as Buenos Aires is now.

It was in Pirámides that Vitoria, now seventy-six years old, grew up. To a young girl, the town was a lively, opulent place to live. Vitoria went to a tiny school, had a group of close girlfriends, and together the sons and daughters of the shopkeepers, shipping men, wagoners, and teacher all played in a cluster on the main beachside street. Vitoria's mother sold knitted and hand-sewn garments to supplement her wagoner husband's income, so the family lived well.

At fifteen Vitoria was forced to move to the campo, away from her friends and the beloved village on the Península. The family was compelled to move because wagons were rapidly being replaced by trucks, so wagoners such as Vitoria's father could no longer make a living.

Vitoria still feels the sharp pain of leaving Pirámides, and her voice rises with wistfulness.

"So my father went to the campo to work on an estancia, and we, the whole family, went with him. We were two brothers: the one you know, Rafael, and one more, and two sisters. There were four of us.

"Ah, life there was very lonesome. Lonesome in the sense that for someone raised in town, like me, it was so different from what I was used to. The campo people were raised out there, in these family groups that visited among themselves and never had any schooling. The little they learned was the little their parents could teach them. The families were very big, and they were very, very, very poor. So, for a person used to something else, it was sad to be in that setting. It was tough to adjust."

Very soon after her family's traumatic move to the campo, at the age of sixteen, Vitoria married the son of the *estanciero*, or estancia owner, for whom her father worked.

"When you married you became independent, so we lived at another sheep station of the same estancia. We sacrificed for twenty years on the campo," says Vitoria Mendizabal de Irazazabal.

The mud estancia house into which the newlyweds moved was sheathed with corrugated tin. The inner mud walls crumbled more each day, and they were pockmarked with huge ragged holes. The previous occupants had built cookfires inside the chimneyless dwelling and just let the smoke blacken the walls and doors. The well-bred young woman was dismayed.

"It was very tough to clean that. Very tough. And my husband had to fix the walls. We painted them and repaired the mud floors. He put in Portland [cement] floors. No, life in the campo before was hard. *Dura.*"

The way she says *dura* makes clear she means hard as granite. The image of the hardness, like an immovable black boulder blocking the bright young woman's energies, is a refrain through her sentences as she lists the ungiving aspects of life in the campo.

"Those years were very hard. The years from 1925 to 1934, more or less, were the worst. We didn't have anything with which to get around. My husband didn't buy the little car until the year 1934.

"I never rode. I was afraid of horses and never got used to riding, so in order to go out we would have to attach horses to a sulky, a cart. We had a sulky, but we used it very little. I went three years without going to Pirámides, and we only went to Madryn in cases of illness. No, those were hard years. Now it is hard for you to stay in the campo a month without coming, but for us in those days, a year between visits seemed like going a lot, because it was so difficult to travel. The roads were made by your very own wheels. You can still see roads like that."

Vitoria was referring to the faint, brushy tracks, with humps down their center, that branch off almost invisibly from the more frequently driven roads of the Península. A veering off onto one of these traces, even now, means flat tires and continual uncertainty as to whether the vehicle or track will give out first.

"We visited the family and the neighbors," she tells me, "but then came twilight, and everyone returned to her own house. Besides, the neighbors weren't, let's say, three or four kilometers away, they were maybe fifteen kilometers away. We didn't have family get-togethers, like other people have, in the campo. It was just a lot to get around because the distances were great. So, you see, we couldn't get into the habit of having parties on holidays, or birthdays, or Christmas, or New Year's. No one did any of that. In the campo, you lose customs. In Pirámides we had all those things, but in the campo we lost them.

"Solitude . . ." Vitoria's sweet voice strains as she tries to make her thoughts absolutely clear. "When the dusk comes and you feel the dryness. And then the fear. I was alone in the house. I was alone at night, too, because my husband might go to town to shop, or for something, and I stayed with the children. Yes, fear. There, anything could happen, and we had to be there.

"When I felt lonely, I used to read. I read and read and read. I read magazines that my mother-in-law sent. She subscribed, back then, to the magazine *Para Ti*. This magazine had everything. It's not like the romance magazines that exist now. It had instructive things. For me, they were wonderful things. Look, when there was a religious conference in Buenos Aires—in 1936, I think it was—the whole thing came out in this magazine. All like it was. So, when someone was coming to our house, my mother-in-law sent me these magazines. And books, too.

"I had a friend who is unforgettable. I don't know if you have heard of her—Rosa—she is the mother-in-law of one of my nieces. She and I were close friends. We raised our children as though they were siblings. Thanks to God, as I say, I had many good friendships. This woman was several years older than I, and she has since died, but she helped me so much. So, so much.

"She lived five kilometers away, and we visited each other. She would come to stay for several days at a time, because, as I already said, it wasn't a question of jumping in the car and going to the neighbor's. Not very frequently, but every so often, she would come to my house for a week, and the next week I would go to hers. It helped a lot. It helped because she was a woman who was also raised in town. It seems that you seek out people like yourself."

Of all this, the beautifully coiffed Vitoria, in her tidy denim dress, in her tidy house in Madryn, said, "I could live in the campo because, really, I was happy with my husband, my family."

From Vitoria's house in the campo, she could see nothing but empty thornland. What occupied the cold, hard, bare room of Vitoria's life in the barren steppe was children. Children were her reply to Patagonia's merciless monotony.

A gift for raising children emerged while Vitoria was herself still a child in Pirámides. This talent was quickly noted and stitched into place by her own mother; one of the first children who came into Vitoria's care was her younger brother, Rafael.

"I raised a brother, Rafael, who was orphaned at age six. I had raised him from the time he was in diapers because my mother was very delicate. I was the one who gave him the bottle, who changed him, who bathed him. I was eleven when he was born. From the time he was born, I was in charge of him, so everyone said it was like he was my son. My mother told me what to do, and I did it.

"Children enchant me."

Vitoria's sentences run together, and her voice rises and falls like a storyteller's, as though the story and the children are attached to one long silk thread. The poised woman suddenly breaks into giggles as she remembers the small ones who tugged at her skirts while she scrubbed her mud house. The list of children she raised seems to go on forever.

"Later, I had nephews at my house—for periods when their mothers were sick and needed to have someone in charge of their children. And after that, I had another nephew who also lost his mother. He stayed with me for a long time in the campo. He also considers me his mother. What do I know? I have always had a lot of patience for children. It is something that you bring with you."

An ostrich-thin woman with an ancient, wrinkled face and prominent, homely, dark-rimmed glasses appeared at the door. Esperanza had a sharp look and was wearing a black-and-white dress.

This sister of Rodolfo's, Gracia's sister-in-law, bustled me off the most elegant street in Puerto Madryn into a pleasant peak-roofed, white and terra-cotta-tiled house. There were several children and young adults moving in and out of the compact living room. The eighty-eight-year-old woman hurried me over to a pair of chairs out of the way of traffic. She moved the chairs up against each other, pushed me down onto one of them, then seated herself next to me and pulled a basket of knitting close with her slipper.

I asked Esperanza how it was to live in the campo when she was young but she waved her long, thin hand, dismissing my question. She aimed her body toward me and spoke very close to my face. Her tone was strident, although her knees were almost touching mine.

"The secret for me is to live with enthusiasm. To not lament. And not to just say it, rather to have it also be true inside. Acceptance helps a lot. To approach all things with eagerness. God helps those who have enthusiasm."

At my insistence, Esperanza told me, "We lived for six years on the Península, in the zone near where the elephant seals are. My husband was looking after a sheep station. When I lived in the campo, you had to work hard. There was no gas stove, no washing machine, no electricity.

"The truth is that in the campo, I had the children almost alone. My husband left every day. Children give you work, but you don't notice the work because with the love you have for them, it goes along without your noticing. Life is a struggle, but if you take it with calm and enthusiasm, it's nice."

The birdlike woman gave me her keys to life in the campo. There were three; the first was fruit.

"We have been here, in town, for forty years now. We still have a campo. My husband used to go back and forth to the campo a lot, but he doesn't travel so much now. We have people there who care for it, but I like to go.

"I like the campo. Bah! In the campo, we have a forest planted around the house. It helps one to live. I like to go because there is a garden there, and fruit. I like to go and make jams. Every year I make jams. I make a lot of quince jam, quince jelly. Now, for example, we are going to go, and I am going to put up plums and make jam. And next month, if I go, I am going to put up apples. Here in town there are never more than peaches, plums, apricots, but in the campo there is some of everything.

"I conserve the fruit for the winter. It is not that I need to do this, rather that I like it. Isn't it like that? That one likes to do things? Life has to have interest. When one loses interest in doing handwork, in taking care of plants, in gathering fruits, then why should one be here anymore? Don't you think?

"Almost my whole life, my biggest kind of food has been fruit. At night, I eat a little bowl of soup, half a bowl, and then four or five fruits."

The second key to life that Esperanza holds close is connected with her belief in enthusiasm.

The tables of the room in which we were sitting were covered with lace coverlets, and there were pillows on the love seat across the way that had been covered with lace, with a darker material behind. The walls of the room were arrayed with pictures and souvenirs, the most prominent of which was a framed needlework tapestry. Esperanza told me she had made the tapestry for a grandchild who was soon to be married. She made one, she said, for each grandchild starting out in marriage. The hanging was bright and cheery—a peaceful village scene with bright red and blue and yellow cottages.

Esperanza grabbed my hand. We were finally on the topic she loved. She motioned to the tapestry. "Can you see it? It's a hamlet. These are the sky and the clouds."

The scene could not have been more unlike a typical view out a Patagonian window. Looking at the tapestry, one might imagine one were in Devon.

Even more important than fruit and imagination, were children, Esperanza's third reply to Patagonia's isolation and sharp wind.

"Now on the Península," she said, "it is almost all lone men. It is a very sad life for these men. It's another thing to live in the campo with four or five children. Children make you happy. You teach them. One does one thing, and one does another, and you're always occupied.

"*Chicos* fill up your life for you," she said.

Esperanza's answer to Patagonia was clear as spring water. For a woman to live in the dry and barren campo, to live at all, she gives birth to children, she plants fruit trees in order to feed those children fruit, and she weaves, knits, and stitches around those children scenes rich and hopeful with plentiful water, greenery, and bucolic peace. She, with her mind and her stories, turns the bristled campo into a bright, daisy-littered Eden.

For me, Patagonia often seemed like an ocean of deprivation. I wandered around on that grim land and couldn't find anything with which to make anything—there were no fruits to arrange in a bowl. I concluded that in Patagonia a woman's urges must be stilled. She couldn't possibly bloom, much less thrive. She could be brave, but bravery was not equal to life.

Then, one day, looking out into the wind, I saw what the women meant.

A little child in a gingham hat appeared in the wind. Her chubby legs were bare. She was repeating a rhyme and wanted to be let in. It came to me: the thing I couldn't understand, as a childless woman, in what the settler women said. The secret to life in Patagonia is to have a child. A woman herself can't flower, so she gives birth in order to fill the void, in order to maintain hope.

In Patagonia, a child running, raw-cheeked, is the lovely, joyous, bouncing thing. Patagonian women are mothers, trees hunched, braving the wind. Their children are pink peaches, orange apricots, and red apples on the sand. Their children are solid and tough, more real than blood.

When I first heard the tale about Loma María, all I could envision was the Welsh woman writhing there among the bushes, Patagonia pricking the woman's flesh and draining all her juices. Only later did the second image come. Along with the blood pooling on the tan earth came the fruit: an infant. María was engaging in the bravest, the only possible, act a woman can make in Patagonia.

Peter and I walked across the campo to Loma María, to the foot of the hill where the Welsh woman's baby was born. The cone was packed with sand, oyster shells, and ancient fish and mammal ribs, like a kind of layer cake. Clumps of thornbushes stood like little domes on the earth surrounding the pinnacle. The cracked ground beneath the bushes was littered with pebbles and rock flakes, and among the scrabble were scattered countless minuscule petrified sharks' teeth. These triangular knives, the size of a woman's tiniest fingernail, were pure and white, like countless ova sprinkled over the earth.

ENGINES

~~~~~~~~~~~~~~~~~~

The vast expanse of paper-flat dryness, in the center of which a little crew toils, has been shocked to a custard yellow by the slamming afternoon sun. The spikes of the low bushes jab into the clear air, as though trying to pierce its light-hearted romping. It is the best of southern Argentine days—brilliant, breezy, warm enough—the land and sky a gold-and-aqua panorama.

In this magnificent arena, I am watching Rafael dip his sheep. He and Roberta, the sick neighbor's wife, and a greenhorn *peón*, all dressed in cobalt-blue coveralls, are working around the dipping trough. Rafael bear-hugs, then heaves five sheep into the brown liquid. His movements are as efficient as those of a killer whale flipping baby sea lions off the nearby coast.

Rafael hurls in five more sheep, engine-efficient, and then stands up straight a moment. He arches and rubs his lower back. He stands tall. His silver pompadour billows grand in the breeze. His Basque-colored hazel eyes, with the heavy glasses before them, follow the line of his jaw to a point out in the empty, arid land. Squinting, the eyes of the sheep rancher pursue the dust plume of a vehicle racing past along the broad dirt road invisible half a mile off across the flats. The man's gaze seems packed with significance.

By the time the seasoned campesino turns back to the dipping trough and mops his brow, the wind has blown apart the dirty cloud of the car's presence, and the campo is again unanimated.

Dipping is one of the critical duties that mark the year of a sheep man. Wedged as it is between the *señalada*, or lamb marking, and the shearing, its timing is always touch and go. This year, dipping has had its drops of panic. Rafael and Roberta were forced to wait two weeks longer than planned for the right kind of weather to start dipping. They needed the air to be *fresquito*, neither too cold nor too hot. ("If it's too cold, the sheep get pneumonia; if it's too hot, they cook.")

As though the vagaries of weather were not enough, Rafael has tossed and turned in his bed at night for fear the *flechillas*, the arrowweeds, would come in thick before he got the sheep herded. Just today the fine, fishhooklike barbs with their long, wispy, blond tails have sprouted in the campo grasses. When in full flower, the venomous little seed darts that assure the reproduction of the Península bunch grasses hide in those grasses and pierce Rafael's bare feet through his rope-soled shoes as he walks over the campo. More important, they embed themselves in the flesh of the sheep in his care. It is critical to a sheep man that he get his sheep herded for dipping before the *flechillas* are out, or the beasts are tortured by the weeds. At the height of the *flechilla* season, the wool bearers must be left free to use their established paths and to gather in the clear spaces around water holes, so they can avoid contact with the *flechillas*. "Sometimes, when you butcher a sheep, the meat is crammed through with them," Rafael's wife, Liliana had told me, "and that can kill an animal."

There is a lore about the dipping, as there is about every event in the sheep year. José, Rafael's neighbor thirty kilometers away, tells a story about a certain Península man who once became so angered by his wife that he threw her in the dipping trough.

The La Entrada sheep dip is a deep, round, concrete tub, big enough to hold five or six swimming sheep. As the dipping rhythm goes, Roberta slops red paint onto the animals' woolly rumps. Rafael heaves the beasts into the pool as they are marked. As the frantic sheep sputter and lunge, bug-eyed, in circles, Pichón, the *peón*, pushes their heads underwater with a long pole that has a metal half-moon on the end. This dousing ensures that every fiber of the animal's wool is coated with the harsh *remedio* or *antisárnico*, a solution that kills ticks and scab.

At one edge of the tank, a ramp leads up and out. One of the crew lifts a wooden panel, which slides up and down over the ramp, after each poolful of sputtering wool balls is thoroughly saturated. The animals stumble up the ramp and enter a holding pen, where they stand still, huffing and dripping. By the time one cohort of treated sheep are in the pen, with the sun yellowing their backs, there are six more sheep, released from the pen on the opposite side, sloshing in the pool. From time to time, without words, the workers switch jobs. The trio is a machine of bent backs, glistening foreheads and upper lips, and strong arms. Rafael and the young *peón* work in tandem, as in tune as two tires on a pickup.

The pace of the work is steady but leisurely thanks to the aching fatigue in the three sets of shoulders. They have already been at this work for several days, dipping around five hundred sheep a day. Rafael and Roberta, as is customary for neighbors, are sharing their workloads, spending alternate days dipping at the two estancias.

Summer is the busiest time on Península estancias: The sheep must be dipped, the wool around their eyes clipped, lot changes must be carried out. "There are no calm days," Rafael says. His tired eyes, during the summer of my talks with him, attested to this truth. And Liliana told me, "I often spend the whole day alone. Yesterday, Rafael left at five, and I didn't see his face again until nine at night."

La Entrada occupies two or three of the enormous lots of desolate, juiceless ground into which Península Valdés is divided.

The buildings of the estancia on which Rafael works are located uncommonly close to the main road, positioned as they are about half a kilometer distant from the one curve in the otherwise arrow-straight, north-south dirt swath. From the road, the low, white, red-roofed cement house, with its small fenced yard, looks insignificant in the immensity of open land. A large sheet metal barn, next to which the crew toils over the sheep dip, stands plain, about a kilometer off to one side. On every compass setting from the settlement, the barren campo, dotted with ankle-high thornbushes, spreads unrumpled to the horizon.

Rafael is *puestero* of La Entrada, and the fact that his title is *puestero* rather than *peón* gives him pride. Rafael's position demonstrates his Buenos Aires employer's belief in him and also allows him to make some money. As *puestero* he receives 25 percent of the estancia's profits. Receiving a percentage, Rafael has told me several times, gives a man the impetus and vigor to go the extra kilometer: to ride the fence lines and mend them or to nurse orphaned lambs. As *puestero* of La Entrada, Rafael is possessor of one of the most coveted jobs on the Península.

When I started visiting him, Rafael had just been given the charge of 1,500 additional sheep. Even with the 3,500 he had had previously, and their yield of 16,000 kilos of wool, he had felt, as he says in characteristic understatement, that he was doing "well enough."

"As for what you earn in the campo, a lot of professionals aren't earning what I am earning here," Rafael impressed on me as we sat together drinking tea in his kitchen. "I earn a lot.

"The owner here is very good and pays well, so I am well situated." This year, 1985, Rafael made two million pesos, about seven hundred dollars a month, a doctor's salary in Argentina at the time. Over the years, by handy management of the erratic Argentine peso, he has come to own three homes in Madryn, a pickup truck, and a car. "We're comfortable. We're doing well," Rafael says.

Rafael has weighed his work in the campo against the occupations of the many sheep men who have moved to Puerto Madryn, the town two to three dirt road hours away. He reckons that the daily wage in the campo is less, but in six months a campo man has much more in his pouch than his fellow in town.

"In town, you live in the present. Nothing more. I never worked in town, but from what I know about this whole system of life, I have a good idea of how it is. Because, for each thing I buy in town, it's three hundred, five hundred pesos, and the daily wage of most of these people can't be much above that, eh? I don't know what the wages are today, because people talk about high salaries, but those with more, those with less, I see that they all go around just on the edge, no more.

"No, no, in the campo you can earn well. With a different life, no? You don't have the movies, you don't have the cafés, you don't have a series of things, but when you go to town, you go with fifty to sixty pesos. Okay, you might be there only three or four days, but at least . . ."

As his life has sewn itself together, Rafael has held only two major *puestero* jobs: at his brother-in-law's estancia and at La Entrada. This unusual happenstance for a sheep man—many such men tend to rove—and the independence and longevity with which he has overseen the estancias are a great source of satisfaction. Rafael shakes his head and laughs, looking around him at the land he stewards. "I came to try it out for a year. For a year, eh?"

Rafael's face is lobster red as he wrestles a huge ewe into the brown sea. Dipping is high-pressure work, and it is a backbreaker. Rafael, though, thirty-seven years a *puestero*, is not afraid of hard work. Work is his fuel, a meal, his elixir.

As I watch the strapping man, it seems his job fits him like a sheep fits into its wool. Rafael is the sort of man who oils the gears of the latifundio system, he is the definition of a sheep man. His self-reliance, honesty, supreme confidence, punishing sense of responsibility, and physical superiority make him a target for any Buenos Aires landowner.

Rafael's work life has had the same diligence, the same relentless clip, as the work around the dip. His career on Península Valdés estancias has rippled, like a stack of dominoes, from nine-year-old asado cook, to odd jobber, to the supreme aim: *puestero*, estancia manager. He is a local success story. The stories that Rafael told me about his boyhood, however, revealed that his accomplishments did not come easily.

Often I arrived for a visit at La Entrada around dusk, when the day's work was winding down. On these visits, when the father of two adult children arrived from the campo, Liliana and I would usually have been chatting for a while in the dimming kitchen, and then the sheep man's wife would light the kerosene lantern.

Soon Rafael would stand in the doorway. For a minute he would lean against the frame, blinking as the light hit his face, the folds of his cheeks, shining with sweat, his mouth still open from exertion. The tall form exuded fitness. The shirttails coming out of his pants, his trousers bunched through the belt loops over his slim waist, his silver bush of hair grander and wilder than when he is fresh, the working man would kiss Liliana and sit down thankfully on the hard chair at the head of the kitchen table, his long legs sprawled in front of him. Then, after Liliana had put the mate in his hand, and in response to my interest, the born storyteller would "put himself to talking."

Once, he reflected on the hard work of his childhood. "My mother died when I was five. Those years were very hard, and those things happened."

When the catastrophe happened, Rafael's father, who had worked a wool transport wagon on the Península, took his grief away to Río Negro, the province to the north, to look for work and left his young son to be raised by his daughters.

"When I was first orphaned I lived in Madryn. I had another sister in Madryn, and she had me for three or four months—that was when I got the little schooling I did—and then she sent me to the campo, to another sister, with a man. I was almost six. They gave me some tiny suitcases and they tied a little string around my neck, with the keys of the suitcases." Rafael gestured to show how small he was and how minuscule the suitcases were. "That was how they sent me to my sister. All alone."

The little boy's trip through the unfamiliar, deserted campo probably took at least fourteen hours. Rafael's sister Vitoria was about nineteen, and three years married, when her small brother appeared at her door.

Rafael grew up poor. While he and his nephew-brothers played among the thornbushes, their stomachs craved raisins, dried peaches, and green vegetables to supplement their diet of mutton.

Once, when he was still very young, Rafael had what he now calls "the day of the olive." He was visiting the Irazazabal estancia, the one ranch on the Península where the exceptional soil could support a huge garden as well as vineyards and fruit and olive trees. Young Rafael decided he would spend the day eating olives. "The problem was I didn't realize you couldn't eat them raw." The serious face broke into a laugh as he said, "So my day got ruined.

"As for our way of playing, the things that interested us were the things we saw around us. Like horses." On Sundays Rafael and the neighbor children, who lived five kilometers away, would play with the horses they had made from broomsticks. "We were a herd. We went off, all of us little *gauchitos*, for round and about. We ran on these horses all over the place."

The only formal schooling Rafael had was the three or so months he got in town just after his mother died. The sheep man's words wended along as he thought about the kind of learning to which he had access. "You know, I didn't have schooling. After those three or four months of primary, I learned for myself in the campo. My sister taught me some, but what stayed with me most was going around learning and correcting myself and trying to find a place for myself. I didn't learn what I did because I had school. I didn't have any."

The farm work provided all the elements of a campo lad's school: hard toil, occasional rewards, rare good teachers, chances for developing high standards of achievement and work habits, and occasional opportunities for a sense of accomplishment. Rafael was a good student. The school of the Patagonian open spaces prepared him well for work on an estancia, and the many aspects of a farmer's round also provided him plenty of fodder for thinking.

During Rafael's boyhood, mail was delivered by a man on a four-wheeled wagonette pulled by three horses. In 1932 he heard his first radio broadcast. The radio in question had huge four-foot-high batteries with power that lasted only minutes. Rafael's brother-in-law's father, Tomás Irazazabal, owned the radio, and he ruled over it like a dictator. Whoever was at the estancia would gather in the old man's kitchen to hear the crackling voices from Comodoro.

"You put it on a few minutes in the morning," Rafael said, chuckling, "and there was no more radio, eh? With those batteries you just got a few minutes' worth." He chuckled again, and then his voice went low, and he puffed like a self-important man as he said, "And when he decided to turn it off, no one listened anymore. No one touched it. Ever."

Picking his way over the sapless years of his youth when he and his sister's family lived on next to no *gita*, Rafael rubbed his thumb and middle finger together, in the Argentine gesture for money. He then pushed toward me a plate of sandwich cookies Liliana had put on the table. "Eat. Eat. You're still young!" he said, and then went on. "Those were very difficult years. We were just barely making it economically."

Once or twice a year Rafael's brother-in-law went to Madryn to put in his food order at the wholesale warehouses, and once or twice a year a man in a truck delivered the "consumables" to the family and the other campo inhabitants. The three or four hundred kilos of provisions arrived in huge crates, which were divided into sections holding different kinds of food. The family bought forty kilos of noodles, four or five seventy-kilo sacks of flour, enormous sacks of crackers, and a giant's quantity of *yerba*, the herb for the ubiquitous campo beverage, mate. "The people from before couldn't do without those. They had to have mate."

The warehouses gave the campo dwellers credit without interest, and every year, when the sheep ranch managers sold the wool, they went to town to pay for the previous year's supplies and put in orders for the year ahead.

During those lean years, the Mendizabal-Irazazabal family ate lots of homemade cakes and delicious homemade bread, and they sometimes had milk and butter from the estancias that had cows. "We ate a lot of meat." Rafael jigged his hand on his stomach. "A lot of meat." On the Península ranches, "meat" means mutton, sheep cooked every conceivable way.

Rafael described, half swearing and shaking his head, the old-style campo medicine. Neighbor women-midwives were fetched by frantic husbands on horses to tend the isolated mothers out in the wastes in their nondescript mud houses. Mothers "brought their babies to the light," as the campo people say, alone.

The campesinos used "flax-flour plasmas" to treat various ailments, and beefsteaks fried in grated sulfur were applied by practiced sheep wives' hands to draw out children's animal stings. For sore throats, the best remedy was a compress of ashes or hot coals.

"They made all these remedies." Rafael's lip curled in disdain for their inefficiency; perhaps he was remembering his mother, who had died young. "Sometimes you were lucky and they saved you. And sometimes, '¡Ciao!' " There was a single doctor in Madryn when Rafael was a boy, but the campesinos could seldom get there, and when they did it was often too late. "No one ever knew what happened.

"And I'll tell you," he asserted, "I wouldn't like anybody to go back to that. I went through all that. It's true that I'm not greatly dissatisfied with what I went through, but it wasn't any way to live, either.

"Then, at age nine," he said, returning to his boyhood activities, "while I still liked toys, they gave me a job. I had the job of going off on a little horse in the morning to the corrals where they were going to treat the livestock for scab. I tended the asado that the men would eat for lunch. At age nine!

"Back in those years, they treated the livestock totally differently. They didn't dip; they treated the animals with applicator bottles of the *remedio*. So my job was to fill the bottles and hand them to each man as he applied the *remedio* to the animals. By the age of fourteen, fifteen, I was already starting to look out for myself with respect to jobs."

At first Rafael worked at the estancia of his brother-in-law, the one who raised him, and then, as he related it to me, "I withdrew from my brother-in-law's side a little, in order to think about how life was."

By eighteen the young Rafael had a brisk working life, where he called his own shots, hiring himself out to do day work. Using his brother-in-law's house as a base, the energetic young man was sought after by all the *puesteros* on the surrounding estancias. "I did shearing jobs, dipping jobs; I'd do anything. But I worked very little as a *peón*," he added.

Rafael liked odd jobbing, and he got rich doing it. While a *peón* might earn a salary of sixty to seventy pesos a month, Rafael could pocket up to six pesos a day.

After being excused from military service because of vision problems, Rafael worked for a little less than a year each at two different estancias. At the end of the second year, at a ranch called La Pamplona, Rafael had set his sights on leaving the Península, traveling six hundred kilometers south to Puerto Deseado to take on a job his brother had found for him, but the brother-in-law to whom he owed everything came to find him and made him an offer he couldn't refuse.

"I told my brother-in-law I was going to leave.

"Okay, he came back two days later, to the *puesto* [sheep station] where I was living, and asked if I hadn't changed my mind. So I told him, no, I hadn't changed my mind. I had decided to go. Then he proposed that I take on his campo, the one my sister now has.

"He says to me, 'Instead of leaving here, go take my place. I'll give you thirty percent,' he says. So I went over to his place. And I was there twenty years."

Because his brother-in-law's estancia was small, with only 1,200 head of sheep, Rafael repaired windmills, drove a truck, and even worked as a wildlife ranger for a time to supplement the slim earnings from the farm.

At the twenty-year mark, Rafael left his brother-in-law's employ and took his current, and second, *puestero* job at Estancia La Entrada, where he has spent the last eighteen years.

"Sometimes I think it's the luck factor," Rafael told me, referring to the many jobs he has been offered. "But you also have to know how to conduct yourself. You have to have a sense of responsibility. José," he said of the venerable old neighbor who lives half an hour away, "is a man who is also earning well. He's a man."

The standards Rafael holds for his performance are fierce. He relishes stories that reveal his stout code of honor, his high standards. As he launched into one of these tales, he motioned to his skinny grandson who was sitting, silent, listening in the shadows. The boy was visiting La Entrada for the week. The pretty-faced boy approached his grandfather, then stood in an attitude of reverence and lit his grandfather's cigarette. The red butt glowed in the gray light.

Then Rafael began.

"When I was a young fellow, I was on an estancia doing day work for a month, a place where there was an Italian in charge. We had finished all the sheep dipping, so then I say to this Italian, I say, 'So now, Don Emiliano, we've finished the work.'

" 'Yes,' he says to me.

" 'Okay, I'm going to leave,' I say to him.

"And he says, 'What do you mean, you're going to go?'

" 'Well, we finished dipping, finished everything, and I'm going to go.'

"He says to me, 'I never told you how much I was going to pay you.' Because, me, I never asked what I would get for my work.

" 'No,' I say to him, 'you never told me what you were paying.'

" 'I was paying you four pesos per day,' he says, 'for the days you dipped, and the days you didn't dip, you were earning at the rate of seventy pesos a month.'

" 'That's fine,' I say to him. 'Thanks.'

" 'And if you stay,' he says, 'I'm going to pay you eighty, and the girls,' he said, because he had two single girls, 'the girls will wash your clothes.'

"And me, always a joking man, I say to him, 'No, Don Emiliano, that's okay. I'll just leave my clothes dirty.' And I left."

I could picture the high-chinned fellow, with his affected breeziness, swaggering out.

After the story he explained, "I worked, but I never asked the wage, eh?" It was clear that this was a key tenet in Rafael's code of conduct. His feeling of manliness hinges on his possession of a solemn dignity, an impeccable honesty, and a dash of chivalry. Charmed landowners fought to have the young Rafael work for them and to pay him more.

"Now I always did like a compliment," Rafael said, beginning another of his ambling stories about himself as a youth. "I always liked a lot of praise. On one estancia where I worked, the boss got up every single morning, every last morning, at three, three-thirty. Can you imagine it? By three this man was on his feet. In those years they had nine thousand and some wool bearers. Almost every day we had a dip going.

"I had an alarm clock and I got up at two in the morning. The rest of the people stayed asleep. Every morning, at two in the morning, I was up," Rafael whispered, as though he were creeping around, trying not to awaken anyone.

"I took a few mates, cooked myself a little steaklet, and I waited. Left the fire going, with hot water, for the others when they got up. And at four, four and a bit, you'd hear the truck that they had start up. And there he came.

"The boss never had to call me. And when he leveled my account he said to me, 'You're the only man I haven't had to call in the morning.' No one has ever had to call me, up to the present. Not one day." Rafael wondered at himself. "How I have this sense of responsibility!"

The *puestero* of La Entrada pulled his callused hand through his luxuriant pompadour. "Sometimes when I go to bed, usually I'm in bed at ten and something, I sleep a deep sleep, until twelve, twelve and something. Then I wake up. And the first thing I do is think over the things I have to do. Like whether I have a windmill on or not. 'Oh, yes.'" Rafael recaptured the way he talks to himself in his bed. "'It's okay. I don't have anything else to do.' And I roll over and sleep again. . . . There are very few days that I go to sleep peacefully, and when I do, it's usually for the siesta. Then I might sleep three hours, and really sleep them. But when I have a worry, you think I'm going to stay asleep? Not even by accident.

"And this grandson of mine is exactly the same way. A boy who doesn't forget even the smallest thing. He wakes up worrying, nervous, afraid he forgot something."

Rafael stubbed out his cigarette, as though stamping down a part of himself. He tried to put into words something he couldn't name. "I feel this . . . I don't want the *patrón* to call attention to me because I have been careless. I don't want the *patrón* to come and find a dry tank or a fallen fence. What I try to do is get ahead of myself, if I can, with the work."

The man with the weather-chiseled face, who paid high dues to earn his present position in this ungiving section of the world, shakes his head when he speaks of the young.

"The young people don't want to pay for the right to the floor, as we call it. They don't want to start from the bottom. They want to come home with a job in charge of an estancia. It can't be. With the value lands have today—many millions of pesos—and the value of wool bearers, these estancias represent immense capitals, so you can't leave just anybody in charge of them."

Rafael believes, in general, that people nowadays work less. The people with whom he grew up had an ingrained sense of responsibility. "I don't find the sense of responsibility that people had before. There is a lack of the man who wants to enslave himself a little."

He conjectures that before, maybe the illiteracy and lack of culture of the people might have produced their greater respect for work and employers. "If a person was a *patrón*, you felt respect. Fear."

At the same time he believes that he was brought up with too great a sense of respect.

"We were raised in a way that was too oppressed. It was too extreme. You went around with fear, too polite. You were timid. They raised us to have this respect for an older person. With these people, I don't know, it always seemed like they were a lot more than you were. If someone told me, 'Today Doctor So-and-so is going to arrive,' oi! God save me! That was something.

"And now it's happened, many times, that we have had conversations with these people and it turns out that we're all equals."

In spite of his views on his own respectfulness, Rafael has drummed into his daughters both respect for elders and respect for work.

"It seems that a lot of *chicos* now are raised too loosely. The parents teach them badly because they don't teach them to be independent. The parents should say to a *chico*, 'Look, these thousand pesos are yours. The others are mine. You have to manage your life with these thousand pesos.' Teach him to make a system for living, give him a form to follow, a sense of discipline.

"We raised two daughters and they studied. My daughters didn't lack anything, ever. But I always counseled them that they had to learn to administer a peso, that they had to think about the fact that we won't be with them all their lives, that they had to look to their futures, and things like this. So, from the time they were very tiny, they began to work, to earn their pesos. If it wasn't a lot for them, I didn't care, because there was an extra peso in the house, see? But they had their fancies like all young girls, and they needed an extra peso. In general, they asked their mother for money, see, but their mother told them, 'You have to ask Papá about it. You ask Papá and he will give it to you.'

"Then they'd say, 'Papá, could you give me five thousand pesos for this, for that?'

"Okay, five thousand, take them. Take five thousand pesos. But you have to pay back those pesos. I don't care if you can't pay me five thousand the first month, or the second, or anything. The day you can't you can't, and that's how it is. But you have to return that money.

"There were a lot of people who said, 'You have some gall to do that with your daughters.' Yes, I have it. And today, one is thirty-three and the other thirty-one, and never, ever, in my life, have they turned their faces to me and said, 'Papá could you pay for me, could you lend me one thousand pesos?' Never. They learned to administer a house. They are both wives who have their children, their husbands. What I did, I see as correct. I feel happy, and I notice that they have appreciation for me. I feel proud of my daughters, and of my grandchildren . . . and of my señora, too." Rafael gave a slurred laugh as he tried to slip that one by, but I caught his eyes darting to his wife. . . .

One afternoon, Rafael and Liliana remarked that they had been married thirty-five years. Rafael leaned back in his chair, stretched, and said offhandedly, "Oh, yes, I did fine until I was twenty-four and I married my señora!"

Liliana laughed and poked him back. "You were twenty-six!"

"There were lots of good women in those days," Rafael continued. "We're talking forty, fifty girls right nearby. So how were you going to choose?"

Rafael disappeared for a few minutes then, and Liliana rose from the table and started chopping vegetables for stew. Her husband returned, stroking his chin, and went over to her by the stove.

"I shaved," he said, standing close to his wife. "I don't know why, but I shaved." Then he came back to the table.

"But, eh? It's amazing how you are drawn to lineage! Because my wife is of Basque descent and I am, too. Look, I am Men-

dizabal, Spanish Basque last name. And she is Bordenave. Spanish Basque."

Rafael proceeded to tell us about his wedding. "Everything
went well until I met my wife," he joked, patting Liliana's arm.
"When I got married, Juan Eriztea gave me a calf. Instead of a
cow, he gave me a calf to eat at the wedding. That, and a
suckling pig. He had three hundred-plus cows. He said to me,
'Rafael, take a pig.' Yes, he loved me.

"We got married on his establishment. My brother-in-law and
sister were there as *puesteros*, so we married there, in the campo.
The whole family was there. And my other brother-in-law, another Irazazabal, did some barbecues *a cuero*. A barbecue *a cuero*
is half a cow barbecued with skin and fur left on. Nice and fat.
We ate like barbarians!"

At the conclusion of my visits, the darkness and wind enfold-
ing us all, the couple would stand at the entrance to their yard.
As I'd get into my car, Rafael would yield to his fatigue, put an
arm around Liliana, and lean into her tenderly, his large figure
undiminished by the frank admission of weariness.

One day early in my friendship with Rafael, he took Peter and
me out across the exposed, cold stretch of barren campo to the
barn to see his new VW-Dodge pickup truck. The Patagonian
ran his hand caressingly from the front globe lights, along the
crown of the sky blue cab, and back along the edge of the shiny
new tailpiece while we stood and admired it. Then he opened
the cab door. There was a glow of soft light from inside the cab,
and he beckoned to us. We saw the spanking clean powder blue
seats, the light that illuminated the keyhole, and the cassette
player that blasted accordion music. The rancher's face had the
same dreamy gaze that it had had as he had watched the car
cross the campo from the dipping trough.

I have never gone in much for vehicles, and it took me a
long time to understand that gaze, and why Rafael had shown
me the Dodge, and what it meant to him. Rafael's meager, isolated childhood gave the bright young boy a passion. From the

time he saw his first dust cloud rising behind a vehicle traversing the barren sweep of his homeland, Rafael was enamored of the internal combustion engine. Cars, and the machines inside them, were his hope and his fascination and the orienting point in his mind for as long as he could remember.

"From the time I was very small, I was distinctive with respect to cars. From the moment I saw my first car, I loved them.

"Back then, *dulce de membrillo* [a thick jellylike dessert made of quince] came in four-kilo cans, so I used to make cars for myself out of those tins.

"I used a broom handle for axles, and then I worked the wheels, you see." The man's fingers manipulated imagined pieces of wood and tin as he explained, "And then I drew myself some long little roads with a string. And then, do you know those little sardine tins? I made a type of little train with those. Hooked one to the other, see? So I had those trains, too. I loved all that.

"And later my brother-in-law bought a car. A car! I will always remember it. A Ford! Aaah! 'Aaah!' they all said, because it had four cylinders. It was the brand Ford-A. Model 1930, around there. Nice little car.

"Ai! How I watched that car all the time. He kept it in the barn. During siesta I'd be awake and I'd keep my eye on the barn. When I saw there was no movement, I'd get in the car. I would sit there and turn the steering wheel." Rafael transformed into a suave and practiced driver, lovingly steering, changing gears with a flick of the wrist. I could easily picture him in a cap, a white scarf, and sleek black driving gloves.

"Then, in the year 1936, my brother-in-law bought a new pickup truck. Zero kilometers. Eight cylinders. I was eleven by that time, twelve, and he taught me to repair the tires. There were a lot of spines and it was hard to come across a day when a tire didn't appear on its rim, so I repaired them. He promised me he was going to teach me to drive, but first I had to learn to fix tires.

"Time passed, but this guy didn't teach me to drive. So,

during siesta, while he was sleeping the siesta, I would go to the barn." Rafael used his voice like an actor, whispering dramatically as he described sneaking into the truck. "The pickup was brand new, and silent. I turned it on. I put it in gear. I moved it forward. Then I moved it back. Inside the barn. Then I left it in the same position. Always in the same position I found it in.

"Then, one day, while we were having lunch, I don't know how, but in the course of the conversation it turned out that he was going to teach me to drive. And I said to him"—Rafael was a swank, cool teenager now—" 'I already know how to drive.'

" 'You already know? Baff!'

" 'If you go on roads, I'm not sure, but drive, yes, I know how.'

" 'I don't believe it.'

" 'Well, I know how.'

"Okay, we stopped eating. So in an instant the pickup was outside the house. 'Come here,' he says, 'so we can see if you know how to drive.' I got in, on the passenger side.

" 'No. Get in the driver's seat,' he says. I sat in the driver's and he sat on the other side.

"He says to me, 'Turn it on.' I turned it on right away.

"He says, 'Okay, move it.' I took hold of the clutch, put it in gear. We started moving.

"And we did two, three turns around the lagoon. He told me to put it in neutral. I put it in neutral, braked. We left again. We came back, parked, parked where the truck had been.

"And he says to my sister, 'He knows how to drive, this one. This guy knows how to drive.' " Rafael laughed deliciously, triumphant. The experience was as alive then as it had been forty-nine years ago.

It is not impossible that Rafael's passion for vehicles welled up through his genes. After all, his father was a wagoner.

Rafael waxed long on the little he knew about the life of the father he last saw when he was barely six. "My father, like other people in those days, had a *chata*, those big cargo wagons that could carry five or six thousand kilos and were pulled by twelve or fourteen horses. The back wheels of some of them could have had a diameter of two hundred and fifty centimeters. Not all of them, but some of them sure did. And in the front they had small wheels—maybe a meter and centimeters, about there, no more. In sandy places, like the dunes over there at Bella Vista, there were times when you had to attach sixteen horses to go in and get out again. These *chatas* were the method of transport people had. They brought in things for settling the campo and the consumables, and they took out the fruits, the wool.

"At that time they shipped the majority of the wool from Pirámides and from Puerto San Román. It would have been very difficult to transport the wool to Puerto Madryn like they do now. Now in those days, the harbor beacons, the buoys, the lights that signal the boats, all these were brought on these horse wagons. Around the years 1910, 1912, and at the time of the seal exploitation, all the transport was done with *chatas*, all the transport of the oil, the skins.

"My father did a lot of that work. I was very small at the time. I think that those people from before worked badly, but they worked hard. Because, do you know what it is to harness twelve horses in the morning, when it is still dark, and then at twelve, say, unharness them again, twelve horses? Let them drift so they can eat a little, and in an hour and a bit go back and harness them up again. Those people worked.

"The mobility problem"—the man shifted on his chair, sitting up, his hand in a fist on the table—"is one of the reasons I wouldn't return to the old days. When my brother-in-law got his own vehicle, we went to visit his relatives, the Irazazabals, a lot, but before that, almost never. If he had to go there to do something, he went by horse. Eighteen leagues. About ninety kilometers. We just stayed at home. We went to town once a year, when we went. It was like that up to the time I was maybe sixteen, seventeen.

"*Mierda* . . ." Rafael rolled the Spanish word for "shit" off his tongue luxuriously, in a soft voice, letting the final syllable fade, and took a long pull on his cigarette. He settled in to ponder the old days in the campo and squinted off somewhere, into the dim light. "Life in the campo was full of sacrifices."

When the Península was first settled, people went everywhere on foot or, if they were lucky, by horse. Even when Rafael was a boy, the indwellers on the peninsula thought nothing of riding to Madryn or Pirámides. The journey by horse through the un-occupied tableland between the Península and Madryn took twenty-five hours. The horsemen left the Península at dawn and arrived in town at first light the following day. He might take along something to nibble in the saddle, but he didn't stop to eat, and he usually rode without pause. "Those were some stu-pendous horses!" Rafael declared, blowing out a smooth stream of smoke that turned into a low whistle.

In the early days on the Península there was virtually no way, except by horse, to get around the grassless countryside. Horse carts, the prized possessions of some families, began to be re-placed around 1923 by the first Fords, but it took the little Model-T's "without exaggerating, ten to twelve hours to get from the Península to Madryn." Rafael wagged his finger lest I conclude that the mere availability of cars made it easy to travel.

"I think the velocity of those little Ford T's was probably between twenty-five and thirty kilometers on these curved roads. And there were also lots of gates, so you had to stop, get out, open the gate, pass through, stop again, and close the gate again. Yes, I'd tell you that you had ten hours of driving cut out for you." Rafael pulled at the coils of loose skin on his neck. "From over there in Punta Norte, where we were, it was a ten-hour trip to Madryn."

Now the gas lamp whirred in the hushed room, and as Rafael described the difficulty of moving around the campo, I began to comprehend why he had, with such hushed excitement, taken us to the barn to see his new pickup. He had to introduce us to an intimate friend, to the source of hope in his life, to the engine of his being, to the interest he held in common with his father.

I should have instantly comprehended Rafael's interest in ve-hicles. I could have taken a clue from my own feelings about vehicles when I was in Patagonia, but it didn't occur to me—a car hater with no mechanical aptitude—to bring them into focus. Our truck was a constant annoyance and therefore a significant being in our life there. Our trips to Madryn on the poor dirt roads took anywhere from two and a half hours to four or five, depending on the number of tires that were punctured along the way. The Industria Argentina tires on our truck had flats every time we ventured out. Each time we left the house we took sleeping bags, matches, canned food, water, and extra *bidones* of petrol, for fear the truck might break down on some especially bleak stretch of road and no one would pass for days. Then there was the strange fact that when I lived in Argentina, I listened for engines and watched the distance for telltale dust plumes. The rare sound of a motor meant company and diversion and a leap in my heartbeat. Motors and vehicles had significance in Patagonia, even for me.

Rafael's genes, childhood, and good mind gave him his passion, and that passion, in turn, handed him a question—the question that is the only loose connection in a life that has been more successful than the young, eager campo boy ever dreamed. Rafael revealed this unanswered question on two or three occasions. I had a sense that I was one of the few with whom he could lift the hood on his secret, for he knew I was a person with dreams and education.

The question first arose when Rafael worked as a park ranger. During this period, he made and sold sandwiches to the occasional tourists who came to visit the remote and strange sea lion colony that he oversaw. The newly married young man drank in ideas and news from the foreigners and city people as they stood munching his sandwiches under the sheet metal lean-to he had fashioned for himself.

Rafael said of the ranger work, "I did it for a year and I liked it a lot. I could have gone on to become more, because this man, Guerrero, the boss, wanted to send me to Buenos Aires to take a course. I would have liked that. It would have been good to get a little more education. It might have been very important for me." He shrugged and shook his head and looked down. Facing one of a Patagonian man's few moments of choice, Rafael accepted a secure *puestero* post rather than going to the city for training. He wondered, looking back, if he was foolish. "I don't know if I'm better off or not."

On a second occasion, Rafael wondered about his intelligence, though he would never call it that. "I have a lot of ideas about a lot of things," he said. "I have always been interested in things—very interested. I always put a lot of attention into everything."

As a young man, Rafael illustrated to himself his powers of learning when a shearing gang was casting around for someone to sharpen the shearing machine.

"They said to me, 'You don't know anything about sharpening, do you?' 'Maybe I do,'" Rafael allowed. "And, yes, I picked up the fork, as they call it, put on the apparatus, and at first it didn't come out too well, but in two or three days it came out."

The man shifted on the hard chair, squared his shoulders, and took a leisurely drag on his cigarette as he told the story. The cinders sparked in the dark kitchen.

"I'm not going to tell you that I should have been a mechanic, but I could sharpen you one of those tools."

A third time he talked about what might have been, Rafael worked out what he thought as he spoke:

"No one taught me much, but I always liked to learn. I was raised well, but I didn't have the chance to study or to be able to go around, see things. Probably because of that, I was left a little . . ." He paused, as if he couldn't find the right word to express his shyness.

"Because by the time I was eighteen, I could have left. I had already made myself independent, you see? But I stayed on with livestock work. I was afraid to leave. It was that kind of fear that something could go wrong for me. Worse than it was already going, see? So I stayed. And I was afraid to say, 'Okay, I am going over near Bahía,' or, 'I'm going someplace.' I was scared that things would be worse for me."

Finally Rafael heaved out his long-hidden dream. "I could have maybe gone into mechanics, and that kind of thing."

Beyond his question about what he might have become if he had had better schooling, I came across another basic source of unease in Rafael's life, rooted in the barren reaches of Patagonia. That unease is evoked at a particular hour in the day: dusk.

Speaking of the scores of *peones* who live alone on the Patagonian estancias, Rafael told me, "I don't know what draws them to this solitude." This man, who knows intimately the lone sheep man's life, seemed truly mystified. His brows knitted together at the top edge of his horn-rimmed glasses. "Because I was alone a lot too from the time I was very young, due to greater forces. Not for long periods, but I have been alone.

"Ai!" Rafael said dramatically, running his hand through his hair. "For me, there is nothing worse than solitude. I don't feel in accord with it at all. It doesn't calm me at all. When I am alone here for four or five days, I sometimes feel even worse in the house than outdoors. I feel strange. Strange. I have never liked solitude, even though I was alone a lot from the time I was very young. I used to be all alone on a *puesto*. With a job here or another job over there, you get through it, but when dusk arrives and you don't have anyone to converse with, no. For me, no. I have never felt comfortable in solitude."

Many times I went to watch Rafael at work on the blustery campo and to sit at his table and hear about his life, sure that I would find the hero of the *American Heritage* books of my childhood: the essence of the strong, independent, self-reliant, self-made man. I wanted to hold self-reliance close, examine it, and then swallow it whole, as I had seen Rafael himself swallow a ewe's heart.

The man I came to know not only had a distaste for the Península's solitude, but he played no bluffs. He faced life square on, felt his fears, and wrestled with the yearnings in his belly. Every day he faced the knowledge that if he had simply been born to a region of the world with paved roads, he could have become a car mechanic. And each day, nevertheless, he revved his engine, chewed the stale bread on the table in front of him. He did not give self-reliance, an uneasy requirement of his life, a thought. To return, after days on the gray, windy campo, to his woman, his daughters, his grandchildren, and his friends, and to love them soundly, was his aim.

There is a thing in every man that makes him want to re-create what he had, to make it into something fine. Rafael sent his daughters to town to school, but he found a way to educate a boy in the way he knew best.

A few months before the *flechilla* season, and before I started visiting him, Rafael had hired on as his *peón* a seventeen-year-old boy from a troubled family of drinkers and card players. His first nights at La Entrada, the young man was too shy to eat with the older couple; he told them he wanted to be alone. When Rafael and Liliana finally coaxed the boy into the house for dinner, he would leave right after the meal, even when Liliana asked him why he didn't stay and watch the TV they had wired up to Rafael's truck. The couple discovered that if they gave the shy boy the radio to keep him company at night after dinner, he would listen, awake, the night through, and he didn't work well without sleep. In the mornings he came very quietly to the house and asked what he should do.

One day we sat around the table with Rafael at José's, and he reported on the young *peón*'s progress. "Sr. Ñoquis . . ." José chuckled when the boy's name came up. José had given him the name because as soon as the young boy had overcome his shyness about eating in the main ranch house, he had revealed a passion for pasta.

"This *chico* loves pasta," Rafael explained to me, chuckling, too. "You should see his face when Liliana says she has made *ñoquis* or *tallarines*. He can't believe his good fortune."

Rafael continued in the low, hesitant voice of a father afraid to say too soon that his son is a man. "So far, up to now, he's doing well. He doesn't look like the type that would work hard.

At first whenever he would stop working, he would clasp his hands behind his back and sink into the wall. Very timid." Rafael spoke more and more urgently, his voice slow, low, dramatic, building suspense. "I told him I would buy him sheets and blankets for Christmas. I told him, 'You have to live like a person.' And he said, '*Bueno*.' He was happy." Rafael's grave farmer's face briefly cracked a grin.

"Yes, up to now, this fellow has been doing well. He worked really hard at the dipping."

I had noticed the thin young man's socks needled with *flechillas* the day I watched the work at the dipping trough, and when I looked back at the dipping area from the house afterward I could just make out the young man's form in the dark. He was sweeping the dipping pens. He swept the barn as well before he came to check in at the house. "He keeps the barn immaculate," Rafael whispered to us later, "but immaculate."

The sixty-year-old man arrived at the punch of his story in a voice low with understatement. Rafael's words, almost choked with significance, strained to hold in his pride in the boy, his pride in the boy he was, his pride in what he, as a man, stood for, and his pleasure at making this offering to the sheep ranch way of life.

"I told the *peón* that I would buy him a bicycle if this keeps up. That way he can go to Pirámides and get around a little. He was tickled.

"I also told him I would teach him to drive, not to take the car out alone, but I'd teach him. He was happy."

The grin on Rafael's serious, drawn, disciplined face took him over. It was deep and broad, with the kind of shine it probably had forty-five years ago when his brother-in-law had said to Vitoria, "Hey, this guy knows how to drive!"

MEAT
~~~~~

The men work in rhythm, their movements notes in an ancient service. Five of the workers make identical motions, in a continuous round. They catch the lambs, grip them tight around the belly, collect the four legs like ends of a bandanna so that just the straining heads and pillow-soft hindquarters of the young animals are vulnerable, and move them along an assembly line of three other men. The silvering crowns and the Basque-style berets of the lifting men bend over the dirty white animals. The broad backs of the men span strong, and the muscles of their brown arms hold easy and taut.

Guillermo Goikoa, in an amber-colored knit beret, and Rafael, with his jacket turned around backward to keep bloodstains off his shirt, are among those hoisting the sheep. They carry the animals to the fence, on the opposite side of which wait the other three men, as if at a bar.

Angel, José's brother-in-law, clips a V shape into the lambs' ears, for La Bonita's mark. Cachorro, José's *peón*, docks the lambs' tails, and José performs the castrations.

In a series of swift hand motions, the slight, gray-haired estancia manager slices off coins of skin at the bottom of the sacks, yanks until the tubes to the testicles break, and then pops out

the balls. He drops the clear, milky eggs into a metal bucket—
they join their cousins soundlessly.

I, craning over the fence from behind to watch the men's
work, can barely contain my urge to plunge my hand into the
bucket of bloody gooseberries and swirl the compote. Wanting
to try everything in the world once, I am dying to submerge my
hand in that bucket, in a bid for anointment in the camaraderie
of men.

As the men work, there are jokes about *cojones*.

Peter, who is helping to catch lambs, says something about
the lambs being left holding the bag.

José joshes back, "When I was younger, eh? I used to bite
them off with my teeth!"

"What do you do with the contents of that bucket?" I ask.

José points a knobbed, blood-speckled finger toward a pack
of dogs flopped out by the *peón*'s quarters. He looks over his
shoulder at me and winks a grinning eye.

"Feed them to the puppies."

The lamb marking, or *señalada*, is, along with the shearing, one
of the culminations in the sheep men's year. Through days upon
days when the cold presses hard into their chests, and the grit
in the wind stings their eyes and cheeks, the sheep men, like
tireless servants, minister to the sheep. They follow the rhythms
of the month and the weather and the needs of the animals.
Enacting pieces of an ancient liturgy, the sheep men venture
into the desolate campo day after day to clip the wool around
the animals' eyes, to check their water tanks, to ride the fence
lines, to let the rams loose among the ewes, to change the herds
from one lot to another, to check on the condition of the wool,
to repair the windmills, to examine the *pasto*, or forage.

The sheep men, whether *dueños*, *puesteros*, or *peones*, are
bound to the sheep in their charge. They are fathers to thousands.

Almost every sheep man I know has nursed an orphaned
lamb in his kitchen and then had the animal follow him around

as though attached to his leg. One campesino I know had a lamb who thought the man's white pickup was its mother. Every sheep man grieves for a sheep gone over a cliff and mourns the carcass of an armadillo-killed lamb.

The men often talk as though the sheep know exactly what is going on, they feel such kinship with the animals they steward. One day, for instance, when Peter commented that all the sheep were lying down, José joked, "They have figured why eat any more if in a few days we are just going to take all that wool they have been growing?"

The Península men's bond to the merinos, the Australian breed with the finest wool in the world, is deepened and regularly reinforced by the fact that they not only breed and raise the sheep, but castrate, butcher, and eat them as well. Their interdependence with the animals is explicit every day.

The first sheep arrived in Argentina from Perú in 1587. The animals thrived on the estancias of the pampas around Buenos Aires, and by 1840 the numbers of sheep were equal to the numbers of cattle raised in the pampas. In 1852 there were seven sheep for every human being; by the late 1880s the ratio had increased to thirty to one. In 1888 Argentina had eighty-seven million sheep—more than any other country in the world. From the 1850s until after 1900, wool was Argentina's great boom export.

At the turn of this century, the wool economy began to stagnate, and sheep ranching slowed in the key regions surrounding Buenos Aires, in favor of the more lucrative cattle ranching. Between 1895 and 1916 thousands upon thousands of sheep were driven south from the pampas into Patagonia, and the sheep population in Buenos Aires province declined from fifty-six million to eighteen million. By 1937, 38 percent of the sheep in the country resided in Patagonia.

The receptivity of the Patagonian campo to sheep varies, depending on the quality of the vegetation and the rainfall, permitting the survival of anywhere from seven hundred to two thousand sheep per league. A league, approximately equal to five kilometers, is a measure of area as well as distance, and the Patagonian estancias are usually measured by this standard. Alternatively, Patagonian landowners account for their estates by hectares, one hectare being 2.47 acres, or 100 meters by 100 meters. In comparison with Australia, Scotland, or other wool-producing regions in Argentina, the number of sheep sustainable on a league of Patagonian soil is extremely low.

To Patagonia, along with the sheep, came immigrants. By 1914 Patagonia had recruited a higher percentage of its population from immigration than any other region, though the cereal belt had much the highest numbers.

In 1914 the population of Patagonia was only eighty thousand. The region, taking up fully one-third of Argentina's huge landmass, held only a little over one percent of its population, with most of that population residing in the northern fruit-growing province of Río Negro. There were few Argentine-born settlers, and aside from a few military and naval personnel and government administrators, shepherds made up the bulk of the occupants.

The sheep and men arrived to a rural social and economic structure very similar to that of northern Argentina. As in other parts of Argentina, ranching in Patagonia was export-oriented and was most effectively carried out on an extensive, low-cost, low-development basis on huge estancias. The Patagonian land, like that of other parts of Argentina, had been given away or sold in huge tracts. The estancias of the south were often even more immense than those of the northern provinces, since the semidesert lands of Patagonia have only one-tenth the sheep carrying capacity of the terrain in Buenos Aires Province. The average estancia in Patagonia in 1948 was 22,157 acres and remains of similar size today. Ninety percent of the ranches in that same year were above average in size, with some estancias virtual kingdoms of 500,000 to 1 million acres.

The estancias of Patagonia have always been buffeted by the ups and downs of the world wool market, the fluctuations of the Argentine wool tax system, the erratic Argentine economy, and the weather. An ex-rancher friend told me that the final straw, which forced him to sell his beloved estancia, was that while the price of wool remained the same for two and a half years, the cost of living in Argentina rose 180 percent. The same friend tells a story about a year on the same estancia when the snow was so deep and long-lasting that he could not ride out to check his sheep for forty-five days. If he had done so, the thick ice crust on top of the snow would have sliced his horse's legs to ribbons. As a consequence of the rare and cruel weather, the rancher's sheep could not find food and over half of them died.

While sheep estancias have always been subject to various capricious and threatening forces, their viability as units of family support has been further diminished in more recent years, due to political processes. In the fifties, for instance, President Perón forced many Patagonian ranches to subdivide, sometimes in the name of land reform, sometimes in blatant favoritism, and usually in an unsystematic fashion and with little regard for the necessities of sheep raising. Some large estancias were confiscated and given away to the landless, while other small estancias, with the minimum of five thousand sheep that made them self-supporting, were cut in half and rendered totally unviable. When in some areas the campo was divided geographically, one estancia owner might be left with a holding with rich land and plenty of water, while the land remaining in his neighbor's hands might be both waterless and of poor quality. In some places now, the smaller estancias' yields are so low that the *puesteros* are wealthier than the *dueños*, whose entire profit margin is eaten up in estancia maintenance.

The average estancia on Península Valdés has 4,000 to 5,000 sheep on approximately six leagues of campo. Many ranches have as few as 2,000 sheep, while there are a handful of large estancias of up to 80,000 head. The pasturage on the Península is of variable quality, and water on the estancias runs from crystalline and sweet, to brackish, to downright salty, to nonexistent. This variability in land quality and water supply accounts for the range in viability of the various land holdings. Most Península estancias are operated by *puesteros*, but many landowners are now shifting over to exclusive employment of *peones*.

It takes capital to run an estancia. The *patrón* covers most estancia maintenance expenses—expenditures for fencing, building repair, shearing shed construction, and the like. The *puestero* pays his own personal expenses and contributes 25 percent for some designated sheep-rearing necessities such as the sheep dip. The *puesteros* manage and live on the estancias, and landowners, often living in the big cities far away, know little about day-to-day operations. In addition to the *puestero* and his family, a *peón*, hired by the *puestero* for a tiny salary, might work and live on the estancia.

As in other parts of Patagonia, the few larger estancias on the Península are run according to "administration farming." The large estancias are broken into smaller units of 5,000 to 25,000 acres that can be managed by *puesteros* or *peones* and their families. An administrator has responsibility for overseeing the whole operation. On the largest farms, there are several levels of staff: the administrator and his support staff, geographical area supervisors, foremen, and *peones*.

The men at the lamb marking were an assortment of neighboring *puesteros* and *peones*, with the owner of La Bonita joining them.

With the coming of the warmer days of September, I spent hours wandering on the campo, wending my way around the low bristle bushes with the odd stiff orange flowers they put out for spring and watching the newborn lambs gambol over the usually barren land.

One day I saw a lamb and a *chulengo*—a newborn guanaco—butting up against each other in play, the one a bouncing fluff on spindly legs, the other a gawky young giraffe. On another day I saw a lamb's tail sticking out of the rear end of a ewe. The poor animal was giving birth in the middle of the road when our truck forced her to waddle off. Her offspring's bloody tail was waving around in the air below her own tail stump even before the lamb had plopped on the ground and taken its first breath.

It is the lamb tails that give zest and friskiness to spring in desolate, monotone Patagonia. The dry, thorny campo is a sea of bouncing and falling lambs with zany tails. Over a foot long, a floppy hank suspended from a stiffer stump, the tails flail and fling themselves around such that they seem possessed of a spirit and independence separate from the rest of the body.

Spring is the time of year that the sheep ranchers of Patagonia hold their *señaladas*. Once the lambs have fattened and gained sure footing on the dry ground, they are ready to be herded in for their christening by the rancher's barn. For Península dwellers, these once-a-year occasions, when neighboring ranchers gather to mark, castrate, and dock the tails of the lambs, are opportunities for celebration.

The *señalada* marks the year, gathers together neighboring families, and ritually binds the campo men to one another and to the animals on which they depend for their subsistence. During the morning's work of the *señalada*, the men toil in unison, in a kind of baptismal hymn. Sweat pours; blood splashes on the colorless ground. At the end of the day's work there are hundreds of marked lambs, a pile of woolly lamb tails, and a bucket of "lamb berries," as I call them.

The men, who began herding the three thousand sheep at five A.M., perform their rites into the afternoon. A fathomless, blank, blue dome of sky sails over their heads and meets their feet at the tan earth. A dry breeze ruffles the collars of their one-piece work suits and instantly dries their brow sweat into a transparent crust.

Around three, the last bloodstained lamb joins its mother in the bawling, animal-crammed pen. The men release the wires holding the gate closed and watch the dust rise as the ovine mothers and babies scramble, in a huge knot, out onto the blank land.

We fifteen or so women and girls have been sitting all morning chatting in Clara's kitchen, eating slices of yellow cake and drinking cups of lukewarm tea.

"There are only eleven hands, so it will be a long time before we eat," the motherly women tell me, pushing crackers and cake in my direction.

I love these times of sitting around with the campo women, who talk about everything under the sun: babies, breast cancer, car wrecks in town, child-tossing sea lions on the beach, sick relatives, we turn them over like pancakes. From time to time, though, I tear myself away from the kitchen, where women customarily stay until the operations are over, because I am keen to watch the men. I want to understand the sheep men's strange communion. I look over the fence and listen to them, observe everything they do, then hurry back to be with the women.

At around one-thirty there is a knock on the door of the house. Clara moves to meet it. There is a glimpse of a man's back and a beret, and a hushed sentence. Clara returns and the women rise, without a word exchanged. We shuffle across the bald patch from the main house to the *peón*'s quarters.

From the sunlit campo we step into a square, clammy room with gray-green paint on its walls. A wood-fired stove squats in a corner, and small green stools are clustered at the walls. A table along one wall is spread with untouched bowls of peanuts, deviled eggs, crackers slathered with tuna, a ham-and-cheese egg tortilla, and cheese and salami cubes brought by the visiting women. At the opposite end of the room, a huge, square, sharp-cornered fireplace occupies the entire base wall. In its maw, over a mat of coals, stand five perfectly barbecued crucifixes of lamb: La Bonita's indoor asado pit.

The asado room is more essential to a campo family's well-being than a shrine to the Virgin Mary. In that simple but grand concrete indentation sizzles the meat that sustains the flesh and the hope of the Argentine country man and woman. The ability to cook and serve an asado gives the humblest campesino a sense of elegance. Unlike so many luxuries, the asado is available to one and all.

"Come on over tomorrow," José tells us, having come by on his way to moving sheep from one pasture to another. "We're going to kill a sheep."

Every asado eaten is a kind of celebration of the riches of the campo and of life. The morning, noon, and evening cookout of the shepherd on the open range has become entrenched as an Argentine tradition. Every Argentine estancia family, except the most poverty stricken, who must barbecue out-of-doors, has a special room for asados, and any occasion is an excuse for the feast.

I have eaten asados all over the campo, each one with the special seasoning of its cook. While torrential rains fell into the blackest of nights on an estancia in the farthest reaches of the Península, Peter and I sat around an asado in an enormous empty barn with a poor ranch family of three. We all sat silently, chewing sheep and month-old bread and drinking wine, and looked out the half-open barn door into the bone-chilling, wet emptiness. I visited that same family at the site of the tiny house they were building in Puerto Madryn. Before any other part of the house, they had built a small asado room. In that room we again shared a meal.

Riding along a dirt road, I have often seen, way off in the desert, a wisp of smoke rising and being torn away in the wind: a sheep man cooking his midday meal.

Following his shepherd forebears, the traveling Argentine often stops at noon for an asado. A truck full of gas canisters pulled over to the side of the road leads to a man in a blue workshirt poking at an asado over a fire under a rare branching tree. A traveling shearing crew of twelve stopped in an unremarkable stretch of plateau are squatting around a couple of crispy *capones*.

We women line up on a bench along the far wall of the drab, closed room, then sit looking at the asado. Upright on their rods, the crispy, purified lambs are silent and omnipresent as idols. There is a murmur of quiet chat as we wait for the men.

Soon, a dignified and solemn ritual takes place. One by one, each sheep man, scrubbed and slicked and changed out of his blood and dirt-stained overalls, materializes in the sky-bright rectangular opening of the dark room. Each man pauses before he steps in, as though giving a silent prayer before entering a chapel.

The women notice each man in turn as he moves across the room to greet, first, the woman of the estancia, Clara. Holding her shoulders, he places kisses on both of her soft, wrinkled cheeks. Then he proceeds respectfully down the bench, double-kissing each of the women and girls, following Argentine custom.

The earliest-arriving men retreat to a far corner or just out the door. As more men assemble, they gather near the fireplace, the *fogón*. Cinzano—vermouth—with soda, is poured for a couple of them. The women flutter and urge their husbands to eat peanuts and cheese from the table.

The men murmur, in deep voices, to the women about the success of the day's work.

"The weather held."

"José counted up six hundred lambs. Not bad."

"This is one of La Bonita's best years, it seems to me."

"Twelve hundred little *cojones* in the bucket, eh?"

In spite of the fact that the sheep do not belong to José, the men know that the old *puestero* derives pride from La Bonita's productivity.

One of the *peones* giggles as Peter comes in. "So, Peter, you've come to eat asado!"

The *peón* swirls the word in his mouth, then sits himself squarely down on a stool at a wall near the other men, bowl belly before him. He pats it playfully, as one would pat the pink belly of a new puppy, indicating he is well ready to eat.

The room is still quiet and hushed, waiting, as at the start of a mass or a dance.

Before long, a fine-boned, lightly built man appears in the

doorway: José. In a gold-and-gray-striped white shirt—one of those worn, clean cottons that is as comfortable as air—and a pair of gray pants, his wet hair combed and his grizzled, sun-scorched face washed clean of sweat and dust, the *puestero*'s figure emanates a spare elegance.

The man's clear gray eyes take in the scene with a fox's quickness. The loose furrows of the seventy-six-year-old face gather into a smile, and the man's torso begins to jiggle. He waves his arm dismissively to the assembled company now turned to greet him and relaxes the gathering in a quiet but sure voice.

"We shear them and we castrate them and we eat them. We do what we want with them!"

There is the first ripple of laughter.

José joins the men who are sitting on a collection of simple benches close to the fire. A *bota*—a wineskin belonging to one of the men—is produced, and the men pass it around. As each man receives the sheep-grease–coated wine bag, he ritually re-arranges the scrap of burlap wound around it, holds the skin up and out, about a foot from his nose, and receives into his open mouth a clear arc of red wine. At the start of the ritual, the men are grave and solemn as they drink, as though a deep and silent ritual confirmation of maleness is being enacted.

José and the other men hold the wineskin high above their mouths and take in the refreshment gustily, as though drinking from a cow's teat. With quiet lust they let the liquid stream into their mouths, a long river of red wine. The plump *bota* is fat-cured, shiny, and smooth from much handling by sheep eaters' hands.

There is a keeper of the *bota*. As the ritual goes, when the keeper is ready for a draught, he picks up the skin and starts it round. Every man receives the bag, and when it gets back to the keeper, he places it on the bench beside him until he is moved for his next drink.

At one point José has his drink and passes the *bota* on, nodding to Peter to try.

Peter manages a smooth, elegant arc into his mouth, and José ushers in the men's attention with his arm. "With this," he says, pointing to the *bota*, "you can't tell who is *norteamericano* and who is *argentino!*"

The men start to lighten up, their voices louder. They begin to make passages to the hors d'oeuvres table. Holding the *bota* in one hand, José makes this pronouncement to whoever is there to hear:

"The first thing Christ drank was wine. So, you see, we celebrate Christ every day!"

He raises the *bota* and takes in a long, overflowing mouthful of wine. The men jostle each other and laugh.

The five sheep in the fireplace are the dominant presence in the room; they occupy the forward position in the mind of every person present. On the platform a little elevated from the floor, they are the regal centerpiece of the campo altar. The sizzling sheep offer communion after a day of toil in the harsh, unforgiving, dry air. The meat is the life infuser, the salvation in the dry plain. Lips wetted, tongues working to contain salivations, we succumb to the savory, heavy atmosphere.

Everyone having taken hors d'oeuvres and drink, Clara breathes into motion. She hands out knives to those women who don't have them, and the eating begins. She encourages us forward to eat.

"¡*Adelante!* Eat! Eat!"

The careful old hands tremble eagerly as she bids us eat in a lilting, hoarse—voiced chant.

"*Come. Come.*"

José says to Peter, "I hope you brought your knife, young'un. He who forgets his knife doesn't eat, eh?"

When Peter pats the sheath sticking jauntily from his pants just above his crotch, José turns to the others and says, "This one's a real criollo, eh?"

A knife, to an Argentine, is as sacred as his balls. The knife that a man chooses to wear and use is a proclamation of his identity, and the knives in an Argentine shop reflect this fact. In the windows of those dark boutiques, there are knives with handles of every conceivable material: armadillo tails, bullhorn, elephant tusk, mara legs, petrified wood, intricately worked silver, and kid leather, and there is every shape of silver blade. Most of the Península men I know carry simple wood-handled knives but with metals that are sharpened and polished to exquisite flashing blades. Without a knife tucked into his pants, a sheep man feels naked, and precise butchery is the mark of a campo man: butchery that is swift and artful is a coin in the armoire of a campo man's self-respect.

When the house is out of meat, José crosses the fifty yards from the house to the barn with purpose in his lithe stride and lowers a skinned sheep that is hanging, pure and clean-looking in its casing of filmy white membrane, by a rope suspended from a rafter in the barn. He takes his knife from its bull-hide sheath, and with a few expert slices he separates half the sheep from its mate.

At the *peón's* quarters, José squats in front of the huge fireplace and carefully composes the bedding for a fire out of grass and paper. He lights a single match to a piece of paper, and the fire flares instantly. Taking utmost care, he gradually adds kindling and then larger chunks of the gnarled campo bushes. He stands the side of mutton, woven from top to bottom with a metal rod, at an angle upright over the flame and lets it roast for a long time over the low fire. He cooks the underside first. After about two hours the knobbed, purple-veined hands turn the rib cage and allow the skin side of the sheep to roast. About ten minutes before it is time to eat, José lays the crispy, sizzling mutton flat over the fire, dousing each side in turn with the spicy tomato-garlic-oregano *chimichurri* sauce.

The time that José gives to his asados is a measure of himself. On days he has been too busy to give an asado his full attention, he warns us about the unevenness of the cooking. "It may be burned, raw; anything is possible!" A favorite phrase of the old campesino seems to come straight from his devotion to both the raising and consumption of sheep. He says, whenever he wishes to indicate that something comes from the heart, "It is from the rib of . . ."

Good asado preparation is so key an aspect to the male service that when campo men gather to work together, one man is assigned the full-time job of cooking the noon meat.

Each man in the chamber has his knife at the ready—the knife used for butchering is the same one the man uses for eating his daily mutton. Each man, in a turn-taking rite, walks up to the fire and cuts off a rib or a piece of shoulder meat, according to his preference. When he is back at his seat, he sets the chunk of meat on a hunk of bread, sprinkles it with *chimichurri* sauce from a wine bottle, puts the open-faced sandwich in his mouth, and, instead of biting with his teeth, cuts off a portion with his knife, a hair breadth from his nose. I imagine this peculiar way of eating—these near misses, this coming perilously close to clipping one's nose—to be a kind of ritual castration, an offering or restitution to all the sheep the man has dismembered.

There are no plates in the room, though every man and woman has a hand-wiping towel on a knee.

The women use their own smaller knives to help themselves to their favorite parts of the sheep, and they eat bites of salad. The salad is not served on plates. Rather, several forks are placed in the communal bowl on a small table in the center of the room, and the hosts and guests all take pieces from the bowl of rare store-bought greens.

The mutton beckons. It is as though it has eyes and heart, calling one toward it. We—the men and the women and the children—gorge, like carnivores at a kill.

Cachorro teases Peter, pulls his hair, challenges him to eat a seventh piece of meat, handing him a large, fatty morsel.

"¡Come, gordo! Eat, fatty!"

Before he serves himself another piece of heart, the short, black-haired *peón* brings me a fat-slathered rib, shaking the hot sauce on it for me, poking it at me in challenge and glee. As I bite, his face shines, triumphant.

I bite again into the finger-burning chunk of meat. Cachorro slurps a cylinder of fat, which slides smooth down his throat. Clara gnaws at, struggles with, and conquers a leg bone. Her patient, deft hand slowly strips it clean as she works and saws with her own small, dull knife.

With the regularity of a liturgy, a long and rhythmic hymn, we walk up, stand before the lambs, make our cuts, and return to our benches time and again. We cut off pieces of meat with slips, slices, and quick thrusts, with shiny, sharp blades. We catch the dripping juice on our curling tongues. We clamp, yank, tear, and chew the meat. We slit the ribs and suck them clean. We grind gristle with our molars, slosh wine in our mouths, and swallow, leaving our lips covered with sheep-fat lipstick. Grease is wiped on the backs of hands; our fingers shine. From time to time one of the men forks up, with the tip of his knife, morsels from the collection of internal organs heaped at the side of the *fogón*. He comes around with offerings of brain, kidney, heart, and intestines.

The room is quiet save for occasional exchanges of soft words, the sound of chewing, and the shuffling of feet. The fire some-times sizzles with dripping fat. Bit by bit, the lambs' backbones become more and more bare.

Watching over us all, unnerving me when I look, is the eye of the lamb itself. The skulls of a couple of lambs are sitting side by side near the fireplace, and the dark eyes of the animals are still luminous in their sockets. When one man helps himself to an eye, I cannot watch him swirl the orb in his mouth.

A suffusion of wine and cooked lamb wafts about the room. The seasoned smell pervades everything, shifting through the air, soaking into the wineglasses, coating the concrete walls and leaving a film of white fat. The fire warms the clammy walls, and they sweat. We remove our sweaters. The asado's smell penetrates our hair, slips silently into our clothes. Peter and I carry it home with us and inhale, noses to our sweaters, for three days afterward.

The meat keeps us, like foxes or weasels who have taken a lamb. The fat greases our insides and lets us meet Patagonia's blustery and parching winds head on, with stout determination. Eating the lamb at the asado, I feel merged with the sheep and the surrounding company. One animal becomes part of another.

On this gaunt flank of land, in the stampeding wind, bands of animals carry out life. Sea lions and sea elephants, penguins and whales sport and fish along the coastline. On the soil, among the bristle bushes, guanacos munch the thorns and hardy grasses; Patagonian gray foxes trot, tuft to tuft, in search of soft-bellied birds and guinea pig–like cuis; pheasantish tinamou forage, dust-bathe, and produce pea green eggs; Darwin's rhea or ostrich stroll; and maras—the local rabbitlike rodents—and skunks, wild cats, and weasels make their rounds.

In stride with these animals ride the sheep men. With them, the men exchange blood and also milk.

At any moment a sheep man may be harvesting one of the animals breathing in the campo beside him. On walks through the rough campo, we often come across wire hoops attached to fences. Asking José about them, we receive the reply, "Cachorro's traps. For the little foxes." One time Peter and I counted forty fox skins and several of mountain cat hanging from the rafters inside José's barn. They had been collected by the *peón* for Buenos Aires women's winter coats.

Once or twice, in campo kitchens, I have eaten huge flat omelets made from a single egg of the Darwin's rhea—one of the strong eggs being equivalent to twelve chicken eggs—and often I have been at houses when the *peón* has just brought home a rhea slaughtered to feed his dogs.

Skins of the llamalike guanacos lie slung over fences like saddles. One hot, gritty summer day, when we had just taken the turn down off the tableland toward our seaside research camp, we came abruptly on Clara's sister and brother-in-law's truck. The vehicle was blocking the road, and the couple stood beside it, the two jolly, bear-shaped people framed against a vista of glittering blue bay. Angel had a long knife in his hand, the blade of which was still wet with blood. After wiping his nose on his sleeve, knife still in hand, the burly campesino approached Peter, arms spread wide, and took him in a full, smothering embrace.

"I just killed a little guanaco," he told us, as though he had plucked a tomato from the garden.

While at any moment a sheep man may be plucking a guanaco or a fox from the campo garden, he may just as likely be nursing or befriending the same animal. Every campo family I know has bottle-fed back to health a guanaco baby caught, injured, and then orphaned by a failed leap over a fence. The tiny Patagonian skunks, more than one campo man has told me, make the sweetest of pets. I have seen one sheep man walking over the campo, exchanging whistles with a flock of knee-high rhea chicks, and I have seen him afterward sitting in his kitchen caressing the feathers of the chicks before him on the table. I have seen an armadillo, said to taste more delicious than chicken, trot behind a sheep man like a dog.

There is a strange understanding of what it is to be alive among men who eat what they love. As citified North Americans, as conservationists who have loved a pet Patagonian fox more than any other animal in the world, we will never quite fathom this. The slaughter of one of the elegant golden-furred llamas brings us sorrow. At the same time, Angel's matter-of-fact, unapologetic earthiness draws us in. We, who enjoy asados with these men, who have ourselves gleefully made a rhea egg pound cake, cannot judge.

I take a look around the surrounding collection of carnivores.

The men sit at the end of the room near the door, near the *fogón*, near the meat. The women are at the back near a little tray of coals, set down for them by the men for heat.

Both sexes talk and laugh. They sit separately some of the time, and now and then husbands move to wives, and vice versa, for visits. There is the hum of gossip.

In this congregation there are people as varied as the other animals on the campo. The members of the gathering possess characters and outlooks that range from the quickness of the Patagonian fox to the gentle stillness of the father mara guarding his burrow of pups.

Grand and pompadoured Rafael sits near the *fogón*, with the cluster around José. He whittles a stick with his knife as he listens to the others and sometimes delivers opinions in a soft, deep voice. His frame, lean and strong as that of a male guanaco, twitches with the constant movement of a man who thrives on deeds. His wife, Liliana, with her gray hair and plain, flowered dress, is constantly asking Clara, "Let me help you with something. Can't I do something, Clara?" She is sweet and dowdy, chockful of goodwill.

Not far off, but aloof, sits the *patrón*, Guerrero, José's boss, the owner of La Bonita. I have not heard a word uttered by the man. He is around forty-five, hair slicked back Italian style, with a beak of a nose. Having come straight from Buenos Aires to attend the *señalada* at his estancia, he seems to be from another planet. He is too well groomed. I know too much about him to like him, though José says only the best of him. Stefanie, his wife, has been striding about all morning, in hand-tooled black cowboy boots she bought in Spain for trips to the Península, showing me the alterations she plans to make on the estancia, complaining about the difficulty of maintaining three houses, and bragging about her daughter, who is a fashion designer in the capital. She tells me her people are from the Basque Provinces in France, where they cook superbly. Her husband is from northern Italy, "where people are tall and blond, with white, white skin. It's very different from the south, where they are dark and short."

Guiseppe, a barrel of a man with white hair, makes jokes to the men in a booming voice while he tucks away a whale's quantity of food. This *puestero* who oversees an estancia fifty kilometers to the north of La Bonita is said to have married his favorite whore. Campo men, we have been told, think whores make excellent wives because they are tough and can endure campo life. Guiseppe's wife, Gloria, heavily made up and wearing a sexy sweater and tight jeans, is outspoken and brash. The smile is a touch familiar, the manner simultaneously frank and friendly. I like her. She tells me she can't wait until her children—ages sixteen, twenty-two, and twenty-four—get married. "Then I'll move to the campo for good. Now, we have to maintain a house in town so the girl can go to school, but once she's finished, *listo!*" She wipes her hands of the children and whisks herself off toward the campo.

Cachorro, the *peón* Guerrero has hired to help José now that he is getting older, sits up near José and argues with every point the older man makes. He brings me a hunk of meat and tells me that all the stuff you read about Indians is lies. "The Indians who lived here did nothing. Only the women worked. The men were laze-abouts. All those arrowheads you find in the campo were made by the women and children. It was like Great Britain used to be when there were ancient tribes. The women did all the work."

An orphan who grew up on the Península, Cachorro is one of the few people I have met here who seems calculating. His laugh is too loud; there is a brash thread in the sound. He wants to be *puestero* of La Bonita. Part of him looks forward to José's death. He is a man with a goal, and everything he does is cultivated to achieve it. He is the emcee of the day. He anticipates everyone's needs, and rushes to execute a task before José can get to it, an efficiency perhaps calculated to impress the *patrón*. He presents himself as an expert on sheep, referring to the days when he worked in a huge stud barn—one of the largest in Patagonia. The striving is also evident in his appearance. He is wearing a white shirt under a V-necked red-and-white-striped sweater, snug jeans, and loafers, but a tousle of curls peeks out from under a jaunty cap. His sun-browned face is handsome and probably draws women, though he, a man of forty-four, has never married.

Angel, Clara's brother-in-law, sits, withdrawn, off to one side of the men. He rests his back against the wall and holds down one Parkinson's-ridden, floppy hand with the other. Once a jolly, well-fed bear, he now seems sad. During the feast, Angel talks only when people approach him. Teresa, his wife, cheery and round and a nonstop talker, gives the scene a sense of hilarity. She pulls everyone's leg and is a great help to Clara. All through the meal she takes Angel bits of egg tortilla—he is forbidden fatty lamb—and Cinzano with soda, then stands beside him, her hand on his shoulder. She whispers to me, as if to explain Angel, that the *pasto* of the small estancia on the Península she and Angel own is not very good. They got only 70 lambs, while this estancia that José manages got 640 or so.

Pablo, the *peón* who has overseen Angel and Teresa's relatively small estancia of only 1,500 sheep for over thirty years, is innocent and simple. His thoughts are kind behind a placid face with flat planes. He has classic Navajo features—a high-bridged, crooked nose, small eyes, smooth terra-cotta skin, no beard, no hair. He is short and square—almost a dwarf—in baggy pants covering bowed legs, corduroy shoes, and cap. A man who does what he's told, lives alone, and is not used to company, he sits on a bench, silent, with his legs crossed.

Up near the men there are various other *peones* and *puesteros* with whom I am not well acquainted. One of them I know to be Guillermo Goikoa, the *puestero* of the estancia just across the dried-up salt lagoon from José's. The handsome man, with a smart cravat at his neck, has with him two wiry sons, one Basque blond and hazel-eyed, the other dark-haired—adopted, the women tell me—who have been running errands for the men all morning. They are good-natured, but they are also scamps. The darker and older one, a soft-eyed, sincere boy of about twelve, tells me he wants to be an architect. He names all the Indian tribes in Argentina. He asks Peter how to build a canoe. When their father tries to round them up to go home, they keep talking to all the adults, who seem to love them, until they hear that there are candies in the pickup. As part of their departure, both boys pass around the circle and kiss each man and woman good-bye. Their cheeks are cream smooth.

Halfway through the asado, a quiet Indian-brown couple and their children arrive. They have come to retrieve from José a couple of rogue sheep from the sheep station they look after. Liliana explains to me that they have just come, as *peones*, to the Península from La Pampa, a province to the north. The brash young estancia manager of one of the largest estancias in the province, who has himself recently come from the capital, believes only northern Argentines have culture and know how to kill themselves with work. He is starting to downgrade all the positions on the sheep stations he oversees from *puesteros* to *peones*, so that they receive salaries instead of a percentage of the profits.

The young pair—neither of them could be over twenty-two— look uncomfortable. They belong among the gauchos of the steamy northern cattle estancias, not in this lonely desolate outreach. The man is dashing, with silver coins on his belt, wide *bombacha* trousers, and a bright scarf at his neck. They say little. The plump, long-haired young mother of two huge-eyed toddlers tells me she misses the north and plans to return to be near her family by the time her children enter school. The women hasten to offer food to her and the children, the men hand the young man the *bota*, and the family joins us.

There is a mix of roles in the room—*patrones, puesteros,* and *peones*—with incomes in descending order ranging from $100,000 to $7,000 to $250 a year. It is only history that has made some men landowners and others employees. As in all other parts of Argentina, the people from earlier-arriving immigrant families ended up with the land, and the later arrivals became their foremen and work hands.

I have always found it remarkable that these Patagonian men so varied in terms of ambition, energy, and outlook can tolerate one another and work side by side as they do. I have come to attribute this mutual tolerance, on the one hand, to the fact that human beings are naturally gregarious animals; hand in hand with this genetic predisposition toward sociality go the facts of life in Patagonia. Plain and simple: Patagonia is so desolate, and one is so seldom in human company, that any comrade is to be treasured. The men are drawn together by the requirements of sheep work and also, perhaps, by the envy and sense of injustice they hold in common.

I have several times visited the barn that holds the prize rams owned by one of the biggest landowners in the region. The septuagenarian landowner himself, a kind and polished man, has taken me into the dark stalls of the barn. There, removing the dumb, massive animal's protective jacket, he has parted the wool of his favorite ram and invited me to admire its texture and evenness and to plunge my fingers into its thicketlike, five-inch, oily depth. Homage paid, I have stood there afterward a moment, observing the inscrutable, prettily groomed ram standing over his ponderous wool-covered duo of softball-sized testes.

Península men have wasted plenty of spit on García, the owner of that ram, a man wealthy by accident of birth, but there is one man who speaks about the inequity with eloquence.

In the dark, crumbling cement room where we gather our stools around the altar, José is in his element. He has eaten little, saying, "I am not one for lamb. I don't like it. For me, I'd just cook the liver and throw the rest away. I am one for mutton. Grown sheep."

Someone mentions García, and José takes in wine from his wineskin, and his tongue loosens.

There is a holy silence that overtakes a scene when José is going to deliver one of his maxims. The slender old man sits up straight, puffs in air, and a subliminal message has us all alert, our ears pricked to catch his quiet words. The men hunch over their meat, silent, looking toward the man nearest the fire. José is spokesman for a clan of wordless men. Uncomfortable with superficiality, he knifes straight into the heart.

"García may be rich," he says, the light of the fire glancing off his weathered red face, "but he can't have a swallow of wine like I can!" The men shuffle and mumble in accord.

José comments on the vastly unequal land ownership system: "I don't know anything about these things, but as I see it, we are a rich country with good land. If we could each have a little bit of it, we could all live well."

José has thought long about the rich estancia owner's child and the poor estancia worker's boy. "A poor *chico* might steal a pair of shoes because he needs them, or a candy because he is hungry. He gets put in prison, and everyone hears about it. A rich *chico* might steal for drugs, or break into a store and steal a bicycle, and you never hear anything. I'm not sure which way is better to grow up."

José tells us what he has heard about the estancias owned by people of British descent in the southern Patagonian provinces, Santa Cruz and Tierra del Fuego. Apparently, he says, they have all the commodities—running water, electricity—and good, humane treatment, but the same problem of low pay. The only problem with the English *patrones*, he has heard, is that they keep their distance from the workers.

"Here, we don't have these benefits of the English estancias to the south of us. My *patrón* can sit down with me and talk, so I don't complain. But these men like García, the big landowners, they are like these Texans in Norteamérica.

"There are two people sitting in one of these bars in Texas. One of the men, a guy from another state, buys the Texan a drink. A little while later, they go home.

"A few days later, the stranger is walking around town and the Texan drives up in a Cadillac. The Texan gets out of the Cadillac, and says, 'Here.'

"The stranger asks, 'Why are you giving me this?'

" 'You bought me a drink, so I bought you a Cadillac.' "

José and the other men chuckle at the foolishness of rich men.

"García thinks that a lot of money is the same thing as a lot of intelligence. They are not the same!" José wags his finger, chuckling.

The seventy-six-year-old man who came from Spain wearing what he owned, who has devoted forty-five years to La Bonita, speaks for all campo men.

"Money, as I see it," he says, "has nothing to do with happiness. When I think about what I have now, I am not any happier than I was when I just lived putting my mat out under a thornbush at night."

José tells the assembled company a joke that he wants us to recognize as the central tenet of his life philosophy.

"There was this Englishman in the north who was traveling

in an area with farms, and he came to a paisano with some goats, resting under a tree.

"He said to the peasant, 'You know what you should do? You should milk those goats instead of eating them, and sell the milk. Then you should buy some sheep and sell the wool. With that money you can buy an estancia. And then, with that money, you can buy trucks to deliver the wool. Then you can buy a factory in Buenos Aires. And then, after that, you can sit back and rest.'

"The paisano replied, 'What do you think I am doing right now?' "

The men murmur assent and pass the *bota* to José.

The women bring out plates piled with small pound cakes, cookies, cream puffs, iced cakes, chocolates, and fruitcakes. Then appear fruits and the three flans Clara has made. The plates of desserts are piled high, toppling and dripping with colorful sugary wealth.

By three the sky is gray, the wind beginning a campaign. Peter has eaten eight pieces of cake, and I have consumed three times my share. The women are piling dishes; there is a hush over the dim room. The men sit with their heads against the concrete walls, dozing.

This slumber of men is overdue. On ordinary days most campo men take siestas. At Angel and Teresa's *señalada*, the women laughed about it as they sloshed the dishes in a pan of water and then dried them with sopping towels.

On that day, about a half hour after the first round of desserts, the women noticed that several of the men had disappeared. José had gotten up earlier and said, "Well, it's about time to go," hoisting up his pants. Clara said she couldn't go until she had helped Teresa do the dishes. Minutes later José was gone. A couple of the women went out to see what had happened to their husbands. The pair reported back that the men were all sleeping in the cabs of their trucks. One told Clara, "José is sleeping with his arms around the wheel and his hat over his eyes." Of one of the little boys, she said, "The little gaucho is sleeping with his uncle, in his uncle's truck." The women laughed and shook their heads about men's need for sleep.

The men in the trucks slept about two hours. Others sat along the walls in a stupor, digesting, tired, sated, with their heads against the wall. Everyone grew quiet, only mentioning how much food they had eaten. We all slumbered by the trays of coals in the dark, cold room.

At about five, as people started to rouse themselves from the heavy half slumber, the women put the cakes on plates and passed them around, and they relighted the gas burner for heating water for mate.

Mate is the Patagonian's coffee or tea. The green caffeinated brew is second only to wine as the prime beverage of the campo men, and campo women drink it constantly, too. The drink is so strong that many North Americans get ill the first time they sample it.

The national Argentine beverage is unique for the manner in which it is imbibed. Mate is served in a decapitated, round-bottomed gourd a little smaller than a tennis ball, and a silver straw is used to suck in the hot drink.

A ritual accompanies the serving of mate. The *yerba*, or mate leaves, are packed into the gourd to about a quarter of the way from the top. The person taking responsibility for the preparation pours enough boiling water onto the leaves to fill the gourd, then draws in the entire amount of the olive-colored liquid through the fiercely hot silver straw, swirls it in his mouth, and spits it out. This is repeated two or three times until the bitterest servings are dispensed with.

Thus prepared, the mate is passed around the assembled company in a customary and ceremonial manner. As with the *bota*, there is a mate keeper who fills the gourd and hands it to the person nearest him. When that person has drained the vessel, he returns it to the server, who replenishes it with hot water from the kettle, and hands it to the next person in the circle.

So the mate goes, like an Indian peace pipe, the movements back and forth inscribing a fan of petals with the keeper at the crown. The ritual provides a sense of communion, somewhat like the sharing of bread in a Basque church and less individualistic and formal than the taking of coffee and tea.

Mate seems a drink concocted for Patagonians. I imagine a surprise encounter between two lonely men, each out with his herd on the vacant wastes; they fashion a fire out of the arms of dried thornbushes and share the brisk, tough brew through a single silver straw.

Everyone in the room wants mate. I watch the men stretch and groan themselves off their benches. They take mate together, standing elbow to elbow.

Sturdy bonds are born on the harsh Patagonian campo. Through the interdependence and collective work required on the sheep stations, and via the shared intake of meat, mate, and wine, bonds between sheep men flower and flame. The ties between the wind-carved men, though, are as unuttered as their work together in the docking pen.

THE IMPORTANCE OF CAKE

The gray-haired woman bends over her bowl, her arms tensed with the work of beating together the sugar and butter. Her brown-tinted glasses shift down her nose a little as her body moves beneath the simple dark dress dotted with flowers. The hot breeze toys with the wisps of her short hair; there is perspiration on her upper lip. At intervals as regular as the ticking of a clock, she raises her eyes from the bowl and through the bright square of window scans the bleak land.

The ranch woman looks out her kitchen window a thousand times a day. Each time her eye skips over a quarter mile of the open, stubbled steppe and sets down on the middistance, where she knows a wide road runs like a dirt river across the wasteland. When the dust of a rare car billows on the road, she leaves her bowl on the kitchen table and stands by the screen door. Her hazel eyes follow the vehicle's passage until the dust plume has vanished. The woman's eyes pursue the vehicle whether it is headed deeper into the Península or hurtling toward Puerto Madryn, but when the car is headed for town, Liliana's body turns unconsciously, as though she is drawn along with the car.

By the time her sheep rancher husband returns home for

lunch, two cakes, one pale yellow, the other bright white and
furred with coconut frosting, stand cooling, glowing, in the hot,
dim kitchen. The drawn curtains luff in the dry breeze—they are
like the filmy chiffon skirts of spring ball gowns—and the fresh
fragrance of the cakes wafts through the air. The cakes sit in
optimistic anticipation, light as a girl's hopes.

It was high summer when I first came to know Liliana, Rafael
Mendizabal's wife, and I was spending those warm months doing
something I had planned for my whole life. At last I was proving
my Emersonian self-reliance in a wild and depriving landscape.
I relished lone walks out on the prickly, desolate land, savoring
the openness, the sense of being totally alone. From time to
time, though, driven by an unarticulated sense that something
was missing, not even knowing I was hungry for conversation,
I would take to the car and go see Liliana.

The yellow-brown land was a slab of hot, bristly pancake, and
brown dust rose in billows as I traveled the roads. The sun
hammered hard on the tin roof of the Renault, and way off
down the road the heat shimmer created the mirage of a blue
lake, backed by fertile hills. As I hurtled down the straight dirt
strip toward Liliana, rabbits bounced away from the prow of the
car, like wheat being threshed.

As I turned the car from the main road onto the quarter-
mile approach road, the older woman was usually silhouetted in
the door frame of the low house.

Liliana kissed me quickly in the heat and hurriedly waved me
into the spare, dark kitchen. I plopped onto my customary chair
at the sponged-clean table and instantly felt settled. The room
was far cooler than the outdoors, with the peach-and-yellow-
blotched gauze curtains drawn.

Liliana cut two big slabs from a cake on the counter and
served two cups of tea, the heavily sugared kind that Argentine
women serve to children.

With her wispy hair brushed back, her plain, thin face, and
the glasses shadowing her light eyes, Liliana had a young girl's

brightness even at fifty-six. Liliana and I relaxed into the empty afternoons.

I liked simply being with Liliana. The campo woman seemed to brim with merriment as she produced plump, light cakes in a rainbow of flavors: lemon, chocolate, peach, and caramel. Gaiety bubbled up in everything she said and did. Liliana was a glass of sparkling tonic about to overflow. On the other hand, there was the woman's faraway gaze. Her eyes wandered regularly to the window and the road.

I desired to soak in Liliana's sense of joy and to understand that faraway look—I wanted to discover their sources.

The enthusiasm that shouts within Liliana, I learned in our talks, was seeded during her girlhood. Her parents gave her a running start on joy, for they christened their newborn daughter with a lilting name that matched her nature. The little girl, born cheery and high-spirited, took life as a promise. She frolicked over the desolate, whiskered land, making the most of every small happening on the estancia that her grandparents, Margarita and Antonio Lasarte, settled in 1900 and that her mother and father later took over.

Liliana and her five siblings frisked about in the empty campo like bunnies. Just as their mother had done, on empty afternoons Liliana and the other children would struggle the five kilometers down to the sea to bray in unison with the penguins, all the while pinching their noses at their stench. When the rare ship ran aground on the coast, the children salvaged the treasure—books and clothes that washed up in the cold tides. Other days the children made huts from the twisted, woody branches of the campo thornbushes and laid over them old, dried guanaco skins. Inside these houses they played for hours.

Sometimes their grandmother sat the children at the kitchen table to recite their letters, and in that fashion they learned "more or less" to read. Liliana's tone quickened at the time she told me about these sessions at the kitchen table. "I loved to read," she said. "And, truth to tell, I wanted to go to school. I wanted to study in Madryn. It cost me air not to be able to go to school!"

While she was of school age, Liliana confided, an old couple in Madryn offered to take her in, at their expense, so that she could attend school there, but her mother turned down the offer.

"To the mamás back then, it didn't seem right to leave girls alone like that, with people who weren't family. But I wanted to go. Ah, me, yes! It cost me lots of tears. I remember how I cried, because I had the dream that my mother would let me go."

In spite of the setback regarding school, Liliana's blithe temperament was irrepressible, but then in the year 1940, when she was eleven, the family was dealt a catastrophe: her father, who had been a well digger in addition to managing Liliana's mother's family's campo, was struck with "infantile paralysis." Liliana's father did not dig another well, and he never spoke again. Her mother's life was instantly transformed into a "sacrifice" and so remained for the next twenty-five years.

When their father became ill, the Bordenave children, who had always helped with the farmwork, redoubled their efforts, their paralyzed father directing them as best he could.

"My older brother was thirteen when it happened, and the others were on a stair step all the way down. There were six of us, so we struggled." The small children learned to collect wood from the campo and to push it home on a little cart, and to surround the sheep when they came to the watering hole, and round them up, herd, and cut them, all on foot, since they didn't have horses. The children carried out all the sheep work, from hand shearing with old-fashioned shears to butchering.

The children carried their father everywhere and helped him manage the attacks to which he was subject. In the evenings Liliana chattered to her mute and crippled father, reporting the day's great accomplishments.

Until the catastrophe, the Bordenave family had had one sole and critical link with the outer world—their truck; but when the tragedy occurred, Liliana's mother sold the truck, because women of the time did not drive and with that sale the family's isolation deepened.

"In those years," Liliana explained, "we were isolated. My family didn't even have a radio. We didn't know anything. We didn't have friends nearby. It was just us. We had very few visitors. Practically no one came. In those years the Península was an island."

In the months of September and October, the family piled into a wagonette and went to the neighbor's to help with the *señalada*, but most of the time the family made its way through long, windy months without any external contact.

"We were born in the campo, and the truth of things is that we were raised there. We didn't have anything. Less than nothing! We never knew anything and we never went anywhere.

"We didn't feel isolated because we were used to it, and we didn't know there was such a thing as getting together with people. In truth, we were half-wild. We were half-surprised when we found ourselves with others. That is how we were raised when we were children." Liliana's gay eyes opened wide and her brows rose as she said this, as if in surprise at her own childhood.

As a campo child, Liliana developed a sense latent in city children: a subliminal awareness of the proximity of another human being, a vestige of the animal urge for contact with any other member of the species. Living on her family's remote estancia near the outer eastern coast, the little campo girl constantly kept an eye on the road and her ears pricked for unusual sounds. She swears that she and her five brothers and sisters could detect a human form threading its way toward them through the thornbushes when it was still kilometers distant. At the time, Liliana had no sense that life held choices—the campo dictated a certain life—and she wouldn't have called her excitement at seeing any human being a longing, but happiness broke out of the little girl whenever a person appeared.

One man who came was Humberto Ramussi, the owner of a "shining *boliche*," a combination bar–general store that used to exist on the Península, who used to come around with his wares. Liliana remembered him as a very agreeable man, and she remembered her excitement at seeing his dust coming down the road. "Ai! When we saw him with his containers of things!"

By her midteens peddlers from stores in town also came around in trucks. They, like Ramussi, bought the fox and guanaco furs that the family had trapped and sold them sneakers, cheeses, "and even natural peaches!" Liliana exclaimed. "And what clothes! Every month they paid us a visit, and got down suitcases and suitcases, and without a single commitment! Sometimes, if we could, we bought something. If not, we left it for the next month, and like that we supplied ourselves."

Liliana slipped into her spontaneous sixteen-year-old self when she recalled the visitor with his car crammed with huge bundles of clothes. "What excitement when they came! And this *gallego*, Patricio Freire, he was known to stay up to three days. I washed his dirty clothes and all that, and I made myself a little bit that way and bought things from him right then and there."

By age nine Liliana was a proficient baker and launderer, and when she was twelve or thirteen she began washing clothes for the sheep men who worked in the surrounding area. They brought their clothes once a week, and with the extra money she accumulated she ordered things from catalogs. When one of the men for whom she laundered gave her a Victrola, the record player became one of the chief joys of her young womanhood. At fifteen, when her parents allowed her and her thirteen-year-old sister to learn to dance, the sisters spent joyous hours after dinner dancing together in the kitchen, their parents on their chairs and the table pushed up against the wall. Later some of the same men brought records to the house and danced with the Bordenave señoritas, again with Liliana's parents sitting off to the side.

Dancing was the passion of Liliana's teen years, and the dancing girl lives on within her as an ardent dream. The mother of grown daughters remembered that Clara, and her sister and brother-in-law, Teresa and Angel, came to her fifteenth birthday party. The families danced and ate lamb until five A.M.

She told another story about dancing at a *señalada* at Clara's brother-in-law's many years before. Angel sent a car with a driver to pick up Liliana's family and another car, driven by Clara's sister, Catalina, to pick up the workers who were cutting metal off the grounded ship, the *Roca*, which had foundered on La Margarita's shores. The only problem was that there were six men and Catalina insisted that the car could only take five. She refused to try to fit in all six, so one man was left behind. "Catalina was *brava*," Liliana said, shaking her hand in a gesture for hardheadedness.

They got to the estancia, ate, and started dancing. At three A.M. the man who had been left behind appeared. He had set out on foot the minute the cars left to travel the twenty-seven kilometers from La Margarita to the Irabis'. "That was how much he wanted to dance!"

At the end of the sheep farm year when the family had sold the wool, Liliana's mother went to Madryn to buy consumables for the year. "She went once a year. And we kids were touched by a desperation to go! And one time one went, and another time another went, and like that. We got to go every six years."

Liliana first laid eyes on her husband-to-be when she was eighteen, strolling with her mother in Madryn. Rafael noticed the pretty young woman, too, asked his mate who she was, and hurried to the dance that evening, hoping Liliana would be there. The two danced, and Rafael began visiting the Bordenave estancia, at first ostensibly to see Liliana's brothers.

"He made friends with my brothers, see. He was very intelligent!" Liliana clutched herself as she laughed at her husband's strategy. "It was all planned. He went around with my brothers, and then we got attached. My brothers would arrange things so we had moments alone. We started going steady and Rafael came once a month, something like that, on a Saturday or a Sunday. First we just talked among all the brothers and sisters. It was all very controlled. We were going steady for two years, and then, toward the end, we could sometimes converse alone."

The wedding took place at La Pamplona, where Rafael was working. Vitoria, Rafael's sister, made the cakes, and Liliana wore an outfit a neighbor had made for her. Vitoria's husband, Carlos Irazazabal, lent the newlyweds his pickup truck for their honeymoon journey to Madryn. "It was romantic! That's the truth!" Liliana loved this memory and giggled merrily as she relayed it to me.

When the young couple took up residence at Carlos's estancia, where they were to live for twenty years, Liliana, who had only lived with her family on La Margarita until then, took along her seven-year-old sister as a companion to help her adjust.

"My sister was with us for a time, for company, because one finds oneself so solitary, with the man leaving and going around. Rafael did all these jobs around the area and I stayed home alone, newly married. My older brother came around regularly on his horse, to check on how we were doing."

Liliana stayed in the wind-shattered house while Rafael did odd jobs, constructing watering troughs and doing fencing for other estancias, and later putted off on a motorbike for long days at the fauna reserve.

As a single woman on her parents' estancia, Liliana had helped with all the outdoor jobs. "When I was single, I sheared with clippers, dipped the sheep, butchered. I did all those things. But with my husband, never, never, never. Up to today, my husband doesn't let me go into the corral to do sheep jobs. No, no.

"I got married in 1949, on the thirty-first of December, and in 1951, about a year and a half later, my first daughter came. It took about a year and nine months, and the other came. One right after the other.

"I had easy births, just like my mother. I never worried about giving birth. People then didn't go to the doctor the way they do now. I didn't do anything about my pregnancies until the seventh month. I didn't get worried or scared because the girls arrived right when I calculated they would."

Liliana gave birth to one of her daughters in a hotel in Madryn and to the other in a house in town rented with her sister-in-law. With the latter, the doctor told her she still had a long wait, but right after he left the baby started coming. Liliana's sister-in-law was so nervous that Liliana had to tell her, "You must be calm. It will be okay," while *she* was giving birth. "The baby was here by the time the doctor returned.

"After my daughters came, my life was busier, more occupied. Then things were different.

"My husband managed the estancia that belonged to his brother-in-law. Since it was a small place, he did all these outside jobs. So he always left at five in the morning and came back at eleven at night. I was with tiny daughters. All day I was alone! The truth is that it was hard."

Up through the toddler years of her daughters, Liliana's life was all of a piece, as predictable and innately satisfying as the life of a country woman can be. She had the good fortune of a fine husband, and the children came easily. Though the longing for society was still there, the children gave her both absorption and delight, and she knew how to live in the oceanic spaces of the Patagonian campo. Still to come was the first ruffle in the smooth sea.

I am in Liliana's spare, clean kitchen on a hot afternoon, and Liliana is teaching me to make empanadas. I had asked her a few weeks earlier to show me how to make the spicy Argentine meat pies that are like meat-and-egg-filled turnovers. The campo woman, an apron over the faded cotton shift that she has remade four times, has already made up the *picadillo*—a mixture of onions and ground beef, oregano and red pepper, and boiled eggs and olives. "If you have time," she tells me, "it is good to make the *picadillo* the day before, to let the spices soak in."

She shows me how to fork together the *masa*—the flour, lard, salt, and water—to make the pastelike dough for the crusts, then rolls out a hunk of the *masa* to form a big rectangle. She presses a bowl into the rectangle over and over again, showing me how to cut the patties. The air is still and peaceful. There is, amazingly, no wind. The cuckoo clock ticks as Liliana works.

On previous visits when I have arrived as Liliana was cutting vegetables for mutton stew, she has dismissed my offers of help, saying, "Oh, Sara, I'm accustomed to being alone and doing everything alone. I make empanadas and *ñoquis* and cakes when no one is here." But today it is clear that she enjoys the presence of another person.

The pile of dough circles grows as we talk. Her hands busy, her body relaxed with the steady pace of the work, the campo woman tells me of the challenge of her life.

At Punta Norte, Liliana's life had hummed along with the care of her little girls; her married life had developed a rhythm to which she was accustomed. When it came time to make a decision about the schooling of her two daughters, though, the cadence broke.

Liliana paced back and forth within the confines of the small rooms of the isolated campo house. "It was a terrible conflict. Terrible, because the family had to separate. It was costly to send the girls to school from the campo. Not costly in the sense of money, because schools have always been free, but costly in the sense that either Rafael and I had to live apart, while the girls and I lived in an extra house in town, or Rafael and I had to live apart from the children while they went to school in town."

The curtains in the window luff a little as a breeze pushes the hot air outside. Liliana stops cutting rounds of dough and sits down. The points of her elbows are on the table as she holds her cheeks in her hands. "At first I sent the oldest daughter to stay with Pepa [the family's nickname for Vitoria], my sister-in-law, for two years, so she could go to school while living with her. Then I had problems finding someone to leave the other one with, so I sent the older one, Marta, to the nun's school in Rawson for two years, and the younger one stayed with her aunt."

Liliana's face becomes a little troubled. "My daughter didn't like the nun school. By the end, she didn't want to know another thing about the little sisters, so I had to take her out. If that hadn't happened, I would probably have sent her a little while longer, but she went for two years and didn't want to go back. She wouldn't go back."

Marta's difficulties at the nun school stemmed from the fact that she had to work in return for her schooling and saw too much in her job as kitchen helper. As the little girl helped the cook peel potatoes, she couldn't help but notice that the girls whose parents could afford full tuition were given eggs and meat, while she and the other ordinary girls ate plain noodles or polenta. She also caught on to the fact that the nuns got more interesting meals.

Perhaps a worse insult to the small girl was the fact that each time Liliana or Vitoria visited Marta and brought her a cake or other baked things, the nuns required her to share the goodies with the other girls. By the next morning the sweet cakes were gone.

Liliana laughs heartily at the memory of her upset daughter. "Oh, she protested! I suppose she said '¡Pucha! Heck! I could have made it last two or three days and now there is nothing left for me!' "

Liliana explains, "There were a lot of poor girls, poor things, who weren't brought anything, so she had to share. It was very hard. It was a struggle. So she got rebellious and didn't want to know anything about staying longer."

After Marta left the nun school, Liliana had to move to town because maintaining the girls away from home was becoming expensive. For the next few years the two girls and their mother lived in Carlos and Vitoria's house. The sweet older couple lent them a room, kitchen, and bathroom.

Liliana's eager eyes become serious for a moment. She brushes a crumb off the bodice of her dress. "When I moved to the pueblo, it was a terrible conflict. But the hardest part was to leave my husband," she says.

On the weekends of the years they lived in town, the three-some often traveled to the campo to see Rafael. They frequently hitched rides with a neighbor, Pocho Zanetta, riding to the campo on Friday afternoons and returning to town on Sundays at dusk. And every twenty days or so Rafael would snatch a night in town, returning to the campo the following day. When he worked as a ranger, he could seldom visit. "It was difficult," Liliana says. "That's the truth."

Just as the campo girl had once fought for the chance to wash the workmen's clothes, the campo woman again adapted to the possibilities of the moment and grabbed the opportunity presented by the need to live in town to add a little to the family income. She got a job at a textile factory.

"In those years I felt an obligation to make a peso, doing whatever it might be. I pledged to make something. Imagine the life the girls had. They were already young women, and everything changed for them when I worked and had my own peso. I could buy them clothes, all that. It was an advantage because it was hard with just what my husband made alone. He was always pulling in, saving, saving, saving. And that's why we have something on the daily level now. We don't have a lot, but the little we have, we have from this kind of sacrifice."

I have the sense as Liliana says this that she could count off the number of work hours, the exact number of pesos, and the number of movies and carnivals forfeited that it took to possess the television, the houses in town, the small luxuries that give her and Rafael's life a measure of grace and security. And I can tell by the perky look in her eyes that she has never known a moment of self-pity.

As Liliana talks on, her voice becomes emphatic and excited. "Sometimes, once I was married, when we went to Madryn, there were dances and orchestras. I always liked them, but Rafael didn't. So later, when I had the chance to take the girls to dances—because in those years mothers took their girls—I always took them. All that I could. Okay, I just sat at a table and was there, but at least I got to watch. And I would go with some companion when I took the girls, and we passed the time. My husband was hardly ever with me, he was almost always in the campo, but when he came, we danced and all that." As Liliana flips an empanada crust onto the pile, I picture her twirling on the dance floor.

Then Liliana's voice tightens as she swings back to the sacrifices required to give her daughters an education and a leg up into their current security—the sacrifices all the campo women of her era had to make.

"I was in Madryn with the girls for three or four years in all, eh? Later, when the girls were older, I came back to the campo and left them there. We had our own house in town by that time, and they lived there, the two of them together.

"Sometimes it was hard for me living away in the campo because I envisioned them all alone, for dinner, for everything, you know? But what can you do? You can't leave your husband alone in the campo, either! It was hard for him. It was really easier for the girls to fend for themselves. There were always relatives going to see them, so in that sense they were accompanied. It was easier for them than for him."

Liliana's voice fluffs with pride. "Marta, my older daughter— she is now thirty-three—became a teacher. She has three children. My younger one, Nancy, has two *chicos* and a good job with the Cooperativa Eléctrica. Both of my daughters earn much more than we did. And thanks to God, both live not too far away, and both have beautiful houses that belong to them. They have cars. The younger one and her trucker husband own a trailer truck and everything. This is a happiness for one, that all goes well, that one's work had good results."

Liliana looks into my eyes as she forms the sentence that changed her life. "It was a sacrifice to be away from my husband," she says, "but then I liked the town. There, one got to interact more with people."

After her time in Madryn, Liliana makes me understand, she returned to Rafael and the campo, but she returned changed. During the first months in town, she had been uneasy living in a new place, but, quickly, her thoughts had shifted. She loved working with the other women in the factory. She loved the to and fro of having neighbors all around her. In Madryn she found that she was made for society, for the pueblo. The small, passionate flame of the zesty campo girl took on a solid shape. The yearnings inside the young girl now had a goal: the dusty, peopled blocks of Puerto Madryn.

Liliana moves to the window and looks across the barren space.

"Here," she says, her back to me, "it is very lonely. It doesn't seem that bad now, but in those years the roads were badly maintained, so you were alone.

"Here in the campo, we get up early," she says as she turns around to sit with me, back at the table again. Her voice becomes wistful and matter-of-fact. The excitement that skipped through her words as she spoke of the town has dropped away.

At six in the morning she is in her bed, sipping mate. She imbibes, by means of the customary lip-searing silver straw, several gourdfuls of the strong brew, and by seven, without fail, she is up. To the ticking of a small German cuckoo clock, so high on the otherwise blank kitchen wall that its peak touches the ceiling, she lights a fire in the small enamel woodstove. She and Rafael breakfast on dry bread and more mate, and as Rafael leaves for the day's sheep work, Liliana starts cleaning and preparing lunch.

Since they have gotten older, and since they no longer have daughters at home, Liliana has tried to serve the main meal, mutton, at noon. This way they eat less in the evening and sleep better at night. When Rafael's day requires only routine chores, they eat lunch at eleven-thirty or quarter to twelve and then "sleep a good siesta" until two-thirty or three. At the end of the nap Liliana gets up first and brings Rafael the mate. Rafael goes out on the campo again until dark. By nine they are eating dinner, very early by Argentine standards. Liliana is surprised by how early they eat. "And for my husband," she exclaims, "sometimes it would be just as well to eat even earlier!"

Liliana knows how to navigate the campo days, but she knows all too intimately their tidal silences.

"Just imagine, my husband leaves these days about eight. When the grandchildren are not here visiting, I am totally alone. What silence! When you have a day alone, you can more or less get through it, but if you get four or five in a row, they are even longer still. You get through the first day okay, more or less, and maybe the second, but then the next ones are . . . You pay too much attention to things, even as far as sleeping."

During the bitter weather—June is the worst month—no one visits the couple, and they only go to town once a month or so. During the months of gray cold, when the winds reach gale force several times a week, she has to fight a tendency to go to bed too early. She makes an effort to knit and carry out other small tasks so as to put off eating dinner until nine, so that she and Rafael go to bed at ten and no earlier. "Otherwise the winter nights make themselves long, no?" She also fends off the urge to oversleep in winter by denying herself a siesta. While Rafael religiously takes his siesta, she makes herself go out for a walk. Her coat flaps and she has to hold her head down as she huddles along, the cold intense and the wind beating at her thin form as it ranges, unbridled, over the open space. She takes "a few rounds" and returns in time to boil water for midafternoon mate with her husband.

On a day when Rafael has been gone since five A.M., helping Roberta, the neighbor, do a round-up, and I am with her, still alone at eight in the evening, Liliana reveals one of the pleasures that helps her dispense with the long, empty days. She lifts a pink crocheted doily that has been covering a small television set. "We have one great advantage here in the plain," she says. "After I do the housework I turn it on. Rafael rigged it up with a truck battery. We get pretty good reception here, and we can even get 'Buenas Noches Argentina,' the news from Buenos Aires." Liliana and Rafael are among the lucky few on the Península who own a television and can get decent reception.

Summer is the good season in the campo. In general, during the warm months, the couple receives more visitors, and ever since they were tiny, Liliana has brought subsets of her five grandchildren to the campo for alternating weeklong visits. All through the summer either the boy cousins or the girl cousins wander free on the surrounding land, on foot, on bicycles, or on horseback, and return to the house each evening exhausted and ready for tea and cake.

On one visit with her, Liliana laughs as she serves me and

the two beautiful, huge-eyed girls not only a lemon cake, but *buñuelitos*, homemade doughnuts. "The grandchildren are a chance for the grandmother to fatten a little!"

Baking is one of the two time-passing activities on which Liliana has come to depend. Cake baking is the answer to any day. On the empty days it is something with which she can occupy herself, a sweet taste in the slowness of the afternoon, a salve when there is no one across the table. Mixing a cake is an expression of hope—for the appearance of visitors. Liliana gets dreamy-eyed as she describes her love for making *pastelitos*—the delicate, jam-filled, deep-fried puff pastries that require hours of dough folding and rolling.

The other activity that anchors Liliana's days is watching the road for a glimpse of other human beings.

"Every day people pass, coming and going, going and coming, and they don't even stop in here," she complains. When she was a child, she tells me, travelers stopped ritually at every house along the route to town, to visit and offer any aid that might be needed.

Liliana tells me that fifty-six years is enough time in the campo. "There comes a time in life to enjoy the fruits of what one has done," she says, and as she does, I realize that I now hold the meaning of the usually cheery woman's faraway look. The regular passage of her eyes to the window is just one man- ifestation of the fact that, by now, the country woman's soul is soaked with a longing to move to town. There is a pause, then Liliana says, "I moved all my plants to Madryn."

Liliana returns to the table, and we begin assembling the empanadas. Working side by side, we dunk our fingertips in a cup of water and wet the edge of each pancake. Then we spoon a lump of *picadillo* into its middle and fold together the two sides of the pastry, forming lumpy half-moons. With the tines of a fork, we mash the edges closed.

Later in the day the two men join us, Rafael back from fid- dling with the mechanism of the windmill under the pounding sun, Peter from getting our three flat tires fixed in Pirámides. In the darkness, by the light of a single kerosene lamp, each of us smothers our longings by eating eight or ten of the savory, deep-fried empanadas.

On a blistering day toward the end of summer, I drive the rutted road forty-five minutes to Liliana's. Rabbits and sheep scatter over the baked flats, dust swirls inside the car.

Today the heat mirage is a broad silver-and-aqua lake backed by brownish green mountains. The scene looks so real that I have to fight the urge to keep driving toward the cool, wet element. I keep blinking myself back to the infinite bristled land.

I arrive with grit sticking to my sweaty arms, my hair dust-tossed like the fluffed feathers of a tinamou, a local bobwhite that has just taken a dust bath. My feet are hot and swollen, and my eyes are smarting from the glare.

As I drive up I see Liliana shoo her grandsons out onto the campo to play. I had told her I would be coming.

For a moment we stand beside my car. Still half in the sway of the mirage, romanticizing the wild beauty of the land, I comment on the blueness of the deep, domed sky. Liliana, not fooled by mirages, says, "It's like when the tourists come. They say, 'How beautiful it is here! How lucky you are to live here!' And we look around and think, It's just dryness . . . dryness. We don't think about it."

Our conversation follows our view onto the sere, vacant, yellow-brown plain. I ask her whether the young people raised on the Península stay on as adults.

"One doesn't know what will happen to the campo"—Liliana shrugs—"because no one wants to work here now." She wipes the beads of sweat off her upper lip with a lacy handkerchief.

Across the stubble we watch the two skinny grandsons set out down a bumpy track on their rattletrap bikes. Liliana tells me, "The *chicos* used to fight all the time over who got to come to *Abuela*'s, but now they know when their times will come all through the summer, and they are content. The boys come, then the girls, always two cousins together.

"The older boy is nine. He was born on the same day as his

girl cousin, the one who loves horses. My daughters were married the same year, and the two first children were born right together. I took one daughter home from the hospital at eleven, and by one the other grandchild was born!

"I have to take advantage of this time because in a couple of years the two grandchildren that are nine won't want to come. They start to have their own commitments, and *chicos* don't like the campo after about thirteen."

Liliana tells me that the boys rode their bikes all the way to the windmill that morning before lunch. They, and the dog way ahead of them, went along the main road, and people who passed in cars waved to them. As they had set out, she'd tried to tell the boys to be careful. They had waved her off.

" '*Abuela*, we already know: look for cars. Don't bike in the road.' Two boys and a dog in the campo, what could people do?"

Moving toward the door, Liliana shakes her head. "Now on the Península there are hardly any children left. All of them have gone because they have gone to school in the pueblo. And the families have begun to leave, to retire from the campo. It's not like before, when we all had big families. Twelve, thirteen children. Incredible," she says tiredly.

Inside, the old burnished red tiles of the kitchen floor glisten from a recent wash. Just inside the doorway, on the floor, Liliana has scattered eight foot-shaped oblongs of flowered cloth to protect the floor. The multicolored patches inspire playfulness. One might dance or hopscotch from patch to patch across the shiny surface. A red gingham patch for my right foot, a blue calico for my left, I skate to my chair.

The table has been cleared from lunch and wiped clean. There is only a crocheted doily in the middle of the table; on the kitchen counter two cakes are cooling. The room is spotless, as though its occupant is about to leave for an indefinite period of time.

"Now in the campo," Liliana continues, "it's all men. The owners are hiring a lot of lone men now. They have hard lives, truth to tell. A lot of them don't have cars, so they have no way to get to town. Imagine having to be out all day, herding, mending fences, and then having to come home at night and cook. Very tiring." She clucks her tongue and shakes her head.

"And in the end they sometimes get half-strange. When they are alone so much, they end up wanting to be alone more, because even if they like people, they aren't used to being with people. People bother them. That's what happens to a person who is alone a lot. And if they get old alone like that, all alone, why should they go on being alone more? The truth is, it's sad."

The woman opens and pours us each a cold tonic from her refrigerator; there is a wonderful cool bubbling sound followed by a fizzing. "Even though a man might have a family, the family stays in town and the man stays in the campo alone. The family might see each other every twenty days, every month, sometimes more. The man goes to town on the weekends and the family comes to the campo if they get a chance. And they live like that."

High on the kitchen cabinet, among old family photos, I notice a ceramic basset hound sitting on its haunches like a totem or a guardian overlooking the kitchen. "It's sad. That's what my husband always says. He has a terror of solitude. Ah, no, no, no! Yes, yes, yes!" Liliana exclaims in the dramatic Argentine fashion.

"If I have to stay alone, I can stay two, three days without anything outside. But him, no! Stay alone? There is no way! He doesn't like it for anything. I don't know why he is like that, but he is that way."

Liliana settles her soft eyes on my face. "Now everyone here is left so alone, no? It seems this way to one."

Having said this, the woman shifts gears and hands me her key to living in the campo. "The only thing is, nowadays generally everyone on the Península has a vehicle and can leave. If one wants to do a quick trip, one can make the whole trip to the pueblo in just one day.

"Truth to tell," Liliana confesses, "I go to Madryn a lot. This time of year, in the summer, I go every two or three days. I just go by myself and come back by myself. Rafael hasn't been to the pueblo for two months, but I go every week."

Liliana puts a plate of sandwich cookies with pink filling on the table—cookies from a shop in Madryn—and we each take one of the treats meant for little girls.

Liliana tells me that her daughters don't come to the campo very often. "The oldest one in particular likes the campo less than less. She comes to visit us, but she doesn't like it here at all. She says the dusk arrives and this solitude descends."

Liliana meets the panting grandsons at the door and pats them off again with cookies in their hands. "Be back in about fifteen minutes so we can prepare to go," she says. Then she returns to the table and dunks a cookie in her tonic, grinning and shaking her head at the shapes of the boys that briefly appeared in the doorway. "We're going to town a little later," she tells me.

Only now do I notice the wrapped packages, tied with string, that are piled on the side table near the door. Rafael, Liliana says, is out riding fence lines. She and the boys will go to the pueblo alone.

"If I could live in Madryn, I would," she says with plain, pure longing. "Yes, yes, yes! The truth is that I have struggled, times back, with my husband, to try to move to Madryn, both of us get jobs there, whatever. Now my husband doesn't want to know anything about this. He is the campo and the campo and the campo. He says, 'Just a little more, just a little more.' He says that before he moves to the pueblo he wants to get pensioned. He says when he retires, he will then see what he will do. And if everything goes well, as thanks to God it has up until now, and God willing, he just lacks four years, and maybe then . . ."

Liliana explains to herself as much as to me, and as she must explain it to her husband. "I was born here. I am from the campo, but Madryn pulls me. Madryn pulls me because I have my house there and I have my plants, and there is community all around. I have my daughters there. I have my grandchildren there. All my brothers and sisters and all the brothers and sisters of my husband are there. So, for me, at the moment, it pulls me a lot to go to Madryn."

Madryn is like a carrot dangling out there, southwest, in the shimmer.

These summer days I have been walking out onto the sere land, being self-sufficient, incessantly demonstrating to myself my North American fortitude. But "the truth is," to use Liliana's words, my need for conversation, for interaction with my kind, dogs me. I zigzag like a rabbit, trying to evade it. Believing I shouldn't need anyone, I deprive myself of contact. My joy is hazed, shimmering off somewhere across a bleakness.

Liliana, on the other hand, billows with her dreams and her hopes. She takes in the grim flank of land, unblinking, and bakes solid lemon cakes. There is clarity in her hazel eyes. She fits into this mean land, but she still yearns. She will not permit her dream to die. She and her culture are certain of her case: the human need for contact, the belief that the greatest fruits of life are social. Like a hunter, she's after what she loves. Her motto is that of a campo fox: "You live in the bare. You pounce on what you can."

Liliana packs the two cakes into baskets. I carry the other parcels for her.

As we walk toward the cars, the boys appear and pop into the back of Liliana's Ford sedan. Just before she steps into the vehicle, Liliana places some cellophane-wrapped candies in my hand.

She trundles down the estancia road and then turns right onto the raised, graveled main road to Puerto Madryn. The minute she hits the broad strip, she guns the engine and roars off in a gleeful cloud of dust.

I am left behind, a dot in the barren campo, with the candy, like a promise, in the palm of my hand.

GUACHO

~~~~~~~~~~~~~~~~~

Rare days, the Patagonian tableland gives forth odd-shaped gems.

You are wandering the desert campo, the wind's whine lonesome, doing a slow and tedious slalom, threading around the knee-high thornbushes, and suddenly, in front of you, on a small patch of exposed earth, is an enormous egg. You stride six paces, and the first egg's twin squats at the toe of a bush. You continue wending around the vicinity and count seventeen eggs dispersed over a quarter-mile circle. A light orb couched beneath a clump of brambles; three hefty eggs clustered in a stand of tough grass; an egg standing grand beside a fossilized oyster shell; a pale green egg left in the open, in a field of black-and-reddish pebbles. You're elated. You're awed. You collect as many as you can carry.

The eggs contain abandoned Darwin's rhea chicks. In the campo a fox or a rider sometimes frightens one of the nesting birds. At the disturbance, the enormous male bird will scramble and flutter up to his full six feet and hastily kick his eggs in every direction. Then, to the extent that a flightless bird can, he flies away on heavy, pounding legs. In other instances the egg scatter is produced when one of the later-arriving female rheas who lay eggs for the single brood male boots out the previously dropped eggs before laying hers in a rhea enactment of survival of the fittest.

The eggs that survive the ostrich boot and hatch are orphans or, as the Argentines say, *guacho*. The wonderful word applies to any wild, unmothered creature raised on the loose. *Guacho*, with the "u" preceding the "a," and pronounced "wacho," is to be distinguished from "gaucho," a similar word with a hard "g" and the "a" preceding the "u," the latter being the term for the cowboys who work on the cattle ranches in northern Argentina. One story has it that, in fact, the pampas cowboys were originally called *guachos*, and by some linguistic mix-up the two letters got flipped.

Most abandoned rhea eggs do not receive the warmth they require in order to hatch and simply pale to bone white under the harsh sun, their contents desiccating away. A few of the eggs, however, may be developed enough, to hatch alone and become living *guachos*. The prehistoric birds chip open their shells and then wander, eyes squinting, into the empty campo.

The *peones* who man the lonely sheep estancias of southern Argentina are another species of Patagonian *guachos*. Many of the lone shepherds are fatherless, motherless, or both, and in some cases even those with living parents have come from families so poor that from the age of eight the boys were forced to raise themselves, out alone on the open range, following sheep.

By the time one of these Patagonian *guacho* boys has his whiskers, the trail of his life is laid. He lives alone in a tiny remote shack, overseeing estancias owned by others. He roams the dusty thornland on horseback or afoot, as unwarmed and unguided as a *guacho* rhea chick.

José's *peón*, Cachorro, was left alone at the age of nine on an estancia where he was working while the owner of the ranch was away. After two weeks the owner hadn't returned, and Cachorro was out of food. Chicken eggs were the last morsels he could find to eat. Finally the sour pangs inside of him were so insistent, Cachorro realized he had to get to town. He mounted a horse, and as he traveled the 120 desolate and tedious kilometers, the boy had to dismount to open and then close thirty-five sheep gates.

Every time I see him, Cachorro tells me, pushing out his chest, eyes mournful, "I grew up *guacho. Soy guacho.*"

A *peón* such as Cachorro will often, in an action of unconscious kinship, gently retrieve a lost rhea egg. He will then try to father it until it hatches, making a nest out of tea bags or putting the egg in his blankets. More than one *peón* has ridden the campo with a gawky, bug-eyed, long-necked, black-and-white-splotched companion loping behind him.

Peones are scattered over Patagonia's vacantness, as insignificant in the 1,600-kilometer backdrop as eggs. Coming across one of them in that oceanic plain can be like finding treasure—one *peón* finding another cooking his noon mutton on a remote rib of campo or a foreigner discovering a *peón* fixing a fence along a hummocky trace when her car has a flat.

Patagonia is a land so vast and barren, she is loneliness itself.

Days when the wind was mad, swirling grit through the window sashes, pounding on the tin roof of the house, beating the sea into a charging froth, and we were trapped indoors, my husband's restless company was never enough. The sea and the wind formed a cage of loneliness. I closed myself in the kitchen and drank cup after cup of hot chocolate, with a litany of names of Cambridge and California friends I longed to see shuttling in my head. Often, by the time the sugar from the chocolate had coated my teeth and I was fed up with my sedentary tendencies, I would think my fanny off the seat of my chair and force my feet out onto the spiny campo behind our seaside house.

I zigzagged into the thornbushes, 1,600 kilometers of unrelieved barrenness stretched before me. I would examine the ground or watch my moving feet rather than expose my vision to the void. On lucky days I might find a pale green rhea egg, a sight to take up space in my mind.

Once in a while on these forays I would spy a thread of black

smoke rising out of nowhere—a *peón*-shepherd cooking his afternoon meal of mutton—or out on the shimmering horizon
there would be the silhouette of a lone horseman on the scrub.

At the beginning, the sight of these *peones* just caused the
pangs to sharpen. The strange, lone shepherds seemed to me
absolutely foreign. I was certain the men, native occupants of
the hostile land, could never offer me any sort of company. I
never approached them when I saw them out on the campo. I
had become fond of the Argentine phrase, *"No hay nada,"* and
I would think to myself, looking at the figure as though he
weren't there, There is nothing here for me. ¡No hay nada! Then
I would return to our house and tell Peter that this time, for
sure, I was going home.

Once, early in my stay in Patagonia, I met a *peón* along an
abandoned road. My journal entry about the encounter reads as
follows:

> For three hours, we see no one. Just before Bajo Caracoles,
> the road curves off a rise down to a dried-up stream dig, or
> arroyo. To our surprise, a tall, thin shepherd appears out of
> the arroyo, silent as an animal, and stands by the road, watching
> as we approach. He is holding a gun. With him are five dogs.
> Three are terriers. One is a gray, friendly-faced sheepdog, the
> last a huge greyhound. The dogs hold close to the man's legs.
> Behind the group is a flock of upland geese.
>   The man is the possessor of a long, thin face. His eyes
> have white blobs in the four corners, and his mud brown
> irises are so dark the pupils are gone. The man's facial skin
> is smooth, dark, and evenly tanned, like purse leather, and
> crow's-feet fan out from the bright eyes. The crow's-feet
> have to fold wide, the *peón*'s skin is so stiff and hardened.
> Beneath a long, straight nose, a thick white mustache hides
> the man's lips. The shepherd wears a cap and a faded blue-
> and-green plaid shirt with cowboy snaps. His britches are
> patched over the patches, and as we pull up beside him, all

I can see from inside the car is his waist. The pants hang down from a flat stomach and hipbones.

We stop the car and the rangy man reaches in the window and shakes both our hands. He then squats on his haunches beside the car, relaxed. Immediately an open grin stations itself on the handsome face. Brown teeth appear below the mustache, and the wrinkles by his shining eyes deepen. It is a deep-cut smile.

When the shepherd speaks, he tells us that he is hunting rhea. He is quick, also, to say that the winter that has just passed was tough. It snowed for three months straight. He was snowed in, "with a *viejo*," for eighty days. "We had plenty of mutton," he says. "We couldn't have died of hunger, but we could have died of cold."

Every time I met a *peón*—such as this ragged man who possessed such strange dignity—the question that haunted me my entire stay in Patagonia arose. How do they survive the loneliness?

In Buenos Aires they have easy answers. You ask a woman dressed in a fur stitched from the pelts of twenty Patagonian gray fox how the *peones* live in the gray solitude, and her answer is ready. She waves her long nails dismissively and repeats one of several pat phrases.

"All a *peón* thinks about is his horse, his mate, and his dog. *Nada más.*"

"Those men are not like you and me. They don't need other people."

"Those men in the campo? They are all screwy. They don't like to be with other people."

Cachorro wore his hair oiled straight back. There was Indian blood trickling through the hue of his skin, and his forty-four-year-old brow was permanently creased from fretting. Cachorro, or "Cub," as he had been called ever since he was orphaned at age ten, read books about sheep. He possessed, in his fresh-painted trunk, two old leather-bound volumes that told him about sheep breeding, and he perused them every night. Cachorro's dream and ambition was to work in the stud barn of a large estancia. One night I met him along the road eight miles from his little house. The five-foot-tall man was walking frantically; torment showed in the rims of his eyes. A troop of horses was loose, and he was determined to catch it, even if it took him a day and a night without food. He would not stop to chat.

Cachorro appreciated the usefulness of horses, and he loved his dogs. His much intermarried sheepdogs, whom he claimed taught each other to herd like champs, were all female. He named them after male Indian chiefs, as though to claim pride in his mixed blood. When I talked with him, Cachorro's fingers were usually fondling the velvet ear of a puppy.

The man's tiny kitchen was impeccable. Every piece of furniture—a large round table, a hand-built, hand-covered chair, a cabinet—was dust free. The concrete floor was as flat and unmarred as a new slab of marble. Tins were lined up soldier file.

On visits, Cachorro offered a choice of mate or tea and then always insisted I have tea. He believed tea was the more delicate beverage, so, naturally, all women would prefer it. He served the tea, lip-searing and fragrant, in a china cup and saucer. He unwrapped a fresh package of cookies for his guest and put them all on a plate. It was as though he were emptying his pockets of all his coins and placing them before me. Cachorro joked about women, and sometimes stretched the truth, but he was all gentleman and generosity.

The *peón* I knew best was Pablo, a bald man who lived on an especially remote inland estancia. Some days when I felt adrift, I would cast about for someone to visit, and I am ashamed to say that Pablo was usually the last one to come to mind. It would suddenly dawn on me that a person lived only thirty kilometers away.

At those junctures I seized the idea of visiting Pablo, grateful for a purpose. I filled the plastic bag of our solar shower with cold water and set it in the sun for two hours. When it was warm I brought it into our concrete Quonset hut, hung the bag, spigot down, from a nail over the drain in the floor of our one room, and bathed joyfully. Swathed in sweaters and wind-breaker, I then ventured out into the gritty wind, grabbing Peter on the way.

The Irabi estancia, which Pablo oversees, stands against a low hill in the center of the Península. A twenty-kilometer rutted trace leads south to the estancia from the wide dirt road that is the main artery on the Península. Three buildings make up the ranch: the large weathered barn; across a patch of dirt, the residence belonging to the *patrones*; and, an afterthought, off to the side of the big house, Pablo's tiny living quarters.

In over eight months I only saw one soul on the road to Pablo's home—the half-mad *peón* from the other estancia along the road who hid behind the windmill or scurried indoors when he saw me coming.

When I arrived at Pablo's spot in the campo, the deserted look of the estancia always struck me. The *patrones*, Angel and Teresa Irabi, Clara's sister and brother-in-law, almost never visited. The big house was shuttered, giving the sense that its eyes were closed, and the gate to its small, weedy garden was clasped tight, as if the place had been packed away and abandoned. Some uncannily quiet chickens skittering among the spindly potted trees next to the big house were the only signs of life. Often, ominous clouds lurked over the low brow of hill, and the only sound was the fierce wind sweeping over the surrounding bleak, flat scrub. There was never any motion around Pablo's shack. The low, white cube, half-hidden under the blowing branches of a trio of hand-planted trees, was mute.

Instants after our motor was turned off, a short, sturdy-bodied man with wide-spaced Indian features would emerge from the gate by his cell, rubbing his eyes. Every time we arrived, Pablo peered at us with a surprised scowl—the screwing-up of his mouth and eyes that made his grin. The old *peón* would then hastily invite us in. We would walk back to the old man's gate, and, pleased, he would shout to Peter over the strong wind, "I thought I heard an auto."

The tiny fenced yard in front of Pablo's two-room house was divided by cement walks into two four-foot by four-foot squares. Each of the garden plots was outlined by neatly arranged up-turned green bottles, but nothing was planted in the dirt squares. Two pairs of worn-out alpargatas with the straw coming out of their soles lay draped over the bottles farthest from the house, like horses put out to pasture. They were the only vegetation in the garden.

Pablo's house was minuscule. The kitchen–sitting room was crowded with its two-person table, a single chair, a cluster of three stools, a gas stove, an enamel woodstove, and a gas burner for heating water. Three hats hung on a rack on the wall: a dusty-looking toque, a leather sheepskin-lined hat with earflaps, and a peaked denim cap. The walls, coated with grease from the frying of mutton, were losing plaster and their dirty green paint. The only thing on them besides the rack of hats was a yellowed auto parts calendar, with pages to be torn off by the day. The metal water bucket, the cabinet with two mate gourds, and the large can of *yerba* were sooted but arranged neatly against the wall. On the little table were two big cooking oil cans, an old dirty radio, two cans of insect spray, and a flashlight. The floor of the room was always swept, and overall the dismal place had a looked-after appearance.

Pablo would open the curtain on the single small window to let in some light as we sat down. Then he would sit on one of the crude stools, set the gas ring in front of him, light the flame, and put the kettle on to boil, each movement slow and delib-erate.

"I was just taking mate," he would inevitably say. "I will take it again with you.

"Do you like it bitter or sweet?" he would then ask—the customary Argentine question.

As he warmed his hands over the kettle, the *peón* would slowly come out of his stupor. He would sit with his short, baggy-panted legs stretched before him, his patched cotton shirt half-open at the middle over his stomach, and pull at his neck-erchief.

The talk was always halting and awkward initially. There were many pauses, as though the lone man didn't know what to say or had forgotten how to speak. He would rub his palm down his face from forehead to mouth, flattening his nose as he went. Then he would rub his spread thumb and forefinger up and down his eyes. With a series of squints and scowls that looked as though he were exercising his facial muscles, he would finally form words.

Pablo always told us first the number of days it had been since he had seen anyone. The brows on his low, slanting fore-head would knot. "Let's see. It's been forty-three days, I don't know. . . ." And he would show us the date on the calendar on which the last visitor came.

One day we shared an asado with Pablo. A pair of truckers had arrived at his doorstep that same morning to buy the estancia's old "sheep of eight teeth," but they had declined the old man's invitation to lunch. They had to hurry back for the horse races in Gaimán.

Just as Peter and I arrived, the truck men had tossed their cigarettes onto the ground and mounted their loose-jointed, dust-covered vehicle. As they ground gears and lurched off, the sheep in the open bins fell onto each other heavily, hoofs scrabbling.

Pablo asked us to have lunch with him. As he did so, his sorrow-brown eyes narrowed, and his forehead became a series of parallel lines. He scratched his ear. When we said we'd love to stay, he grinned like a boy given a skateboard.

"It's all ready," he explained as he led us to the meat shed in the shade of some dry-looking trees. He opened the door of the outhouselike closet made of cast-off boards and from the hook on which it was suspended took down the freshly butch-ered rib cage of a ewe. Following his custom, the shepherd had listened to the radio messages the night before, as the wind whistled through the tin roof, and heard that the truckers were coming. He had risen early to butcher a fat ewe in honor of their visit. The slab of meat was an honest red and white, packaged in the animal's own transparent cellophane.

We lunched with Pablo in the long asado room in one of the outbuildings. In the bare room was a long table, covered with an old oilcloth and lined by benches. A cupboard held plates and cups. The fire in the asado pit had already been neatly laid— a stack of pieces of gnarled wood. Pablo wove a long iron skewer through the two-foot slab of meat, lit the fire over the brushwood, and leaned the meat, just so, over the fire.

We talked food as Pablo poked the fire and turned the crucifix of mutton.

"Right, the other day I made an asado. I had it for lunch, then I ate it for dinner, and the next day I ate it for breakfast and for lunch. I had asado at midday, as well."

He usually ate the meat cold after the first meal, said the old man of over seventy-five years. "All except for winter. In winter, it creates cold to eat cold food. In the winter I like something hot at night, so I always make *puchero*—a stew—at night, because, you see, the days are very short and one has much to do, and the nights are long, so there is time to make *puchero*, or whatever thing one wants. I make asados, *puchero*, stew with potatoes, some kind of mash, some kind of chop in the frying pan, like that—I cut it up like this, two or three chops, and I cut up an onion over them, and then I throw in two chicken eggs."

A researcher I know once lived with the forty-year-old *peón* who inhabited an estancia four leagues from Pablo. Pocho, the younger *peón*, had five meals in his eating repertoire. Try as the researcher might to tempt him with a lettuce leaf or a mutton steak with gravy, Pocho's lips would not part for anything but asado; *estofado*, a mutton stew with potatoes cut up big; *guiso*, a mutton stew with potatoes cut up small; thin fried mutton steaks; or mutton roasted in the oven. The man's appetite was as bound as his movements.

Pablo told us he loves pasta—*ñoquis* or *tallarines*—but those were things women made. He loved the cakes and breads and empanadas that Teresa, Clara's sister, made when she came, and he loved pancakes with *dulce de leche*, the sweet Argentine milk jam.

As we chewed the savory meat, Pablo spoke of some of his habits. He took water in his wine as he ate his asado, then undiluted wine at the end of a meal.

He commented after we had all tucked away a quantity of mutton, "When one is alone, one eats when one is hungry, at whatever hour. One often eats early. When one is alone, one eats, and in a little while, one goes to bed."

The man looked down at his fingers and went on, "What do I know, it seems that at some times one eats more than other times. It seems that when one is accompanied, one eats more. It looks like I ate almost this whole asado today. When there are people, maybe because one talks, it's different. One is more distracted, and one eats more?"

During our visits, the old man spoke nonstop. Dammed-up words, relentless as the wind, jerked out of him until he was spent. Half thinking to himself, half speaking aloud, short sentences burst from his mouth. It was as though he had had the breath knocked out of him but was compelled to speak nonetheless. His voice moved systematically from one thought to the next, halting to consider every topic over which he had mulled since he'd last had a visitor.

"What will happen to José? *No sé. No sé.* He has been at La Bonita, must be, nearly forty years. Nearly. Now he's sick. *Pobre.* Poor man. And Clara, the wife, can't stay in the campo. Can't stay in the campo. She's old already. The campo is not a good place for the old ones."

Elena, the Irabis' thirty-four-year-old daughter, who sometimes came to the estancia on holidays, was usually among his thoughts. "Elena says Bruno misses the campo. Bruno must be two, eighteen months, two years, something like that . . . They live in the capital. Here, there's more *libertad*, she says. . . . In Buenos Aires, the boy goes on the balcony and waves to the cars. He can't go outside on the street, because there are too many cars. It's sad for the *chico*. Elena says he has more freedom here. To play. Those things. When he comes, I take him to the barn. To see the old wagons. . . ."

The litany would proceed for several hours, Pablo pausing only for me to interject, *"Pobre,"* and, *"Qué cosa,"* and, *"Qué lindo."* And then, at last, the old man would tire and fall silent, as though he had said all that he had in him.

For Pablo and other lone sheep men memory performs a function beyond its usual safekeeping of information and experience. Memory is called upon to populate a life as empty as a jar. Each of the past exchanges a *peón* has had with other human beings is a living part of his present—the interactions are banked, like rare coins, in his memory.

Pablo told us about a fishing trip. His brow flickered concern, the trip present in his mind. "Angel and I went fishing. Over in San Román. We didn't catch many fish. There weren't many fish that year. We came home early. We were going to stay a week. Stayed three days . . . no fish.

"Let's see . . ." He paused. "Must be seven years ago Angel and I went to San Román."

The *patrón*, Angel, has supplied Pablo for over thirty years with the *peón*'s every diverting event, his every smidgeon of social interaction, his every luxury. Dependence on the *patrón* is the rock-bottom truth of Pablo's life. His relationship to the Irabis is a source of pleasure, but also of hurt and frustration, the latter by now well blended with resignation. When Pablo has an urge to make *buñuelitos*, a kind of doughnut, and he is out of baking powder, he once told us, he must wait until the Irabis come so he can ask them to buy him some in town. The wait may be four months.

Pablo told us the story of his getting hired by the Irabis.

"It was fate," the *peón* recounted. "It wasn't that I knew Angel. I knew his cousin, Javier.

"At the time I was working where the asphalt ends now, as a *peón*, and I had decided that I wasn't going to work in the campo anymore. I wanted to work in the pueblo, or with a shearing crew, or find a place as *puestero*. I wouldn't have come here, because I had decided to work in the pueblo, but I did it for Javier. If Angel had come to my door alone, I wouldn't have come here, because I didn't know him. But it happened that just after I quit my job, I met Javier and he asked, 'Are you still working at So-and-so's?' and I said, 'No. I left there.'

"That afternoon Angel went to Javier and asked, 'You don't happen to know anyone who might be able to work as a *peón*? My *peón* left today.'

"The next day Angel and Javier came to my door and Javier said, 'Angel needs a *peón* and I recommended you.' So I went because it was Javier." Pablo's sense that he had had no choice in directing his life was palpable.

The times that the Irabis have taken Pablo with them to the beach, to stay with them in their trailer—an Easter custom they maintained until Angel became ill with Parkinson's—are engraved on Pablo's mind as some of his best moments. He described to us several times the net they used to catch fish and the hundreds of anchovies they captured.

Whether or not Pablo visits his mother on the Christmas holidays hinges totally on the Irabis' plans. "Usually I stay here. It depends on them. They usually spend Christmas in Madryn, not here in the campo, so if I went to the pueblo, too, there would be no one here to look after the sheep. Sometimes the Exteberris take me to Pirámides for the night. At least there, there is something different—a dance or something."

Sometimes, Pablo told us one bitter cold day, he eats the estancia's chickens (chicken is a luxury in Patagonia). "And I don't ask anyone's permission, either," the old man noted quietly. This was the only glimmer of defiance I ever sensed in the man, but as Pablo spoke his back remained slumped.

I often left Pablo asking myself, "Why do the *peones* take it?"

Rafael, the well-established, securely married manager of the sizable estancia La Entrada, pondered the lot of *peones* one day.

"I think it is hard for all these lone men," he said. "By our way of thinking, we see it as a hard life. But I would say to you, for them it's not so hard. There are a lot of people, I'm not sure why"—Rafael seemed to be straining—"who like this solitude. They like the campo because they like this solitude. They are happy that way.

"I knew a man of Italian descent who died three months ago," he went on. "A blond man. The more he could be alone, the better. He lived for twenty-six or twenty-seven years on one *puesto*. Alone. Now, you'd go to visit him and he was very pleasant. He lived very clean. The house was impeccable, and he would invite you to stay. He'd invite you to lie down on a bed with sheets, and he'd serve you chicken.

"But that would last one day or two. Then you would observe that he wanted to be alone. Alone. Night. Day. Months. Alone. I have known many cases like this."

A restless businessman in Puerto Madryn envies the *peones* their freedom from wives and children and jobs. He once set me straight on *peón* loneliness and dependence.

"You ask me how the *peones* can live so alone like that? They're happier than you and I. Because they don't have ambitions. They're happy just being with the animals and doing daily things. It is the people in town who want a new TV and a new this and that, who are unhappy. No, no, the *peones* are happy."

Cachorro, another *peón* who lives utterly alone, was one of the men that Pedro, the businessman, pointed to as an example of a contented *peón*. "That man," said Pedro, "for example. Look at him over there at La Bonita. He is *perfectamente contento*."

The one time I saw a light-hearted glint streak from Cachorro's loneliness-bruised eyes and an impish grin overtake his face, he was sitting on a folding chair across from a *peón* who had come to help herd. When I peered through his doorway, and the swart, tough man got up to extend his hand and beckon me in, he was chuckling at something the other man had said. And when he introduced me to the fellow, he slapped him on the back, with a grin about to break his face, and said *"Mi compañero."* The two were sitting on opposite sides of a table so small, their knees might have been touching. The two *peones* were eating identical heaps of stew.

Pocho is another man who was described to me, by people who do not live his life, as perfectly happy. A man with a shy smile, inhabiting a bare house in the center of a low, bleak stretch of campo, Pocho had almost no words. He used one room of his four-room dwelling as a pantry. On the shelf in the utterly bare concrete room, there was a heap of onions, a tumble of old oranges, a bag of *yerba* for mate, and several ancient boxes of noodles. A burlap sack of potatoes leaned against the shelf, and onionskins littered the dirty floor.

Pocho's life fit in a tin bucket. From the well outside the house, his bucket drew water. When one set of clothes got dirty, Pocho stuffed them into his metal bucket and soaked them for two days in a soup of hard soap and water. He could have carried his possessions—his extra clothes and his kettle for boiling water for mate—in the bucket. And at lamb markings, the same metal pail received the testicles of the infant rams as they were castrated, one after another.

The researcher who lived with Pocho for a time and got sick of his five dinners said the youngish *peón* spoke often of getting a woman *bien gordita*, and he looked forward to his quarterly trips to town as a way of finding such a woman. A full month before each trip, Pocho began to get nervous. He made big plans.

The researcher transported Pocho to town for a couple of his breaks. On the day of one of these trips, Pocho put his pay in his front pocket. By the time they reached the town limits, the dark-haired, sturdy young man was so nervous he couldn't speak. His brows were so furrowed they hid his eyes. The researcher let him out on the street with the bar where the *peones* went, and his housemate stood awkwardly along the roadside until the researcher pulled away.

When the researcher picked him up the next day for the return trip to the campo, Pocho was morose. He had been so nervous about the woman that he had gotten drunk. A mu-

chacho at the bar had made him an appointment with a woman,
but he had been so drunk, he'd missed it. That fact had so
depressed him that he had spent all his money buying more
vermouth.

About halfway into the return journey, Pocho perked up. He
settled comfortably onto his seat, and he took the vow many
peones take on returning to the campo. "I will never go to town
again. I just drink. I can't manage it."

Six months after my friend left Pocho's estancia, I happened
to be passing through that grim and dusty spot. When the *peón*
shuffled out of the house, he had on the researcher's cast-off
sneakers and old blue jeans.

Pablo believes that being a *peón*, for all its sadness, has its bless-
ings. He and other *peones* often count them out.

"For saving pesos, being a *peón* is the best there is," Pablo
told us. "It's much better to be a *peón* than to live in town. The
owners give you your food—noodles, onions, mate, meat—and a
house. In Madryn there are always people who are hungry. And
in town you always lose. Your money is in your hand. At the
end of the month you have to pay the meat man, the bread man,
and if you have three or four *chicos*, you don't have enough.
Besides, there are more temptations there. Here, the owners
give you all you need. Living here in the campo, you can save
to buy a piece of land or a house. I have land in Trelew. I want
to build a small barn on it. I already have a shed there for
keeping things. And I have my house in Madryn. It cost one
hundred and fifty pesos. That was money in those days. But I
bought it about twenty years ago."

Pablo took pride in his independence. He considered himself
lucky when he compared his lot with that of the *peones* on a
large estancia on the Península who have little decision-making
power. "On that place, the *peones* don't do a thing until the
manager tells them to dip the sheep, or shear, or herd. They are
very demoralized. Dispirited. They won't bother to skin even
one dead sheep." Taking the time to skin dead sheep found on

the campo, a nasty job, is the local measure of a conscientious sheep man.

"They also don't herd carefully. Lots of animals are left in the pasture when they herd, and don't get shorn. At La Angostura last year, they missed over one hundred animals."

As *peón*, Pablo manages the shearing and other major jobs on the ranch and gains satisfaction from those tasks. He feeds the chickens and collects their eggs in the morning. Later in the day, he checks on the windmills to assure that they are functioning, to see that water is entering the sheep troughs, and to make sure no animals have fallen in and drowned. He uses the sulky Angel built to collect the thorny branches of the campo brush that fuel his cookstove. During the summer months, after the sheep are sheared, he has to herd them to the corral once a month to clip the wool around their eyes. This is done so that the wool doesn't block the sheep's vision. Pablo takes these tasks seriously, if perfunctorily, even after twenty-seven years.

Pablo is as familiar with sheep work as with his own body. I once watched him dividing sheep. The old man stood calmly in a corral of jostling sheep. He separated the animals expertly, casually, just shifting his body into the way when enough sheep had gone into the next pen. Each time he got exactly the right number.

A man does what he knows. He takes up what life has dealt him. But a lump formed in my throat each time I watched Pablo cross the patch of beaten sand between his cubicle and the barn to find his horse. When he rides home from the campo at dusk—the wind biting and peach streaks in the flat, faraway sky— there is no soul in the vicinity to share his meal. He opens the door to the tiny indoor world and creeps into a silent gray room.

Pablo was raised in the Sierra Grande, in Río Negro Province, just to the north of Chubut Province. One of three boys and seven girls, Pablo spent his childhood herding the family's sheep and goats in the open, unfenced range. He and his brothers departed the family's tiny house early in the morning. They rounded up the livestock and followed them, on horseback, with their dogs, as the animals grazed in the direction of the wind. "The sheep in those days were tame because you were with them all day," Pablo marveled.

Life was backbreaking. The whole family helped to shear the sheep by hand, with hand shears. The family had only about five hundred sheep, as opposed to the Irabis, who have twenty-five hundred. His family was also "known to have," as Pablo put it, as many as two hundred goats. His father also kept a few cows. All the animals were raised for their meat. The family ate goat more often than mutton and had lamb on Christmas. In the winter they ate mares and cows. Pablo's mother baked bread in an outdoor mud oven.

As Pablo remembered it, his family had plenty of visitors and suffered none of the loneliness he has since experienced. "Out there, there were a lot of settlers. A lot of people went around by horse. There were a lot of families, and also a lot of relatives. All my aunts and uncles were there around us. I had one aunt who had a big family. A great number of *chicos*. She was known to come with the *chicos* and stay one day, or two, or three." A trip to Madryn from the Sierra took two days by wagonette, with an overnight in the open campo.

Pablo had no schooling and never learned to drive. The family had an old wreck of a car that had to be abandoned before he got his turn at the wheel. This deficit had ramifications for Pablo's adult life, preventing him from being able to get out to see people. "It's a shame," Pablo told us. "If they could have bought something that drove well, I could have learned to drive when I was a *chico*, too."

Pablo left home at age twenty to look for work. "I worked for people there, near home. Later, when I was twenty-five or so, my brother got married and decided to stay there, on my father's campo, with the livestock. Since the campo yielded too little for all, I left." At age twenty-five, cast off from the campo he loved and knew, Pablo began to find work for himself in the lands around Madryn.

"I worked a lot over there in the campo, outside, off the Península. I worked all around. I worked in a lot of parts, and then I came here to the Península, and I just stayed. I came here to the Irabis in 1956. I've been here twenty-seven years. I stayed and stayed. Already I'm an old campesino."

Pablo squinted and scratched his face and commented with regret, "What are you going to do? How rapidly the years go! Now they go sooner than before. Before, it seemed that there were so many years left for leaving."

Pablo believes that he is too old to be in the campo anymore. Having drawn this conclusion, he is surveying back over his life.

He regrets that he missed out on an opportunity to buy a small campo from a widowed woman in Madryn because he had committed himself to working for Angel.

"If that hadn't happened, I would have had a nice piece of campo in Mirasol. It was a campo for goats, because it was open, unfenced campo. In Mirasol, everyone has goats. The little white goat has a lot of value. They sell goats for holiday meals. A goat might even have more value than a lamb by now."

And there is another stinging loss that lurks in Pablo's gray matter—the selling of his family's campo.

"After my brother decided to leave my family's campo, they sold it. That campo should never have been sold outside the family since we were all raised there. . . . They should have sold it to me. But since there were so many brothers and sisters, one pulling for one side and one for the other, and no one could agree on what to do, they sold it to someone else.

"I would have been secure for the whole journey if they had sold it to me. I would have just stayed there. It was a big enough capital. That little campo had a thousand and some animals. And everyone knew me around there. It was good, that campo.

"At least they should have left it for my old mother to live there. She could have paid for a woman to be at her side, and then she would have left it to me. The whole affair was a shame.

In the end, I didn't stay there on the campo. So now I am left without the bread and without the cake."

When I left Pablo, I often felt choked. At departures the old man wore his frown-grin and began to stare at the earth even before we left. His parting words were always, "Greetings to them."

Driving away from Pablo, I felt my own loneliness condense and overflow. For a few hours afterward I felt calm. I set my own impatient loneliness beside Pablo's vulnerable dignity. I set my frivolous loneliness beside the *guacho* rheas' and *guacho peón* boys' courageous forays into the void. For a period, it would be clear to me that loneliness is only conquered in Patagonia if you soak in it, go deep as you can into the wind and withdrawal, and sway there.

The campo's honest starkness, streaked on its barely perceptible ridges with sun, always looked magnificent to me after visits with *peones*. In part, like Pablo, all I needed was a scrap of another's life to chew on for the empty land to flush peach and lime.

Toward the end of my time on the Península, I took a long wander south, deeper into Patagonia. As I drove lumps of old horse dung were like mileposts, or cairns, on the path. I watched for them, plucking my courage at the sight of each deposit, at the sure evidence that a *peón* had made it through that patch before. By the time I left Patagonia, I knew how to make a feast of little. I could spot a rhea egg, and the scribbled smoke of a *peón*'s fire, from a great distance.

THE PEARL

~~~~~~~~~~~~~~~~~~~~

On one of our early supply trips to Puerto Madryn, we saw an evil-looking, brown-snouted wild dog draped dead over a mound of earth beside the road. The dog seemed to me an appropriate guardian for the dusty, wind-whacked town.

Puerto Madryn is positioned in the northwest corner of Golfo Nuevo, just twenty minutes by car from the isthmus that leads onto Península Valdés. The small port has been the primary supply depot for the sheep ranchers of the Península ever since the ranches were first established. Driving south from the town of Patagones on Ruta 3, the main north-south route along the Argentine coast, the traveler passes through 450 kilometers of barren Patagonian campo before reaching Madryn, the next real town on the half-dirt, half-asphalt road. And from Madryn it is another sixty monotonous kilometers to the next settlement, Trelew. From Madryn's beach one looks, through the opening in Golfo Nuevo, across a wild and vacant ocean for ten thousand miles—halfway around the globe—to the next closest landmass, Tasmania.

Puerto Madryn is a grid of dusty graveled streets, bounded on one side by Avenida Roca, a broad paved road that parallels the sea. From the avenue, the streets trundle perpendicularly inland twenty blocks or so. The town so looked to by the Península people is marked by a complete absence of vegetation. The low, cube-shaped concrete-and-sheet-metal buildings, shuttered to keep out wind, cold, and sun, sit in rubble. Many of the wind-weakened buildings have large gouges out of the walls and seem about to crumble in on themselves, and the pavements of both streets and sidewalks have long ago cracked and heaved in response to the regular assaults of frigid gales. The town's blocks are a testament to the advantages of zoning: a humble concrete-block home sits beside the half-finished tile-roofed "chalet" of a doctor who is planning to make a venture in the south, and beside the chalet sits a grubby tire repair shop. The farther inland one goes, the humbler the neighborhoods become, finally petering out into barrios of sheet metal and cardboard shanties, mud roads, and garbage heaps with black-backed gulls and iridescent black giant petrels circling overhead. A wind-blown trail of garbage from the barrios trickles off across the barren scrub toward the sandy cliffs that back the town.

Puerto Madryn was named for Sir Jones Love Parry, the Welsh baron of Madryn. Parry was one of the leaders of the group of Welsh pioneers that put ashore in 1865 at the current site of the Patagonian township and went on to settle Chubut Province.

Madryn was initially nothing more than a few corrugated tin supply warehouses and shacks hastily erected in the scrub near the sea. Early campo settlers journeyed to these warehouses in sulkies and wagons to supply themselves with four or five sacks of flour, potatoes, and *yerba*—provisions that would last them a year. From the 1880s to the 1940s, Madryn was even smaller than Puerto Pirámides, the tiny salt- and wool-shipping village on the Península itself.

In the mid-1950s all Argentine towns located below the 42nd parallel were, for a short while, declared free ports, and with the designation Madryn enjoyed a growth spurt. Cars and light engines began to be sold from Madryn's warehouses, and a handful of textile firms, taking advantage of the low taxes in the *paralelo* towns, set up factories in Madryn. The firms, which produced such items as socks and stockings made of artificial fibers, employed women from the campo as seamstresses.

After less than a decade, however, the warehouses and factories closed (taxes crept up again once Madryn was no longer a free port), and Madryn's population folded in with them. Only around 1973, when the foundation was dug for Aluar (an aluminum plant that uses electricity from a dam seven hundred kilometers to the west to transform raw imported aluminum into ingots), did the population of the town begin to increase and did the Argentine government's injunction to the people to move south to *"Poblar la Patagonia"* begin to be followed.

In 1971 Madryn had a population of six thousand. In 1978 and 1979, when we were first there, the town was little larger than that. By the time Peter and I left after our second stay, in 1985, the Madrynenses boasted that the Patagonian town, now claiming twenty-eight thousand inhabitants, was the site of "the most important demographic explosion in the country."

Like all Península dwellers, Peter and I made monthly supply runs to Madryn. We regarded Madryn as a place of little interest, and we looked on these obligatory trips to, and the hours spent in, the little town as a tiresome necessity. To pass even a day away from the high-soaring albatrosses, the lumbering whales, and the gleaming dolphins out in the wide, pristine bay bothered us, and the journey from the Whale Camp to Madryn seemed increasingly tedious as the months passed. For an hour and forty-five minutes we traveled the raised dirt road through the flat, changeless thornland. Finally, having crossed the isthmus, we would reach the Madryn cutoff and turn left onto a road so seldom graded that the ridges in the gravel made the car shudder uncontrollably. This road led us gradually down the escarpment from the bristly tableland to the town at the northwest edge of Golfo Nuevo.

At a point in the slow descent toward the sea, not far from a gull-encircled garbage dump, the austere, broad gulf and the town would first come into sight. In the foreground were the cranes and hulking buildings of Aluar. Beyond the buildings of the plant—the huge, barrellike, gray warehouse and the quarter-mile-long, armlike conduit leading out from it onto a quarter-mile-long black shipping dock—we spied the low, blocklike buildings of the little Patagonian town.

Once in among the concrete-and-dust blocks of houses and shops, we dashed, like people in a footrace, to accomplish errands before the noon to four siesta. First we dropped the flat tires at the *gomería*, then we deposited the gas canisters for our stove, space heater, and lights to be refilled at the natural-gas man's. We roared to the tour leader, who exchanged our dollars for pesos, to four or five shops to collect enough C-cell batteries to keep our tape recorder going for the next month, and to the stationery store for the dust-covered, dog-eared pads of paper and binders so old their seams were cracked. Just before lunch, always hoping for a shipment of peanut butter, we waited in a long line for our aging mail.

At lunch, usually in a pizzeria with metal and Formica tables, we wolfed down sandwiches made of breaded minute steaks and fried eggs, drank orange Fanta, and hungrily read our letters. After a cheek-chilling walk along the grim and blustery sea, the strand empty save for, perhaps, a small boy kicking rocks or a dog sniffing at a discarded plastic jug, we climbed back into our truck to wait out the remainder of the siesta. In the truck, parked near a statue that we had never even bothered to look at, we tapped our fingers and grew increasingly annoyed at the inefficiency of a country whose shops were closed for four hours in the middle of the day.

At four sharp we were at the door of the greengrocer's. There we filled plastic-mesh sacks with cabbages, onions, potatoes, withered apples, and a few luxuries like eggplant and lettuce to be eaten the first week back at camp. Then we hastened to the *supermercado* for dried milk, soup mixes, beans, sugar, and flour. We bought only essentials, priding ourselves on our Muir-like simplicity, as well as working with a slender budget. Sometimes we allowed ourselves a package of *mantecol*—a peanut-y dessert like halvah.

On earlier trips it did not occur to us to visit anyone while in Madryn. Our sole aim, as we banged through town, was to get back to the noble, pure life in the wilderness.

By eight or nine, exhausted and relieved that we had made it through another day of town, we would steer the car once again up the rise past Aluar and continue out onto the Península.

As we drove away into the unlit darkness, out onto the yawning campo, feeling the cold wind blowing her dust up through the seams of the truck, we would turn on the radio to listen to "the messages for the rural population." Between the messages emitted out of the blackness—"Alicia San Martín, your brother is out of danger in the hospital in the pueblo. . . .

"Angel Irabi, your truck parts have arrived in the pueblo. . . . —the lips of the radio announcer would caressingly roll out the extravagant slogan of the station:

"¡PUERTO MADRYN—LA PERLA DE LA PATAGONIA!"

A wilderness snob, I laughed at hearing the dust-dredged, homely little settlement compared to a pearl. Gradually, however, like sand duning up in my consciousness, both the town and campo people I came to know through interviewing, and my own experiences, taught me that you cannot judge the value of a town, any more than a book, by its cover. Its beauty depends entirely on your frame of reference.

It was Marta, Rafael and Liliana's daughter, who gave me the meaning of Madryn for Península people.

Marta and her family live in a small concrete house on one of the residential streets on the outskirts of Madryn. The exterior of the house is fresh and inviting, with new white paint and a tidy, gated entry. The house sits almost on top of the concrete sidewalk. Unlike in many Madryn homes, whose occupants keep the shutters on their big picture windows closed, giving the interior an insular quality, in Marta's home the shutters are left part way up, to let in the sun.

When I arrived for my first visit with Marta, one of her sons, a boy I had seen pedaling a bicycle across the campo near Rafael and Liliana's house, opened the door and then hurried to get his mother. The thin woman came out of the kitchen where she had been working, cutting up the beef for the noon meal alongside a well-groomed older woman in an apron. The washing machine was churning, and the attractive older woman kept working as Marta hurried from the kitchen to greet me, wiping her hands quickly on a towel. She dispatched a brief sentence back to the older woman as she closed the kitchen door behind her and had me sit down on a chair in the main room where I had been standing. She then moved the three children, who were coloring and playing with Lego blocks on the floor around the coffee table, back to the dining table at the rear of the room, gave them some crayons and paper, and told them she was going to be occupied for a while. Three obedient heads bent down over the table.

Marta sat down next to me on one of the dark-striped chairs in the living room area where she could keep an eye on the children. The chairs, severe and uncomfortable even though they had high backs and deep foam seats, were functional and modern like all the furnishings in the room. Though unornamented, the living room seemed comfortably lived in and thoroughly used.

Marta's face showed colors and strains from both her family lines. There was something like Liliana in the overall pattern of Marta's features, but the younger woman's coloring was darker and her eyes were dark brown. They had the deep, serious quality that pooled in the eyes of her father and his older sister, Vitoria. Lines traveled from Marta's inner eyes down along her nose, then curved toward her ears, giving the thirty-three-year-old woman's face a worried look. The skirts and shirts Marta employed to cover her spare frame had the no-nonsense style that matched her efficient, practical cast of mind.

Marta was the devoted and organized mastermind behind a family of five and was also a committed professional—a teacher. Raised her first few years in the campo, Liliana and Rafael's daughter was now a confirmed town dweller. Her life possessed a pace and routine entirely different from her mother's in the campo, and her reference point, if she had one beyond Madryn, was Buenos Aires rather than the Península.

"On a typical working day," Marta said as she set out a blueprint of her life in Madryn for me in neat, frank prose, "we have breakfast at seven in the morning, neaten up the house, and the three children and I go to school. My husband goes to work at eight in the morning. He works at Aluar, the aluminum plant. He goes in at eight in the morning and returns to the house at twelve.

"We eat lunch at twelve and my husband goes back to work at one and we all go, too. Then at five in the afternoon we come home and my husband arrives at five-thirty. The *chicos* have *la leche* [the term used for an afternoon snack of milk and cookies], and then they have other activities. For instance, Pablo goes to basketball three times a week and my daughter goes twice a week to painting class. So I take them, and I return home. Then I have to go back and pick them up. I have a full schedule, with them." Marta's voice was hoarse but gentle, her words succinct. Everything about the woman was unadorned. "Then later," she concluded, "we prepare dinner, rest a little, and begin the next day in the same way."

I noted to myself that there was no mention from the young woman of her own need for rest.

As if she could read my thoughts, Marta leaned forward on her chair to explain why she liked the clip of her life. Her tone was that of a professional well informed about the problems that run rampant in big cities and used to outlining her points clearly. She anticipated my North American obsession with stress without my voicing it.

"It's not such a rushed life, not as agitated as in the big cities, because we have things closer to us. That is to say, it takes me ten minutes to get to work, while in the big cities I would have to leave an hour before, and take two buses, to get to work on time. It is also much calmer here. But, in general, time is pretty well occupied for all of us. And there isn't much free time left over for us to notice that time is passing. That is to say, all of a sudden you realize that the week is finished, the month, the year, and you don't know how."

As we talked, Marta kept tabs on the meal making in the kitchen and the children's activities. She was expert at focusing in the midst of distraction.

"How well it works out to have both working," she went on, after suggesting that one of the children get out another set of crayons, "depends a lot on the couple. That is to say, when the schedules of both leave some time open so that the couple can share moments together, then I don't think it is a serious problem. The problem arises when the schedules are contradictory. You find couples who only see each other on weekends, even though they live in the same house all week, because no part of their schedules coincide. This, to me, is extreme.

"I always try to arrange our schedules so that the family can keep being together—so that we all sit down to eat at the table at noon, so that we have a bit of time in the afternoon to have tea, or some mate, or whatever it might be. We might just talk for half an hour, but at least we have time together.

"If you don't have that, you don't share with the *chicos* enough, and you don't know their problems or anything. You lose communication in the family. And that can bring problems later."

The girl and the two younger boys, aged nine, eight, and six and a half, sneaked glances at me from time to time, then turned and colored furiously when I caught their eyes.

A smile lit up the young woman's careworn face when she caught me looking over at the busy shoulders and intent faces. "I love children," she said. "That's why I had three in a row. They're only thirty-six months apart!

"I didn't work while the children were little," she said. "After the girl was born, and until the smallest one was four, I didn't work. I think they needed me a lot. There were three of them and they were very small, and I didn't have the inclination to leave them. I couldn't have left them with a feeling of tranquillity. I thought it was more important for me to be here with them during that time than for me to work. I didn't feel any need to work outside, either, because I was so busy with them that the time flew without my realizing it.

"Nowadays most women work," Marta went on in her informative manner. "Many work for economic reasons. Others work so that they aren't in the house all day, no? The women don't feel bored at home, but I think they feel a need to do something, something different from the rhythm of the house—in order not to become dull. They work at things they like, at something which contributes economically, too, but the most important thing to them is to do something that they like."

In our conversation about her dual-career family, Marta allowed that some husbands don't want their wives to work but said that this more traditional idea was changing quickly in response to necessity. In many Madryn households a family can no longer survive without two salaries, she explained, so it is becoming common for both members of a couple to work.

Marta's son, named for Rafael, the boy whom I had watched light his grandfather's cigarette, had at some point worked his way across the room and was now sitting on a chair across from his mother, playing quietly with the tools in a tin box. The controlled plinking of tools, and the other children's quiet discussion, backed the conversation Marta and I were having. The house was filled with the gentle, muffled din of constant movement and industry. Chopping and footfalls came from the kitchen, along with the swishing of the washer.

Having evaluated her son's presence near us, Marta settled her hands in her lap and told me about her schooling. For a short time Marta was a homesick pupil at the nuns' school in Rawson, and later she attended primary school in Madryn. She was one of the many children from campo families whose schooling required that the parents live apart much of the year.

"While I went to school I lived with my mamá and my sister here in Madryn, and my father went on living in the campo. This living apart from fathers still goes on now with families from the campo. During the school year, they bring the wife and children to town. The mother sends the *chicos* to school, and the father comes to visit them every twenty days or so, depending on the resources they have. There are some families with better economic resources who travel every weekend, for example, to be with the men in the campo, but in my time my papá came to visit every fifteen to twenty days, was with us two to three days, and went back to the campo."

The self-disciplined young woman, with her assumption that schooling is worth much sacrifice, minimized the impact of such a separation. As a little girl, her father's absence was a fact handed to her. "For us, not living with my father was normal. It was just like that.

"On the other hand, I think that this kind of separation would be very hard for my children, because they are accustomed to having their father continuously in the nucleus. But for us, it was normal. We were here and we just saw Papá from time to time. We just shared summer with him.

"The situation was much harder for my parents than for us. Now, come to think of it, of all of us, the one who felt the separation the most was Papá, who was left alone in the campo. He had to do everything: cook, wash his clothes, take care of the house. He was almost always alone. Sometimes he had a *peón* with him, but most of the time he was alone.

"In the time of my parents, it was practically impossible for people who lived in the campo to come to school. There were two primary schools here in Madryn at the time. And in Pirámides there was a school also, but the school was mainly for the people who lived there, not for the people from the campo. The biggest obstacle was that the people in the campo didn't have vehicles. The only way they had of moving around was by horse or horse-drawn carts, and the roads were very bad, so it was practically impossible to go to school."

Marta moved easily to the next paragraph, giving order to her history lesson.

"The campo people who came from a good economic level contracted directly with a teacher and brought him to the campo to teach their children to read and write. All that mattered to them was reading, writing, adding, subtracting, nothing more—they didn't worry about other aspects of education. That is to say, in a period of about nine to ten months all the children in the house were taught to read, write, and do figures, and that was it. Done.

"In other homes where they couldn't afford to bring in a tutor, if there was someone in the family who knew how to read and write, that person taught the children in the house. For example, my grandmother taught my mamá. And my grandmother learned from her mother."

Marta returned to her own experiences. "My school in Madryn—it is the one between Sarmiento and Gales streets—is very old. All the schools in Madryn are old," Marta said with pride. "The school where I am working just had its fiftieth anniversary!

"I have good memories of my time in school. By the time I went it was a modern type of education. They didn't put you in penance. They didn't hit you, or any of those things that existed in the old days.

"I wasn't ever an outstanding student, but I always liked to study, and then later I liked my profession. I finished primary school in Madryn and did part of my secondary school in Madryn and part in Trelew.

"I wanted to be a teacher." Marta put emphasis on the word *teacher*, an identity that was almost magical for her. "And at that time there was no teaching program in Madryn." She explained that she was only able to do three years of her teacher's training in Madryn and had no option but to go to Trelew for the last two years of the course. The teenager commuted to Trelew daily—it was over an hour each way—leaving Madryn at six-thirty in the morning and returning at two forty-five in the afternoon.

Marta's tone lightened, and I could hear her smile in her voice as she told me about her girlhood delight in teaching her playmates. "I always say that being a teacher was born in me. Before I had even gone to school I knew that I was going to be a teacher. Always. Always."

After finishing teacher training, there being no posts in Madryn, Marta took a position in the village of Telsen in the interior of the province. For three years she lived and worked in the tiny hamlet, in a locale of extreme isolation.

"I liked Telsen. It was, more or less, like living in the campo, when you are in the middle of emptiness. It was a totally different way of life for me. I lived with two other young teachers. We shared the house and worked together. The three of us felt that we were doing what we liked; we felt independent. We were also sort of caught up in the idealism of seventeen-year-olds, when you still think you can do what you love and change the world.

"As a teacher there, I tried to show the *chicos* things that I had seen and they had not. There were *chicos* there, for instance, who didn't even know what an airplane was. Planes never flew over that area, so they had never seen a flying airplane! Things like that. So I tried to show the children things about the world through drawings and through talking with them and telling them stories."

As Marta spoke, it occurred to me that Liliana had been an insulated, knowledge-hungry campo child, just like those her daughter was describing.

"I was in Telsen for three years and then I came back to Madryn to work, and from then on I've been here. I got married three years after I returned."

Little Rafael's hammering had intensified into a steady din, and the other children were beginning to squabble. Marta somehow smoothed the waters, then returned to her chair near me.

As she sat down she told me that television was at the root of many of the current learning difficulties among Argentine students. In the days before television people read a lot; today her students seldom reach for books. They often have spelling and writing problems because they don't read. "It's very rare at this moment to find little ones in sixth or seventh grade who write short stories or things like that, which they did before."

Marta's sentiments regarding TV were all too familiar. The opinions of this Puerto Madryn woman living on the edge of the desolate Patagonian steppe could easily have sprung from the lips of an upper-middle-class mother in Boston.

"Television has caused all this," Marta continued. "But then, also, the way of life has changed. Before, children in primary school went to school, and the other hours were left for playing, reading, and doing their homework. Now, no. Today everyone lives in a hurry. The grown-ups and the *chicos*. After school the children go to do some sport, or go to study painting, or to a theater class. They all have special activities after school. So when they want to reflect, there isn't time left. But this is the fault of grown-ups. We go around in a rush, so we try to keep them busy, too."

Marta beckoned to her daughter, the nine-year-old whose long hair fell from a cloth headband, whom I had seen out in the field behind Liliana's house chasing a horse. Her beautiful eyes sparkling at me in recognition, the sturdy young girl approached her mother. She had a broad face with a petulant, jutting underjaw and was very leggy and tall for her age. Breast nubs were already pushing behind the blouse she was outgrowing. I commented on how grown-up the girl seemed. "Yes, but she's only nine," said Marta firmly, as though reiterating that fact to both herself and her daughter, and that said, she sent her out with a woven plastic shopping bag to buy oranges and bread.

Marta sat back on her chair and spoke, for a time, about her child-rearing beliefs. Her body relaxed a degree or two, but her voice remained crisp and became strident as she talked on. "I think that you should raise children with a truthful perspective, show them what life is really like. Not raise a child in a very special world which he will have to give up someday in the future. If you always give a child what he wants, he will have a lot of disappointment when he is older, because life is not like that. What purpose would it serve to give my children all that they want, at great sacrifice on my part, when they are not going to get all they want later in life? They are always going to have limits.

"I think that you have to really prepare your child, in the best way possible, for the world that we are living in. I hope that things will be much better in the future, but how do you know if they are going to be or not?"

As Marta elaborated on her philosophy of realism, I began to see before me a young woman who had experienced disappointment, who had learned to grit her teeth, and whose foremost purpose was to help her children build defenses against similar suffering.

"As a parent, you should show children how things are at all levels," Marta asserted. "Above all, at the economic level. They have to learn that there are some people in very good economic positions, and some people with very bad economic positions, and that they are in the middle, and not to complain. It's better if they can rise above where they are, but they should never forget that they must also help those who are below."

Marta held the fatalistic views of the many townspeople I had met whose hopes had been deflated time and again by the never-ending Argentine economic plight. Their pessimism, chiseled by economic realities, was warranted, and they were wise in cautioning their children.

Marta went on with her unromantic hopes for her children. "For my children, I want, first, for them to do something they like. Something that will make them happy. But at the same time something that will help them make a road for themselves in life. I don't wish so much that they be something like doctors or engineers, but that they do something that they like, and that really will be a tool for a job for them.

"I would like them, at least, to finish secondary school. If they want to go on to the university level, good, better, but what really interests me is secondary. For the boys, I am interested in the technical courses in secondary school. Those are what most qualify men at the moment, and give them a wide field of action. These specialized, technical studies are things like mechanics, construction and plan drawing, chemistry, lathe work, electricity, machinery, computers, communications. Those kinds of studies, to my way of thinking, are what most capacitate, above all, the boys.

"I would like my daughter to finish one of the secondary-level careers, like secretarial studies or teaching, so that if she doesn't want to pursue something else, at least she has those qualifications.

"As for the university level," Marta said, "I don't hope for my children to go to the university, though I would not stop them if they wanted to go. The university serves some well, others not. We live a long way from the big university centers, so a lot of times sending a child to university requires a very big financial sacrifice from parents, and also sacrifices on the part of the student himself, since he has to live far from his parents and undertake the six or seven years of study required.

"I'm not sure university is always worth it. At this moment, for example, there are lots of professionals in each area, and there aren't enough jobs. So, suddenly, you come across an engineer driving a taxi, for example, or one who has a kiosk. You could go through all the years of sacrifice demanded by a university education and then have nowhere to be employed. This is the employment problem that is occurring at this moment with the Argentines. An economic problem. I think that with time a person who is competent is always able to find work." Marta then stated one of the sad truths about being Argentine: "But sometimes it is not within his own country."

A car honked from the street. Marta went to the front door, leaned out, and waved to someone. Her sister had come by, on her way to the market, to see if Marta needed any vegetables. Marta motioned that she didn't.

"For my parents the moral values were the most important," she continued. "Most important was that we got what we got through the sacrifice of work, and that we got it without stepping on anyone and without taking from others what belonged to them. Very important to my parents was that we knew how to earn, how to obtain things for ourselves, and not to envy those who had more. You have to learn to be happy with what you have."

As Marta spoke I could hear Rafael's deep voice patiently explaining to the serious little girl why she had to pay her father back the money she had borrowed to buy a candy.

"Then, for them, above all things was honesty. And to have values that are truly important, not crave little things that seem very important to us today but which we won't even notice tomorrow."

Marta's account of her parents' views swiftly melted into her own beliefs. "To maintain good conduct through one's own life is the best one can show one's children, don't you think? To work for what one wants, and do what one can with one's work, and to always do it with responsibility, with the best of oneself." When Marta issued this life motto, her father's story about getting up early in order to please his boss flashed into my thoughts.

Marta became thoughtful as she considered something she probably didn't often articulate. "I always say that my parents were very intelligent, because even though they never had opportunities to study or to go to school, they saw to it that we got those things. People with less intelligence might not have done that. If they were able to live without education, why try to give education to us?"

As the young woman spoke, her two parents materialized in my mind. The lusty little campo girl who wept and pleaded with her mother to find a way to send her to school. The young man puzzled by his native talents and making the most of them with the few opportunities he had on the Península.

Thinking of her mother's solitary life in the campo, I asked Marta, who was not much older than I, whether she had a good sense of community in Madryn.

"Here in Madryn I have friends from school, friends from work, and also people I know through my husband's work. I have visiting relationships with a lot of people. We get together to talk—not every day, because we all have our obligations—but regularly.

"Then, we visit among the family regularly, like with my parents' families. My husband's family lives in Rosario, so my husband's mother, my mother-in-law, comes to spend a period with us each year and then goes back." Marta gestured toward the kitchen, where I could see the older woman cutting up onions through a crack in the door. "That's my mother-in-law. She's with us now for a month."

Marta told me she was eternally grateful that she was not destined to a life in the campo, as her mother was. "My life has been very easy compared with my mother's life. That is to say, I have a house where I have cold and hot water, where I have electrical appliances, and heat, and all these things that my mother and grandmother didn't have in the campo. They had to carry their water. They had to put water in a big pot and heat it up just to take a bath. Very different from my life." As Marta described the requirements of her mother's life, it was apparent that the prospect of carrying out the many tasks of survival in the campo were all too vivid and all too grim to the daughter.

Marta shifted on her chair as she brought into focus her own experiences in the campo. "When I was a little girl, most children lived in the campo only until they were six. I, however, only lived in the campo until I was four years old. After that age, my sister and I only went to the campo in the summers.

"By the time I lived in the campo you could travel to the pueblo every twenty days. Each house had a vehicle with which they could move around, and a radio, so people on the Península had better communication. Everyone had cars, so we could visit the neighbors. But, at any rate, I was in the campo only a short time because when the time to go to school arrived, we left the campo.

"I never liked the campo." Marta's brows knotted over her pond brown eyes. "The campo gives me a deep feeling of loneliness. I like to live in places where there are people with whom I can communicate and visit.

"The campo has always given me sensations of loneliness. Even at age four I preferred to come to live with an aunt here in Madryn rather than continue to live in the campo. So, from the time I was tiny, I never liked the campo." Vitoria was the aunt who took in the decided little four-year-old. Liliana's sugar cakes apparently couldn't make sweet for young Marta the thorny, hard cake of the campo. The silence pierced her, as it continues to pierce into her father.

"Now I like to go to the campo for the weekend with my children and husband, and at those times I really enjoy the solitude, the tranquillity that the campo supplies, but I wouldn't like to live there. It's too lonely.

"On the other hand, my children like the campo. They like it because there, they get to do things that are different. They have another life rhythm. The enjoy the break from their schedule. They get to ride horses. They enjoy the tranquillity of being able to ride bicycles without having to look every which way to see if a car is coming. In the campo, they can feel that there are no dangers from anything—everything is for them. And, also, in the campo they have their grandmother, who makes them cakes."

I compared the children now sitting on hard chairs, trying to get their legs comfortable, manipulating Legos and crayons, with the breathless, free-racing grandchildren I had seen at Liliana's.

"Besides"—Marta put on her teacher's hat—"being in the campo is a way to learn about nature. In the campo, the *chicos* enjoy seeing the animals. The child who never leaves the city never sees a wild animal. In contrast, the child in the campo almost lives with the guanacos, rabbits, owls, and all these things that you see so close."

Marta's mother-in-law came in and asked if she should start cutting up the pepper. Marta nodded, and I knew I should be going soon.

Before I could, Marta delivered, with fierce intensity, her thoughts on the future of the Península. "The whole way of life in the campo must be restructured. If they want people to live on the estancias, they are going to have to offer to campo people the things that have been lacking, up to this time, in my province.

"The provinces of Buenos Aires and Santa Cruz are totally different. There, in the campo, the houses are really comfortable, and the people have the same commodities that are offered in the cities. In the province of Buenos Aires, the campo houses have telephones and television.

"A person who lives and works in the campo needs to be able to communicate at any moment, whenever he needs to, so that he doesn't feel isolated, so that he doesn't have to feel that he lives in a different kind of place, farther away, remote, more alone than anywhere else. I think this is the only way that they will be able to get people to live permanently in the campo.

"If nothing changes," Marta declared, "if the way of life in the campo doesn't change, they are not going to have anyone who will go there. A moment will arrive when no one will want to go to the campo."

Marta folded her hands and concluded our conversation with thoughts about her mother and father. She encapsulated the dilemma of the older couple who now inhabits the campo. "I think that at this moment my mother would like to come live here. Because we are here. Her two daughters are here and her five grandchildren, too. She has her whole family group here, no? But the campo is also the place she has lived her whole life, so she might come here and find that she likes it better there. She doesn't feel bad where she is.

"On the other hand, there is my papá. There is a man who wouldn't like to leave the campo. He wants to keep on living there."

Marta holds her knowledge of the two places, Puerto Madryn and the Península, in the dark wells of her eyes. She looks off toward the rough, prickled, baked ground on which her father toils and envisions her light-spirited mother cooking in the silent, dark house. She sees grayness. She feels the loneliness in her bones.

In her own house in the pueblo, she sees, in the kitchen, the woman with whom she has the pleasure of sharing the daily work, she hears the excited voices of her children, the frequent knocks at the door. The smells of a huge meal cooking enter her nostrils. Marta's days in town are a feast for the senses and the mind, a colored contrast to Liliana's monotone days on the campo.

During the visit, my identification with Marta was immediate. Unlike the campo women, Marta had a busy and complicated life, much like mine in North America. In her concerns and routines, I found confirmed the outlines of my life there. I even felt myself hackle instinctively as Marta and I tried to intermesh our busy schedules for a future get-together, just as I did when my best friend in Cambridge told me she could fit me in for a cup of tea two weeks from now between five and five-thirty.

Marta, however, taught me something only a person who has experienced profound social isolation can convey: the inestimable value of the nearby presence of other human beings. Marta and the other campo-born pueblo dwellers treasured other human beings and human companionship with a keenness uncommon among North Americans. They were family-centered and openly mother-loving in a way that made them seem solid and chockful of common sense. Through my talks I was forced, in spite of my romance about the independent pioneer woman, to see that the women living in the pueblo were far more satisfied than the women still living in the campo, and that this was because pueblo women could see people.

As for myself, over time a sense of the unutterable emptiness of the campo grew inside of me, gnawing out a cavity, a chasm, deep inside my belly. I began to realize that while I loved living with the basics—an outhouse, a Coleman stove, the sea right there, silence at night—I also loved conversation. One day I chewed and swallowed my need-nobody hat.

With the new hollow in my gut, with the new eyes it lent me, the shapes and outlines of Madryn began to metamorphose. On one trip there, I suddenly discovered that I was fond of Madryn. I liked it, simply as a center of human hubbub. As time went on I found myself secretly glad when our Industria Argentina tires blew so that we had reason to go to the pueblo early. With my new sight, during our later months in Patagonia, our visits to Madryn began to change.

Trying to tidy up for a trip to the pueblo, I would shower, wielding the hose from our solar-heated water bag while squatting over the drain in a corner of the hut, and then I would put on my best shirt and my gray pants. It would occur to me that I looked very unfashionable. Tugging at my hair to make the ends go under, I would grab the last cracker on the shelf, close the door to our burrow, and climb in the car with Peter.

At the sight of the octopuslike Aluar, I'd feel my spirits rise. By now the town had sprawled up the hill toward the overlook, and buildings were going up every day to accommodate the steady influx of migrants from the north.

The first thing we would do was stop at the gas station, where we savored a sense of arrival. Peter would chat with the man pumping gas as though he were his best friend, as though he had just arrived from a yearlong ocean voyage. Then we would drop in on a friend or go to see an acquaintance I wanted to interview. The talk that was exchanged, often through coffee and lunch and into the siesta hours beyond, became the food on which I throve. Madryn came to be a place where I had the ready and supreme pleasure of taking in others' experiences and perspectives. Hearing the Patagonians talk, whether in the pueblo or in the campo, soothed me. The to and fro of voices gave me, as it did them, a sense that I lived in a warm, animated, inhabited world, rather than a windy emptiness.

I grew to love even the shops of Madryn—the incongruous mixes of items, the shopkeepers who never seemed to know what they had. One hardware store we loved to explore carried not only enamel buckets, rope, and wire, but fresh chicken eggs. I once came upon a store that sold primarily cake decoration supplies—special molds for making cakes in the shape of little houses and trains and plastic people for activities on tops of the cakes—it must have been one of Liliana's dream havens. We became acquainted with several shops that carried rotisseried snacks, empanadas, and candies. I poked in clothing shops that displayed only six dresses, in odd sizes, from Buenos Aires, piles of thin cotton campo housedresses, and an assortment of cheap, dusty shoes. The household shops with plastic tablecloths, plastic tubs, and cheap striped towels intrigued me. Once in a while we bought gifts in a telephone-booth–size shop with gaucho crafts from the north—hand-stamped leather belts and Indian weavings.

As we roamed, we found on doors of warehouses signs that designated the entrance to a notary, a bank, or a lawyer. We discovered, sprinkled through town, the auto parts stores, tire repair shops, car repair places, and the several hole-in-the-wall shops that filled the natural-gas and kerosene canisters so essential to campo heating and lighting, as well as the bakeries that sold not only French-style bread, but long-lasting crackers and breads for the campo, the butchers' shops with goat meat and lambs and chickens hanging from hooks in the windows, and greengrocers such as our favorite, "The Happy Carrot." We often joined the throng at the Cabina Telefónica and waited restlessly for a line to the United States.

On Madryn's main street there was a record shop, a movie theater, and two confiterías that faced each other, both filled with men taking *cafecítos*. Sometimes we stopped for a *café con leche*. I even took up the habit of buying gossip magazines and read about Princess Caroline to bone up for my conversations with campo women. At the kiosks where I got the magazines, I also bought my beloved *alfajores*—my favorite Argentine sweets made of chocolate and cookies sandwiched together.

On later visits, richer by the fact of inflation, we took ourselves out at noon to the Club Náutico, the best restaurant in town, an establishment with white tablecloths and pert waiters, where we feasted on paella, scallops roquefort, and Pedro Moreno, a fancy ice cream topped with chocolate. We stayed overnight in the Hotel Yanco, in a room overlooking the gloomy sea. There, in the simple double bed, we felt as luxurious as we would have felt at the Georges V.

Before leaving town, we accomplished what was ostensibly our main purpose for being there and spent hours at the two supermarkets in town: La Anónima and Supermercado Madryn.

At Supermercado Madryn the commodities were arranged neatly, from right to left. Aisle 1: various kinds of crackers and cookies, detergents and soaps, and toilet paper; aisle 2: cleaning supplies and sponges, flours (including pea and bean flour), beans and dried soups, baking supplies, and rice and pudding mixes; aisle 3: vats of *dulce de leche*, cartons of jelly, a case of processed foil-wrapped cheeses, boxes of long-lasting milk, and eggs; aisle 4: soda drinks and mineral water. On the floor of the fourth aisle, the leftmost, sat large basket jugs of red table wine; carousels of spices, candies, and bouillons were arranged near the front of the store. At the back were three counters: one for vegetables, one for cheeses, and one for meat. The foods were ordered from a clerk, who selected, weighed, and wrapped each item and kept a tally on a sheet of paper to be taken to the checkout counter.

We usually pushed two shopping carts through the store or else a single one piled so high that things toppled to the floor every time we moved it. As we came gradually to forget the extravagance of an American supermarket, Supermercado Madryn began to seem like heaven. I loved watching the prepossessing Argentine women who squabbled with the vegetable clerk over the state of his tomatoes, shrieked with laughter with the friends they happened on in the wine section, and jostled each other companionably. Trying to sound as though I, too, knew the exact number of kilos of onions I needed, I felt like one of a tribe of pueblo women.

From time to time, on very special days, we took tea with friends at a wonderful Welsh tea house recently opened on Avenida Roca. There, in a small room of perhaps eight tables, with dark wooden beams and flowered burgundy wallpaper, we escaped to a warm, rich, cozied world. The bosomy proprietress, in tweed skirt, Shetland sweater, elegant scarf, and hose, promoted the illusion. She wore a string of pearls. Tea and cream and sugar and napkins and tea strainer all appeared on a silver tray. On the white tablecloth were placed blue-and-white Industria Argentina dishes showing British farmhouse scenes. From them we consumed *torta negra*—Welsh fruitcake—toast, and scones. The graceful tea and the loud, animated Spanish conversation filled every cranny in my body.

It was only when Señora Jones—she pronounced it "Joan-es" in Spanish—slipped through the curtain into the kitchen that we glimpsed the other side of where we really were. There behind the curtain was the campo kitchen: a plain, cheap table with benches around it, a horde of dirty-faced children, a jumble of grubby cases of soda pop, and a dog, not unlike the one on the heap of dirt we had seen years before, slinking at the edge of the room.

Living on the Península, I came to love Madryn for herself, and by the end of our stay in Patagonia, we often took to sitting at lunchtime at the foot of the statue on the beachside promenade. The monument, we discovered, was a depiction of a lovely woman in a shawl and long flowing dress. The plaques at her feet told us she was erected in 1965 to commemorate the one-hundredth anniversary of the arrival of the Welsh settlers, the first colonists of Chubut. The Welsh woman was lovely. Her hair was coiled neatly in a bun, her eye possessed a faraway look, and there was purpose in her stride.

With time I came to think of the brave, determined woman, instead of the dead cur, as the guardian of Madryn, and on our monthly journeys, when we would pause at the crest of the hill to overlook the town, this was what I saw: a white concrete pueblo, shocked by sun, shining like a pearl beside a pristine sea.

FAT

~~~~

As we make our approach to the Goikoa estancia across the parched, flat ground, two boys are out in the vehicle-worn, horse-trampled area between the barn and the house. Hugo, the younger boy, a dishwater-blond nine-year-old, is seated atop a Model-A Ford planted under a couple of spindly trees. Jorge, the adopted twelve-year-old with Indian blood, is kicking a ball of rhea dung across the dirt.

The Goikoa family lives across a salt pan—and through three gates—from Clara and José. The distance from one house to the other is only about two kilometers across the open steppe, a rarity on the Península.

Hours spent in the Goikoa family kitchen transport a visitor back in time to the 1930s when the estancias of Península Valdés were in their heyday. With the Goikoas, one of the few families with young children that remains on the Península and one of even fewer who cleave to the old ways, you gain a sense of the flourishing family life that used to prevail on Península estancias. The Goikoa kitchen, jammed and ajabber with full-fleshed bodies aged from one month to over eighty, fosters a vision of the

Península as a bountiful land of fat and honey. The amicable, fertile campo family seems to tap a rich vein of syrup in the dry, sandy ground.

As we drive nearer to the boys, I can already taste the honey. I am eager to be charmed once again.

We inch up to the barn, and the boys flail out of their occupations, gallop toward the car, and mill beside us like a pair of dogs. They bang the car and call out to us with cocked heads. When my husband gets out of the car, they yell, "Peter!" grab his arms, and hang on to him. Hugo lays his head against Peter's side, bursting with his admiration for grown men, and walks him toward the house. Both he and Jorge, who is running ahead, wave to me insistently. "Come into the house! Come into the house!"

Both boys have a slogging gait—an imitation of the swagger of the gauchos of northern Argentina whom they admire. Their trousers drag on the ground at their heels, and one hand of each boy is constantly hitching up his overlarge pants at the back.

Emilia Goikoa de Lasalde, the boys' mother, appears at the doorstep and beckons us toward the house.

The Goikoa house, two hundred feet across the scrub from the barn where we have parked, is sheltered by big trees. Built by the fanciful landowner for whom Guillermo works as *puestero*, the house is surrounded by a low brick wall, topped at intervals by concrete turrets. A band of yard about fifteen feet wide fringes the perimeter of the house. Its bare ground is broken up by concrete pots stuck deep in the ground, from which rise healthy slender trees. The dirt garden, when I first saw it, reminded me of the grounds of a Buddhist temple; I imagined the dirt to be swept each day by a monk until on closer inspection I saw the plastic toys scattered among the trees.

The house itself, a decorative combination of brick and concrete, has overhanging, shade-endowing eaves. The exterior of the house, like the tiny yard, brings to mind houses in the Orient, but in the doorway hangs a Spanish plastic curtain made of gay yellow plastic strips.

The boys leave Peter's side and race up to Emilia. She hugs them to her large bosom, one at each side, the trio filling the doorway just as would a mother bear and two cubs. The campo woman, dressed in a cotton, uniformlike dress with buttons down the front, happily invites us to lunch. "All I have is noodles," she says, turning to lead us into the kitchen.

We sit at the end of the table as the large woman moves around her domain.

In an offset alcove at the back of the room is a bank holding the sink and cabinets and counters. The stove is at one end of the alcove, the sink at the other. The one large window in the cooking area looks outward onto the scraggly rangeland to the rear of the house. The larger portion of the room is almost totally occupied by the giant-size table at which we sit. Two large windows near the table frame shapes of trees in the courtyard, their drooping branches blurred by the gauzy, pastel-colored curtains, which are drawn. The room feels rich, shaded and darkened by the flowery curtains, and the long table seems to promise feasting.

Emilia flings her dishcloth over her shoulder and moves quickly around the small space, getting lunch. She deftly chops up a large pile of lettuce and then divides the pile in two, putting several handfuls of greens in two bowls. She cuts up a basketball of *galleta*—the hard-crusted campo bread—and throws the ragged pieces in a dish. While she works she smokes extralong cigarettes, a strangely sophisticated touch in such an earthy, unadorned globe of a woman, and wipes her hands hastily on her apron, in habit, between each job.

I ask questions about Emilia's family, the Lasaldes, and about that of her husband, Guillermo Goikoa. Guillermo is the offspring of a Goikoa and an Olazar and is thus one of Clara's relatives. The Goikoa and Lasalde clans are legendary on the Península, so Emilia finds it logical that I want to hear about them—she is proud of her family and that of her husband.

"Guillermo and I were raised on the Península," she says.
"And we're still here. We are one of the only families like this.
Both my family and Guillermo's were early settlers. He is one
of fifteen children and I am one of eleven, so you see, the people
around here are almost all relatives of ours, by one manner or
another!

"Guillermo and I were neighbors as *chicos.* I was born and
raised at Punta Buenos Aires. The estancia was then called La
Siberia. My mamá gave birth to all of us out there, with a woman
at her side. Mamá never had much time to watch over us. She
was a woman with work to do all the time. Guillermo was raised
at La Hermosa. His father was *puestero* at La Hermosa for fifty
years, and then Guillermo took over. Guillermo has worked on
the place for forty-one years. He was born there, and stayed
there."

Emilia, forty-five, and Guillermo, fifty-eight now, got to know
each other, Emilia says, because all the families back then attended the neighboring *señaladas.* Emilia lived with Guillermo at
La Hermosa for many years, until Guillermo received the charge
of the Lizarza estancia where they are now. "From here now,
Guillermo goes on managing the estancia his father managed
before him."

Hugo and Jorge grin, ear to ear, elbows on the table, as their
mother talks about the family to which they belong.

"We have only one child who is ours—ours natural," Emilia
says, "but I have raised lots of little ones."

With this, Emilia winks at Jorge, who looks straight into the
gray eyes above the woman's ruddy cheeks. The boy nods vigorously and again grins as if his cheeks will split.

Emilia took in the smooth-skinned, chocolate-eyed lad as an
infant, when his unwed mother couldn't care for him. She has
reared him as her own son.

Hugo, the rascally nine-year-old whom everyone calls "El Galenso"—"The Welsh Boy"—because he is so fair, punches his
adopted brother in the arm.

Ignoring Hugo, Emilia says, "Beside these two, I raised Diana,
too." Diana, Emilia's niece, began living with Emilia and Gui-

llermo when she was a year old in order to provide temporary relief to Emilia's brother and his wife, Juana, who were giving birth to daughters in rapid succession. When Diana was about two and a half and Emilia lost an infant daughter, Diana stayed on, and Emilia raised her as her own. Diana is now twenty-two.

"I have these *chicos*," Emilia says, "but I really have a lot more family in the house, because Guillermo and I are from big families. We always have lots of relatives here with us in the campo.

"Last night we had fifteen people at the dinner table, and the night before, fourteen. It's very rare that it's just Guillermo and me and the boys around the table."

As if on cue, people begin to appear in the kitchen.

Diana, a petite, dark-haired, delicately pretty woman with a bundle of baby in her arms, slips in. She is trailed by her skinny little six- and seven-year-old daughters. An older woman is also with them.

The young mother places the infant in a basket that I just now notice to the side of the table. We all stand around looking at the peaceful, sleeping child. The tiny, scrunch-faced baby has gold earrings hanging from her miniature ears and a queenly name: Angélica Victoria. A cylindrical, pointed ivory object on a blue ribbon is hanging around her neck.

The older woman tells me, "It's a dog's tooth. My son also wore it. It is going around the family. It's a tradition of the *antiguos*—to prevent teething pain."

As we separate to let the child rest, Diana grins at me. "These are my two mamás," she says happily in a soft voice. She points to Emilia and says, "She raised me. She pampered me, I should really say, and," she says, pointing to Juana, the other middle-aged woman, "she is my natural mother." The young woman beams as though everyone ought to have her good fortune.

Juana's sleek-headed five-year-old son comes in. There is a sudden scraping of chairs, and Hugo and Jorge race outside with him to play with trucks under a tree in the courtyard.

The women now set to work laying the table. They add three more leaves and spread out an enormous plastic tablecloth. Emilia puts out a jumble of tan glass bowls and tosses four or five big serving spoons on the table. Diana and Juana lay out forks and knives, in long rows, on both sides of the long plank. I count fourteen places. Chairs appear out of nowhere.

Diana turns to Peter and me. "One campo family once had a three-meter table!"

Emilia stops to wipe her hand on her apron and take a puff of her cigarette. She looks as satisfied as a hen.

Soon, much of the clan has arrived, and children are lined up like pins along one side of the table. Hearty Emilia, who is moving around the kitchen swiftly now, announces, "I hope you like noodles."

From behind the children, two big casseroles of yellow noodles, topped with tomato sauce with bits of mutton in it, are plunked down on either end of the plank. Between them is a bowl of cooked mutton ribs from the night before. Everyone serves themselves noodles and bread and either wine or orange drink. The women pour out the latter for the children, who begin to slurp their noodles, to jostle each other, and to poke elbows. Hugo shouts, "*¡Abuela!*"

I turn to look, and a stout, thick-legged old woman, with raven-hued hair and golden hoops in her ears, comes through the doorway. Julia, Emilia's mother, limps, crooked-stepped, up to the table, mumbling, "I know one woman who is so unwell, she can't even walk, *pobrecita*, poor thing."

Julia then proceeds from person to person along the table, poking a rib, squeezing an arm, chucking an elbow, as though taking little bits of skin from the different members of her family. At one of her stops around the rectangle, she takes a piece of bread and stuffs bits of it into her mouth. Crumbs fall from her lips as she goes on with her pinchings and greetings.

Noticing me, she points a pudgy finger at Juana's five-year-old son and says, "That's a grandson." She nods her chin at Hugo and Jorge and says, "Those, too."

Hugo squirms, pleased, as though his bottom is crawling with ants, and Jorge looks shyly at his noodles.

Julia motions to the beautiful little girls whose heads reach not far above the table, who are watching quietly from big, brown, level eyes. "And those are great-grandchildren," she says.

Emilia finds her mother a place to sit down. The old woman wedges into her place, and we all plow into our luscious noodles. For a few instants there are no sounds save the slurping of noodles, the gulping of liquids, the crunching of bread, and the scraping of the children's stools. Each of the heavyset women eats two or three bowlfuls of the yellow pasta. We all eat heartily like bears at a carcass.

Suddenly Guillermo appears in the room and stands beside Emilia at the end of the table near the cooking area. The *peón* is close behind, and he sits, wordless, in a chair off to the side and begins devouring an enormous plate of food.

Guillermo is handsome. The well-respected *puestero* has salt-and-pepper hair and a deeply tanned face, and he is tall and strong, with huge hands. The deep bags under his soft, light eyes give him the sad look of a hound. He wears the spanking white shirt that is the mark of a dignified campo man.

Still without having said anything, Guillermo places a platter of pieces of freshly barbecued lamb on the table—leftovers from the hired workers' noon meal. Emilia rises from her chair and has her husband sit in her place.

A subtle grin crosses his lips as Guillermo sits down, but he says nothing. He looks tired. The *puestero* offers sweat in return for his mutton, managing four or five sheep stations and over 6,500 animals. He spoons noodles onto his plate and three hunks of lamb. He says almost nothing as he chews, but when he speaks to Emilia, asking for more wine or bread, his speech is fast and clipped.

Emilia stands, cutting up the lamb. She just rips the searing, greasy hunk of meat, using a knife and her fingers skillfully but roughly, like a sow bear. She stands during the remainder of the meal, giving instructions to the eaters.

"Run the lettuce around. Run the bread around."

Whenever Emilia passes behind her husband, or beside him, as she serves the food or moves around the kitchen, she gives his shoulders a squeeze with both of her hands, in nonverbal, physical appreciation of him. He calls her "Emma."

I comment that I am amazed that there are fourteen people at the lunch table. The people in the room rumble with pleasure at my comment, like one body, one large animal.

Emilia says, "This is not anything. Just my family, without Guillermo's, is so big that we can almost never all be together. We wouldn't fit into any house. We wouldn't even fit into the barn!"

She continues, "Even at Mamá's eightieth birthday party there were people missing, though all of her living children were there."

Emilia goes on to tell us that the family just had a huge fiesta at New Year's. Jorge played the bongo drums, accompanying his father and another relative who were playing accordions, and they danced through the night until four A.M. They had to stay the night in Pirámides, where the party took place, because it rained so hard and the roads were impassable.

The noodle platters are almost empty, and the children are asking for dessert. Julia, who has giggled from time to time at various comments, rises like a whale's head out of water when I again remark on the size of this booming family. A monologue issues from the great-grandmother in a crackly voice.

"We had big families back in those times. I brought to light eleven *chicos*. I have more than seventy grandchildren, if you count the great-grandchildren."

I ask about the settler families on the Península, and about her childhood. The children sit quiet, respectful, looking on from eyes like planets.

"The people from before on the Península? There are none of the old settlers left. They have all died. It could be that one is left. Could be. The children have been left with the property.

"Before, on the estancias, they hardly hired *peones*. The people from the house worked, the owners themselves did the work. It was different before. All the children helped on the place.

"The *chicos* are different now. Nowadays the *chicos* don't respect their parents. They are all mischievous and talk back to their parents. When visitors come, the *chicos* sit here, and for every word spoken by the adults, they have ten. Children used to sit quietly and stay in the background. We were quiet around adults. We had to do everything they told us, without a word, or they would bring out the stick. We had to mind, or there was the stick, and we knew it."

As Julia speaks, Hugo and Jorge soak in their grandmother's words. Hugo, out of his seat, leaning on the table, twisting his body and feet, is watching Julia with fascination. At one point he disappears and brings back a slingshot and plays with it as he listens. The boy is so utterly absorbed in his grandmother's thoughts, he wets his lips with his tongue and rubs his lips together intently as he watches her.

"I am almost eighty-two," she is saying. "I have had a good life. I raised all my children in the campo. Eight of them were born there, and all my children have come out well. But I have suffered."

Julia heaves a big bosom sigh, and her voice begins to sing— a long, hoarse, heaving lament. "I come from a big family. But now I just have one brother left. I had four brothers, but only one is left to me. I have two sisters, and both have died. In my family we were several, but now they are all dead, *pobrecitos. Pobrecita gente.* Poor little people." Julia looks down at her breast and heaves.

"Two of my sons died," she says, and she begins to cry, open as a bird.

Angélica whimpers from her basket, and Diana picks up Julia's thirty-first great-grandchild.

When Julia recomposes herself—she does so quickly, since she is given to free outbursts of tears—the *chicos* and the women remark about how old Julia is, but how young she looks. She looks about sixty. She has eager, bright eyes, and only a few white hairs inhabit her jet black head.

Julia giggles and primps her curls, saying, "But you should have seen my husband's hair. It was white as flour!"

Jorge pipes up. His voice has pride in it. "*Abuela* must be one of the oldest on the Península!"

Julia names some other old ones, counting them on her fingers, but then pronounces each one dead. "Pedro was eighty-five, but he died, *pobre*." She looks up from her thinking. "They have all died."

"*Abuela,*" says Hugo, "I bet you're going to live to be a hundred and forty!"

The grandmother shakes her head vigorously, with sadness in her rounded shoulders. "God will decide that," she says, and she closes her eyes.

Emilia serves coffee in special blue demitasse cups with white insides. The children bolt their canned peaches, and as Hugo and Jorge rush for the door, knocking into chairs, Julia comments about Jorge, "That one works like a man, *pobrecito*," and about Hugo, whom we see doing a cartwheel out the window, "That one is a laze-about. He would ride his horse all day if we let him. He loves horses."

Peter and I sit and sip the syrupy-sweet coffee with the women. Guillermo has long since slipped out to the barn to saddle up for an afternoon of herding. Angélica Victoria has awakened and is handed between the moon-size women. Diana hums. As I listen to her sweet, high voice, I ponder what it is that so draws me to this campo family.

What I love about being with the Goikoas is that, when we visit, there is no fanfare. We simply sink against the family bosom. We become a part of the warmth and bustle, just another pair of young bears crowded into the Goikoa den. At the Goikoas' no one fusses over me; my presence is unremarkable and unremarked upon, unlike in my own close nuclear family. The sense of being invisible bestows profound comfort. I go into the Goikoa kitchen and I am a grown-up child, talking or watching as I feel moved, and no one takes particular notice of what I do or don't do.

Emilia so adores teasing Peter that she has made us the butt of a joke, and this joke has become part of the family lore. Every time we visit she teases my tall, blond husband mercilessly about the way, the day we first met her, lost on a road, he had used hand gestures, not yet knowing the word in Spanish for "faucet." Any assembled company unfailingly finds Emilia's imitation hilarious.

Hauling our sated bodies off our chairs, Peter and I say that we must get going. We mention that we will stop in at Clara and José's on the way out, and a chorus sings out.

"What neighbors!" says Julia.

"What good people!" says Juana.

"What luck to have such people for neighbors!" says Diana.

Emilia just shakes her head, as if there aren't words.

The ranch woman kisses us, holding a dish that she is drying, and says, "Come back next week. Come stay all day. Come in the morning for mate. Then stay for lunch. And then stay for dinner."

Julia, who walks us to the door on her round, puffed feet, kisses us both good-bye in proper Argentine style, on both cheeks. "Come again anytime, dearie," she says to me, "to talk!"

As we step into the yard, Hugo appears from behind the house, as if he has been hiding all this time, and dashes to the car ahead of us like a half-grown cub.

The day I first met Emilia, the shearing crew was at the estancia. The settlement was a whirlwind of swirling dust and running sheep, and Emilia was hard at work.

As we drove up, she appeared at the door of the huge barn. She was wearing a light-colored apron over a dark skirt, and the apron was billowing in the wind. She beckoned us into the building, squinting as she tried to place our unknown faces. "You're the *chicos* from the Whale Camp, aren't you?" she said as she guided us to a place where we could gape at the roaring frenzy of sights and sounds in the barn. Hundreds of sheep were bawling in an animal orchestra, while sweating men toiled and dashed every which way.

Centered in the dance hall–size building was "La Máquina," a Model-A Ford truck modified decades before into a mobile, self-contained shearing machine. From a bar six feet above the body of the truck descended long, jointed, swinging metal legs like the legs of a spider. These appendages transferred power from the ancient truck motor to the shearers toiling on the floor. About eight shearers worked furiously on each side of the chassis of the old vehicle, attacking the bulging-eyed sheep. The car, which faced us as we watched, was dark green and one-eyed—only one of its large, ancient headlights was still in place.

The car, held stationary with blocks on the floor, chugged along in the semidarkness, its motor toiling away. Workers raced along the corridors, called *playas*, or beaches, behind the shearers, grabbing the huge piles of wool falling from the backs and tender undersides of the animals like participants in a relay race. Each *playero* hurled the fleece he had picked up onto a waiting table. The pom-poms of wool bounced toward us, one after another, as we watched, and the *playeros* ran back and forth behind the shearers. The armfuls of wool arced forth like flying suns, the fleeces so light and bright they caught the rays of sunlight coming from the door and lit up the whole scene.

Another set of men, the *envellonadores*, or fleecebundlers, hastily grabbed the mounds of fleece from the receiving table, folded each fleece into itself, and placed it on spread burlap squares on the floor.

Each fleece was a fluffy ball about two and a half feet in diameter, and the *envellonadores* were constantly grabbing at the outer edges of the tumbling wool mounds as they transported them, to keep the fleeces together. Their actions were identical to those of a person trying to keep a dozen socks from falling off the top of a pile of laundry.

The men organized about eighteen fleeces on each burlap square, then strained to tie up the four corners crosswise. They knelt on the bundles, the *lienzos de lana*, punching the wool down, the muscles of their backs and arms tightening as they strove to pull together the kitty-corner ends. Once the four corners of a *lienzo* were tied, they overturned the bundle onto another square of burlap, this one of double thickness, and tied the second cloth. After successfully tightening the last layer of the *lienzo*, the *envellonadores* heaved the heavy, solid package over to the scale, where Emilia was waiting to execute her part of the operation.

Each time a bundle was heaved onto the scale, Emilia interrupted her explanations of the events and took up a series of repeated actions. She rattled the weights on the ancient scale until they registered level, she locked the metal bar in place, then inscribed the digits neatly on the next line in her book. This precise bookkeeping was essential, perhaps the most important task at the shearing, for in that book were revealed the fruits of the year's labor.

Under the high roof of the barn, the stout ranch woman stood prepossessing as a queen in her dusty loafers. Firm on her heels, a serious look on her face, she tapped the weights of the scale gently, to ensure precision.

Emilia was wearing a dark, plain skirt, and all through the day the bib of her apron was flopped down, the neckstrings hanging loose. She obviously hadn't brushed her hair since her five A.M. rising and looked both dowdy and totally natural, at ease. Purposeful, busy, vital at her work, straightforward as she spoke with the men, the unpretentious woman radiated satisfaction.

At the scale, Emilia told us, "This year the wool is clean—clean, but too light. Because it isn't dirty, it isn't heavy, and it won't fetch as good a price."

Emilia went on to say that at this estancia, there were 2,300 sheep to be sheared, but that the sheep from the neighboring ranch were also being sheared, and that ranch had 4,000 and some. Seven hundred of the 6,300 animals were left to be sheared.

"My husband," she said proudly, "is in charge of five sheep stations, so we have been through a lot of shearing already this year!"

As Emilia had led us into the barn, we had passed through a long, dark corridor formed by two walls of piled wool bundles. Each of the facing walls was about twenty feet high, fifteen feet wide, and thirty feet long. The surface of the walls, made up of hundreds of separate *lienzos*, had the look of an immense quilt but was rock hard to the touch.

On the day of the shearing, we witnessed Emilia in her once-a-year official capacity as accountant for the estancia. Most days we spent with her, though, she was involved in the occupation most natural to herself—the rearing of young animals. Babies of any kind did for Emilia; she was not particular about species.

Before I ever met Emilia, Clara had told me that Emilia was known for taking in children. In campo families of the settlers' days, Clara said, women took in children no matter what age the women themselves happened to be, and Emilia maintained the tradition. Emilia's life was for raising creatures smaller than herself.

One burning afternoon, for about half an hour, we went off with Jorge to see a tinamou nest. By the time we got back, Emilia, to whom love was synonymous with feeding, was deep-frying *churros*—long fluted doughnuts similar to crullers.

Peter and I sat like an older batch of children, with Jorge and with Hugo, who always materialized at moments to his belly's advantage, and with Diana's two girls, while Emilia brought to the table plate after plate of sugared *churros* from the pot over the stove and had us drink milk-tea. She periodically sent Hugo off with plates of the doughnuts, covered with cloths, for Guillermo in the barn and for Diana in the next-door house.

At one point Emilia came to the table, pushed Hugo off his chair, sat down herself, and then took the scamp of a boy onto her ample lap. He stayed there, grinning and gobbling *churros*, until he got heavy, at which point Emilia playfully shoved him off.

At the table, the little girls were a perfect complement to the boys. Dark-featured, with large luminous eyes and shoulder-length hair, they leaned their chins on the table and grinned quietly at Emilia, saying not a word. Emilia twinkled back, eating them up. They were delicate, skinny things, and Emilia plied them with food. She kept putting out additional plates of doughnuts for them and served them more milky tea without asking them if they wished more.

The older one finally nibbled a doughnut and said, "I don't want more."

Emilia replied, matter-of-fact, "Don't eat more."

After stuffing ourselves with *churros*, Emilia said, "Why not come see my garden?"

We trooped out to the garden behind an outbuilding, where Emilia showed us the rows of parsley, beets, onions, garlic, lettuce, and radishes that she had planted. She pointed out the kale that was going to seed to feed the family for the third time that season. It was a serious garden.

Emilia watered with the slow hose that led from the cistern and then had her granddaughter take over. She told us that, contrary to what most campesinos told us, it was easy to have a garden. "It's good soil. It just needs water," she said.

We went on to feed the chickens. Emilia ground some corn in an ancient grinder with a rusted wheel and a funnel at the top. Jorge asked to throw it to the chickens. There were scads of baby chicks with brown feathers beginning to spike out of their downy backs. She told us that by eight months they would be laying.

Walking around her garden, looking at the green fronds poking from the poor-looking soil, with children's voices chirping all around me, I felt like plopping myself in the garden and remaining there for the rest of the season. I would eat lettuce, and every day the children would come and sprinkle me with water.

Emilia's sons have been reared with the rheas and armadillos in the campo as their mother was, and this about them is unusual. They have been able to live the old-style campo boyhood, while at the same time commuting, during the school year, to the tiny Pirámides school.

Emilia mothers the boys with affectionate, no-nonsense love, and the boys have the same disarming cublike mixture of toughness and affection possessed by their mother. Emilia told me once that each boy thinks she loves the other better. "That's boys!" She laughed. But her nine-year-old and twelve-year-old, equally beloved by her, keep polar opposite orientations to life.

Hugo, Emilia's "natural" son, is a contrast to his darker, adopted brother. He has soft blue eyes and is fair-complexioned. While his brother races from place to place, Hugo lounges around. His dead-straight, brown-blond hair is cut to go to the side, so that when his bangs fall in his face, they angle down toward one ear, adding to his mischievous look.

The day Emilia was making *churros*, Hugo was leaning his head on his crossed arms on the table. He was wearing his knitted beret and a filthy, food-smudged shirt, and Emilia told him to go change. He continued, without a word, to lounge on the tabletop, his bright face sporting an impish grin and shining eyes. Emilia scolded Hugo all afternoon, telling him to stop leaning on the table, telling him to change his clothes, to take off his beret, to take the doughnuts to his father. He ignored her and did as he pleased. Emilia scowled, but the glow of love was in her eyes.

One day during the sheep-dipping season, we were visiting Clara and José, and Hugo was at La Bonita helping out with the dipping. Both boys help out their father with any and all the estancia tasks when they are not at school, and during lulls they often race over to help their old neighbors. Clara told me that she keeps a supply of soft drinks on hand for the boys, who affectionately call José by the term for uncle, *"Tío."*

That day, Hugo worked with boundless enthusiasm. He herded the sheep into the dipping arena, rushing them forward in a cloud of dust by shaking a rattle made of an oil can filled with pebbles.

Clara served orange soda and beer halfway through the morning. Most of the men had soda, and José had a beer. Hugo tired at one point during the proceedings and sat down to sneak a few swigs of José's beer. The boy worked most often in the sheep-launching pen, from which the men hurled the sheep into the trough of antimange, the most strenuous of jobs. The small boy sought out the lambs, since they were lighter for him. He would grab a leg, then work the animal across the pen, pushing and poking and dragging it any way he could until he had it in a position from which to push it into the bath.

He worked breathless with pleasure. Clara told me Hugo was happy because he was out of school that day owing to a teacher's strike. She whispered to me that Hugo liked to work, because José paid him something. "And I know *Tío* will pay me right away," he had told her.

Hugo accepted a soda from Clara as he set out across the campo for home, saying, "We don't have anything at home." The boy departed with his yellow knit shirt blotched with the red antimange liquid. "It comes out with gasoline," Clara assured me.

For all his man-work, Hugo was also a baby. The boy with all the swagger often sat on a wicker high chair at the dining table, claiming his position as baby of the family. After lunch one day, when only the grown women were around, he defied one of Emilia's orders and demanded a cup of tea from her.

"Make it yourself," she said.

He made himself the tea and pulled the high chair over beside his mother. He then sat down and slopped and sloshed hunks of bread in the tea, gobbling them hungrily. Defiant as he was, he sat as close as he could get to Emilia, often gazing up at her. The son and the mother, sitting shoulder to shoulder, made a portrait of private, comfortable intimacy.

Jorge is a contrast to Hugo both in looks and in earnestness. His skin is milk chocolate, and his almond-shaped eyes have centers so dark and bright, they appear pupilless. They shine like deep brown gems. When we arrive, he comes up and offers his baby-soft cheek for us to kiss. For the friendly greeting, the adopted boy shyly bends his head sideways as though about to slink away. He arrives everywhere breathless, as if he has just come from doing something grand. An alert, observant fellow, he has an insatiable curiosity and motivation to learn, and he absorbs everything.

During the summer Jorge rides as much as he can, galloping out on the dry ground. The boy is enamored of the life of the campo man and participates in it to the maximum. He once eagerly showed us a photo of his father on a horse, with two rheas in the foreground eating meat. The photo was staged and artificially colored: Guillermo's shirt lime green, the meat bright red, and the ground a pale green. The picture had been torn and glued back together and occupied a place of honor on the kitchen sideboard, along with a flag and some statues.

Another day Jorge took us out to demonstrate his expertise at riding. He rode bareback slipping on and off the horse as if it were nothing. Afterward he took us into the barn, where he showed us the saddle that belonged to his dead uncle. He lovingly stroked all the layers of the *recado*, an Argentine range man's many-layered saddle that converts into a bed at dusk—the slab of felt, the pair of brushed sheepskins that form top and bottom layers, the hand-tooled leathers, and the huge round leather stirrups with the words *Dios Nos Salve* tooled on them. He also brought down the bridle and lassos his uncle had made.

The boy's face shone with worship as he told us that the night his uncle died, he had called Jorge's father to him and given him a knife made of silver and gold and also a wide gaucho belt fashioned of leather and gold and silver coins. The uncle once told Jorge, "If I ever find a man who can work leather as well as I can, I'll kill him."

Jorge next showed us the *boleadoras* that José had given to him. He said he and Hugo had been out trying to catch rheas and guanacos with them but hadn't succeeded yet.

As we returned to the house, Jorge told us that his uncle used to play the guitar at dances with his father. "My father played the accordion and then there would be a bongo player and a singer. Now Hugo and I play the bongo and sing. You should come to a dance."

As we crossed the dirt yard, Jorge picked up a rooster that was in our path, put it under his arm, and strolled on into the house. "We raised him in the kitchen to be a pet," he said, beaming. "He goes with me everywhere."

Back in the house, the boy got down his accordion and put on a tape of his father playing mournful old campo tunes. Later, when Peter went to take pictures of the house and the old Ford, Jorge got the guitar, accordion, and bongo, fetched Hugo and Diana's daughters, and the four children hammed it up for the picture. The young campo-bred voices sent melodious, melancholic songs into the windy air.

Emilia's boys go to school in Pirámides. During the school season, she drives them there each day for the afternoon session which starts at one. The drive is just a little over twenty minutes in decent weather—"not bad." Emilia stays in the seaside village until school is out at five, tending to her little *ranchito*. She doesn't visit while in Pirámides, she says, she just waits to return to the campo.

For Emilia, a woman who thrives on campo life, the topic of schooling is fraught with turmoil. All campo families are hit with difficult choices when their children reach school age, but for Emilia, who is not taken with the pueblo, the conflict is particularly acute.

She has been lucky that the estancia to which Guillermo is attached is as close to Pirámides as it is. Generations of mothers on the Península have wept over the lack of schools in the campo and endured all variety of family hardship and separation in order to give their children the gift of education. A move to Madryn would be too much for a stout-hearted farm woman like Emilia. At the end of summer she sighed to us, "These are my last two weeks of freedom! Then we have to start going to Pirámides again."

Then she quickly redoubled, saying, "It is worth it, though. This is much better than my moving to Madryn with the boys. This way, except for in the winter when the roads are muddy, the whole family can stay together, and eat together at night." Emilia's real preference, however, would be to spend her days on the campo with her *chicos*, feeding chickens, cooking, and helping out with the sheep work.

Juana and Diana, like many Península women, indicate that

they believe the sacrifices on behalf of schooling for their *chicos* are at least halfway worth it.

"My daughters finished primary school, and then they quit," Juana tells me. "They were all intelligent, but they didn't want to study anymore.

"It seems that all my daughters have regrets now. Since getting married, they have all been regretful about not having kept on studying. In the campo, we didn't have much to give them, but we always wanted them to keep studying."

Diana confirms Juana's assessment. "I didn't finish my schooling because I didn't want to. More than once I have regretted that decision.

"Now, I would love to go to school. If it were then now, and if I could keep studying, I would. I don't know why I quit. I think that today without any school you are not anything. You have to live as a dishwasher, speaking frankly, because nothing else is available.

"If I had more education, I would like to . . . What do I know? Have a good job with some business or do something useful, pursue a career, maybe, like architecture. That's nice. That, I love. I also would love to study languages. That's beautiful."

Emilia, though, is deeply ambivalent about the importance of schooling, and her conflict runs through whatever she says about it. At the shearing she told me, "The boys like to be able to be on the campo, and help with the work. These days, for instance, I can't take them to school, because of the shearing. We all have to help."

Emilia went on to say that she thought it was silly to send *chicos* to school who don't want to go. She told us of a nephew who dropped out when he was almost finished, and what a waste it had been for everyone. "It's a waste to send them if they don't want to go. They don't do anything, and repeat grades. Some people are born for school, and others not."

She told us that she never went to school, implying that life could be good without it. Some of her younger siblings were able to attend school, but there was no school available to her when she was young. "Lots of campo children don't continue on in secondary school," she asserted. "They don't need it for campo work, and it doesn't help them in the campo."

Another stage in the Goikoa boys' schooling is fast approaching for Emilia, since Jorge will finish the last grade available at the Pirámides school next year. The ranch woman's face becomes sad and knotted as her mind treks across the implications.

Jorge loves school, and every time we saw him he told us about how he loved math and drawing and how much he wanted to be an architect.

He tells anyone who will listen that he wants to go on in school. He is campaigning. Whenever Emilia is around and he speaks of his love for school, she looks dubious, shakes her head, and says, looking sad, "We'll see how he feels in a year. He still has another year to decide. He likes the campo a lot, too. But if he wants to go, I won't say no. He can live with his uncle in Madryn."

As for Hugo, Emilia has a different story. "This other one doesn't study. He's half-lazy. El Galenso's last report card said, 'Do better on your letters and do better on your conduct.' He just doesn't like school. He's intelligent, but he doesn't want to study. He gets into trouble because the other *chicos*, the ones who aren't intelligent, don't work, and then he doesn't work. He talks back to the teacher. Jorge isn't like that. He wants Hugo to behave in class."

When I asked Jorge whether he liked school or the campo better, he looked at the ground and twisted on his heels. "Both things," he said looking tortured. It is clear that he would miss the campo and his mother if he went to town, but equally undeniable that the drive is in him.

Hugo says, "Papá says he'll send one of us to school, and keep the other one for the campo."

Jorge unfailingly pipes up, "I am going to be the one to go to school."

And Hugo counters, "I'm for the campo."

Between them, they divide the campo family's dilemma.

One sleepy afternoon when I visit Emilia, she leads me through the plastic-stripped curtain into the kitchen, and there is Diana, sitting up very straight at the table, with curlers in her hair. The table before her is plain and clean, except for a bottle of hair-curling fluid and a pile of worn hardback Argentine history books. Emilia bids me to sit down and goes back to giving Diana, who is visiting that weekend from Madryn, a permanent. There is no shyness at all about the curlers, and the homey scene continues as if I am just part of it. Juana, also visiting, leans against the kitchen sink and watches. Her hair has already been done, and she has a scarf tied around her head.

As I sit at the table, family members wander in and out. The small kitchen is like a way station, with people of every age (except for middle-aged men, who are helping at a shearing somewhere) coming in on different errands. Diana's tiny infant daughter lies sleeping in a buggy in the corner. Diana sits thumbing through the old history books, looking for answers to questions for a history contest in a magazine, while Emilia pulls at her hair. Julia shambles in after a few minutes and plunks down beside me. Jorge runs in and out, breathless. Flies buzz around an open bottle of orange soda on the kitchen counter.

The women seem easy and lazy, ready for banter. I ask them about the relative merits of the pueblo and the campo.

Emilia jumps to answer my question. "I wouldn't change the Península for anywhere. I don't want to travel. I like just going around the campo to places I know.

"Here, there is no schedule. If it rains, we stay indoors. In the pueblo you have to work even if it's bad weather. Here it is more *tranquilo*. Besides, here we have everything. We have meat right here, while people in the pueblo have to buy it. Have you seen the price of lamb lately? Our relatives come every weekend, just to eat lamb."

Emilia grins down to Diana. "My husband never wants to do

anything or go anywhere on Saturdays because Diana comes to visit on Saturdays. He always says to me, 'No, we can't go there today, Diana is coming.' "

Emilia paints fluid on another strand of Diana's hair and says she gets bored immediately when she goes to town. "We only go to town when we need something. We're not people with a fixed schedule. Sometimes we don't go for two weeks, and then, other periods, we go every two or three days. I don't like the city. What do I know? I get bored. I can't get used to it since I was brought up in the campo. I just like the campo. There's nothing to do in the city, while in the campo I always have things to do. I have everything.

"And we don't get lonely in the campo. We just visit people all over the Península—that's how we are. We also have to go around, regularly, to all of Guillermo's *puestos*, so we see a lot of people.

"Besides, we always have people here, too. At our *señalada* this year—you should have come, Sarita—there were more than a hundred people!"

Then she shakes her head as she pats Diana's curlers. "But you can't get young people to work in the campo anymore. Diana likes the campo, but she lives in Madryn for the *chicos'* schooling. All you find now, on the *puestos*, are old ones and men living alone. The young people are all for the pueblo. They want to live in town . . . what do I know?—for the movies, the theaters, that kind of thing. I don't know what will happen in the campo when these old ones die.

"These old ones are the ones who love the campo. It's like José. He is facing the question of whether or not to move to the pueblo now that he is old. He has no interest in leaving the campo, even if it threatens his health.

"It was the same with my brother—Juana's husband, Diana's papá—who died a year ago. He said the day he had to move to the pueblo, it would kill him. And my husband says the same thing.

"Guillermo says, 'I wouldn't live in the pueblo, not even if I were crazy!' "

Sitting in the bustling kitchen of the Goikoa-Lasalde clan, I believe Guillermo and the rest of them are right. It is crazy even to consider living anywhere in the world but way out on an estancia in the open sweeps of Península. For a few minutes the Goikoas convince me—despite the undeniable signs of disintegration, despite all the weighty evidence to the contrary—that the bountiful family life that sprang into being on the sheep ranches in the 1880s and quickly attained a glorious vigor will reproduce itself well into the twenty-first century. For a few lovely and precious moments, I am able to sustain a vision of generation after generation of warm, fat Goikoa children and mothers frolicking on the estancias of the Península. The jolly, welcoming families of Península Valdés will not, after all, vanish into the Patagonian wind, like insignificant shreds of wool.

On the day we left the Península for good, we were unable to resist dropping by the Goikoas' one last time.

The boys accompanied us to our car, after we hugged the mother bear a last time. As we walked to our parking spot by the barn, Jorge pointed to my feet and then to his own. We both had on black alpargatas—the rope-soled campo shoes. His caramel-brown face lit up, sweet and grinning. "Adidas!"

As we stood by the car, Hugo bargained with Peter, "If you lend me the money, I'll buy you some gum for your trip," and he thrust a sculpture he had made out of a mussel shell into Peter's hand.

As Peter put the car in gear, El Galenso said, out of the blue, "Greetings to the bears!" And when we were slow on the uptake, he added, "You have them in Norteamérica, don't you?"

DUSK

~~~~~~

During an aerial survey early in our second stay on Península Valdés, Peter and I spotted an enormous flattened carcass on a beach of the outer coast. The forty-five-foot whale lay sprawled flat, one or two ribs protruding through the loose black skin that seemed only draped over the bones. In the surf, just off the beach where the dead whale lay, there was a huge right whale cow, lying on her back with her calf floating on her belly between her flippers. The carcass looked as though it might have been dropped from a plane. Near the tail, intestines spilled out of a four-foot hole where the whale had exploded, to release its death gases. Peter marked the location of the carcass on the map.

We walk the campo.

Out among the the thornbushes, we come across a dead lamb. The skyward eye of the young sheep is missing—plucked out, like a gumdrop, by a gull.

At a fence line we come across a mara—one of the strange rodents that look like a dog-rabbit cross—in a trap. The animal had chewed off one of its legs in an effort to free itself before it died.

A dead eagle is lying in the middle of a road. It is a stiff husk with a fierce, empty eye. As I squat for a closer look, a sudden strange breeze picks up the bird case and rushes it off, like a balloon, across the plain.

At the northern tip of the Península, one of the places we walk, there is a mass open grave. Literally miles and miles of coastline are carpeted with the bleached bones of elephant seals and sea lions slaughtered and boiled at midcentury.

Walking around the Whale Camp, our friend Pedro Ramírez found two human skulls, polished and bleached to a heavenly white. One was nestled between two green stabbing bushes. The other, embedded in the earth, showed only a snowy round peeking from the baked ground.

The grounds around our house are decorated with bones. An enormous wooden bin off to the side of the building is filled with bones judged priceless and hauled to the house from far and wide by various researchers, children, and tourists. A sei whale skull, abandoned before it reached the house, lies low behind a bush along the eroded driveway. The bony beak of an odd, platypus-shaped whale points airward out of the bin. Ribs, flipper bones, and mandibles stretch the box to overflowing, an enormous bouquet of bone flowers.

The Patagonian earth is composed of layers and layers of human and animal bones. In a ceaseless fossilization process that allows the skeletons of whole animals to stay intact, a film of sand covers a generation of bones and lays the base for the next decade of animals. In my mind, for perhaps a kilometer down into the earth there are generations of whole guanaco skeletons in the slump of death, fox skulls, Indian skulls, shark teeth, oysters, settler rib cages, and entire forty-five-foot whale skeletons. I imagine the whole of Patagonia as supported by the humped skeleton backs of dead whales. If we dug and swept, and dug and swept, I feel sure that is what we would find: kilometers and kilometers of whales, head to tail, head to tail.

Strewn over the Patagonian steppe along with the bones are roofless shacks and rotting vehicles, the leavings of families who tried to fashion a life in Patagonia and got their fences knocked down, their shacks crushed, and their sheep frozen, and who finally surrendered to hopelessness, went to town, or died. Set down among the bones and overturned trucks, a few wind-crumbled sheep stations remain inhabited. An old couple or a lone *peón* stands within the houses, watching the wind lash at the earth and wishing for a child's song.

The old campesinos in their low-lying houses on the vacant, windswept ranges of the Península have a mournful and heaving two-line lament that they chant when they stare off across the scrubland that is their home, into the future.

"There are no children in the campo anymore," they begin. Then they finish the dirge: "They have all gone to the town."

Rafael belongs to the Península chorus that intones the emp-tying of the campo, those who mourn the now abandoned sheep stations that used to hum with activity and resonate with the high chirps of children's voices.

"Before, there were more families in the campo. It was very tough to find a piece of campo that didn't have a couple with four, three, five, or more children, because before, families were larger. Where I was raised, near Punta Norte, a pretty small contour, there were at least eight families, and in those eight families there must have been more than forty children. Between Punta San Román and a little farther along, there were twenty children in two families. There was one family that had thirteen children. We even had a soccer team, made up of the *chicos* in our area. There were eleven players and we still had *chicos* left over."

The *señaladas* were gay during Rafael's youth, while nowadays they are quiet affairs, with older people lining the walls of the cold, bare cement rooms. When Rafael was a child, scores of people arrived for the day's working and feasting, and the ten or fifteen fellows of about eighteen to twenty would play soccer and dance with the fifteen or so girls of the same ages.

In place of the sixty or more people in the Punta Norte region, Rafael reports, there are now about twelve souls. At the

Telechea place, where there was once a couple with four daughters, there is now a lone man. At a place farther west there were seven people; now there is one. The twelve or thirteen Goikoa siblings and their parents have been replaced by one person, perhaps two. At Punta Buenos Aires, where the Lasaldes raised eleven sturdy children, Rafael believes there is now one *peón*. Toward Punta San Román, Iriarte raised his family of thirteen. There is no one on that piece of campo now.

"It is like that everywhere." Rafael's tanned fingers play with the cables on his blue, hand-knit sweater. "All these places have been left unpopulated. All of them. The children came of age and withdrew. Couples left, and young people don't want to come back here. All, all of the children left. No one stayed. *Chicos* like me became adults and then they went to seek their futures. They went looking for their comforts.

"And now there's no one left on the Península. Lone men remain. It's all lone men."

Wanting to understand the absence of children in the campo, I asked campesinos all over the Península for their perspectives on the phenomenon.

A priority in my mind, as I pursued the question of the departure of the young, was an interview with José. I knew that the old campesino, with seventy-six years under his belt, would see through to the core of the situation, but I kept putting off going to see him.

In part this was due to my assumption that there was plenty of time ahead for long discussion. The more weighty reason, however, was that I was tormented both by intense desire to interview José and by an excruciating shyness about approaching him. I was afraid he would be uncomfortable if I asked to interview him since he constantly belittled the significance of his life. I cared like mad what he thought of me and dreaded offending him in even the tiniest way. Even though our friendship was composed of a snappy back-and-forth, I felt such a keen hesitancy that I nearly didn't interview him. When I did get up my courage to talk with him, he was the most gentle and serious, the most earnest of all.

~~~

There was a windmill set on top of the barn at La Bonita that pumped water into the water tanks for the sheep. It was a rusty pair of wings with a ladder of weathered boards leading up one leg of its teepeelike stand. On the bright spring day that I finally went to see José, we spied the old *puestero* as we approached the settlement. He was standing at the top of the teetering windmill, one leg wrapped around the top of the tripod, tinkering with the blades.

There was a warm, caressing breeze that day, and Clara's lilacs were waving their creamy purple fronds from the spindly bush in front of the house.

We found Clara skulking back in the recesses of the kitchen, unable to watch José, quaking and furious. "I told him he would fall. I told him he would fall. It's dangerous. He is more than seventy-six years old, José!" She shook her finger and clucked her tongue.

José soon came to greet us with a wide smile on his face and his cap on backward, looking like Lindbergh stepping down from *The Spirit of St. Louis.*

"Hi, young one, how are you?" he said, clapping Peter on the back.

José's high spirits made us trust in his essential well-being. He had me convinced he was in fine fettle.

Clara prepared tea for us, and José took mate. I gave Clara the banana bread I had brought, and she bustled off to fetch a plate and some *dulce de leche* to spread on top of the bread.

Nervous and eager to get to the questions that occupied me, I blurted out my purpose for visiting. Mentioning the campesinos' sighs about the childless campo houses, I told José that I wanted to hear his thoughts about life on the Península, how it was changing, and why all the young people were leaving.

Hearing my words, he sat down across from me, folded his hands before him on the table, and said, "I hope I can answer your questions." He endowed the meeting with the air of an honored and solemn occasion. Crossing his graceful, thin legs, he emptied the gourd of maté in his hand and offered me his analysis.

"What do I know?" he began. "I believe that yes, things are changing, because when I first came to know these parts, there were whole families in all the houses. But the problem was, those *chicos* didn't receive sufficient instruction.

"By my way of seeing, I think that people are rising nowadays by moving to town. It is not that they are moving to the pueblo because they like it there, but rather because they want their *chicos* to be in school. They want to put their children on a par with the rest of the people in the nation, and in the campo they can't get instruction. Because here on the Península, in the past, there were many who didn't go to school. Some completed first grade, or second, but with much sacrifice, eh? And now, parents from the Península are putting in a lot of effort so that their *chicos* can have some instruction. They go to the pueblo and buy a little house—the government lends campo families the money to buy one house in a town—all so the *chicos* can have some instruction.

"All the campo people want their children to have more education than they had. It is because they have all been, not ignorant, but without sufficient instruction, and they recognize that they have to give their children an education. So that they can develop themselves for a better life tomorrow, eh?"

"Do the *chicos* return to the campo?" I asked.

"No, no, no, no, no. Not one of the *chicos* comes back to the campo. All of them make their way along staying in the pueblo and arranging things for themselves with a job in an office, or in a grocery store, or in another place. The campo doesn't attract them," said a man who had devoted his life to the campo.

"Why?"

"Why? Because here in the campo the only thing you have is a radio, and there, in the pueblo, you have conversation with other young fellows. You can go to the movies on a Saturday, go to a soccer match every Sunday.

"I don't think it is an economic thing, because, economically, you live better in the campo. I don't believe people earn more in the city. But, as the saying goes, bread isn't the only thing that comes from London, eh? You need other things just as much as money. Economically you live better here, but culturally you live better in town. This is what I see. Because these families in the town, I don't believe they can go to the grocery and fill the cart with everything they need. They have to restrain themselves."

"But what will happen here in the campo if they all go to the city?" I asked.

"This is what we all ask ourselves," José said. "This is what all the people are asking themselves. 'But what is going to happen?' "

"It seems as though in the old days the campo people were happy," I said. "How did those generations before entertain themselves?"

"*Bueno,*" said José, ready with the next explanation. "It is that before, Madryn was nothing. It was just a center where carts and sulkies gathered, all of them coming from the surrounding countryside. People traveled from here, from the center of the Península, to Madryn, which was a port, to supply themselves for the whole year. They bought four or five sacks of flour, five or six sacks of potatoes, and that was it. They came back to the Península, and then they got together out here, the whole family, neighbor with neighbor. They visited among themselves on the campo. Back then, they visited more than now. From my way of seeing, they were happy."

"And were you happy?"

"I am always the same." The old campesino chuckled. "I am always the same. I put myself to this and I am happy, and nothing more. I live here in the campo more tranquilly than in the town. If the town had some kind of occupation for me, or something like that, we would see how it was, eh? But in town I get tired, I get bored. . . . I prefer this work here.

"Madryn has changed a lot," he said. "There are so many outsiders now that I don't even recognize the people on the streets. It is no longer a little supply depot.

"As for me, I have never been in a confitería, and I never want to go in one. In Madryn now, at three A.M., you see it is all dark inside, and you see muchachos and muchachas in there together. I don't know what they do in there."

Clara, who was sitting opposite José at the other end of the table, piped up, "It is just like with magazines, now that we have democracy. A friend of mine has to read every magazine her thirteen-year-old brings home to make sure it's all right. And she watches all the children's television programs to see how they are. What does a child of thirteen know?"

José added, "For me, between newspapers, television, and radio, I prefer newspapers. As for television, what little I have seen of it, the programs are all for children, and *we* don't understand them!"

Clara, who dreamed of having a television, switched the subject and told us all about Luis and Sara's new blender and curtains. Then she mentioned a hair dryer that a friend had bought. She lit up, enthralled with the gadget. "What a beautiful thing!"

José shook his finger, laughing at his wife. "All these things you can buy in the shops—things that enter through the eyes, no more!"

"But in Madryn, what things cost!" Clara said. "It is disgraceful. A skirt costs five thousand pesos! Emilia went to Madryn and returned red in the face—the prices. They charge whatever they want! And the gas prices! I liked the life of before better. Before, a pair of pretty sneakers cost you just sixty centavos, and there weren't the taxes that exist now."

José said, "People are getting poorer and poorer, and the prices are going up. I don't know anything about these things, but that's how I see it."

I commented that I knew of a seventeen-year-old girl from an estancia, working at a shop in town, who spent seventy dollars on a pair of pants while she made only one hundred and forty a month.

"*Exactamente,*" said José.

Clara turned to me and gave me her view of town.

"Look, for me," she said, "I am as content here as in the

town, because I am accustomed to it here. But, to me, the town is nicer. I would like to live in town. Me, yes. But José is different. It is because he is not a man that is going to go to the confitería and have a cup of something. No, he doesn't like that, that city kind of life. Now, if he could leave Madryn, spend some time on the farm in Gaimán, spend another little while in Madryn, and go back and forth like that, changing around, maybe he would like that. But he is not a man that is going to go to a bar for a drink. And from there, what are you going to do?"

While Clara and I talked about her love of seeing all the people in town, Peter and José chatted at the other end of the big table. Then, all at once, the climate in the room shifted and we all turned to José as he prepared to share a joke.

"I have a friend," José announced, "who tells his wife that she must be ready to leave by a certain hour whenever they are in town. If she isn't ready at that time, he leaves without her and she has to find a way to the campo with a neighbor or someone!"

José chuckled, his eyes twinkling, and Clara beamed fondly. José's torso bounced up and down. "I told Clara, 'I should do that with you!'"

We finished a second round of tea and banana bread, and Peter and José went off in the truck to see if the men were coming with the herd. The sheep were to have the wool around their eyes clipped the next day.

Once the men left, Clara drew her chair near mine and spoke in confidence. She told me that José had a bad cough. He'd caught cold, she said, from going to rescue some sheep that were stranded on the beach below the cliffs. He had also been outside in a rainstorm at the time of the La Bonita shearing. "He shouldn't do those things," she said. She looked worried.

To me, José had never looked heartier. He filled out the tartan-plaid L. L. Bean shirt one of the researchers we knew had given him. His cheeks, his nose, and the shirt were all ruddy.

Still, I thought over the things Clara had said, adding a few more details each time I saw her, about José's health. The very first day we had arrived back on the Península, she had taken me into the pantry and told me about an operation he had had the year before.

"Oh, but it has been hard, Sara ... with this one," she said of her husband. "I was so afraid. He is already well on in years. He was very bad, and we went to the doctor, and he wanted to operate immediately. José didn't want to let him do it. He said he had things to do back on the estancia.

"And I could tell that the doctor who would do the operation disagreed with one of the others, so I went in and said, 'Doctor, I want you to tell me the truth.'

"They said, 'It is serious, señora.'

"And I said, 'If you find anything, I want you to sew him back up and I'll take him to Buenos Aires.'

"They said, 'Señora, you must have faith.'

"Oh, the pain he was in! The night before, he screamed and he cried from the pain, my husband! He was crying from the pain, he was walking around, but he didn't want me to take him to the doctor. I took him at five A.M., sweetie.

"It has been a bad time. It was very bad." She leaned even closer to me as she said this and shook her head. She was whispering, her back bent way over toward me, her head low, a finger drifting to her lips lest José hear her somewhere out on the campo.

Clara had always complained about José's eating. He was one of those rare people with little desire for food, except as kindling.

"He eats meat," Clara told me on many visits. "He eats meat, all kinds, but just a little. And even though the doctor says it's healthier, he won't eat my soups for me if I remove the fat. As for sweet things, no. He won't touch them. When we're at his relatives' and they have cakes, I sit beside him and he slips them to me. This sister-in-law of José's, the one who just died? She said José was never one for eating much. Never. But now he eats even less."

The two men came into the kitchen. The herd was almost to La Bonita, they reported.

Peter told me later that while he had spotted the men on horseback from about a kilometer away, José wasn't able to see them. He had told Peter that he couldn't see as well as he used to. "Every once in a while," he had said, "a little cloud goes across my eyes."

José summed up the drive with the hearty words, "Well, at least we gave the truck a little air."

At the table José returned to his assessment of his life on the Península. Holding a cigarette vertically between his thumb and forefinger, he told a story that we were intended to recognize as his creed.

"Once there were three old friends that met on a street for the first time in over fifty years.

"The first man said, 'Look at me. I've lived to be ninety because I haven't taken a drink in fifty years. I have never gambled, smoked, or fooled around with women, either.'

"The second man said, 'Well, look at me. I'm a man of moderation. I've smoked a little, gone with women a little, and drunk a little for fifty years. That's the secret to old age and health.'

"The third man boasted, 'Well, I've lived the best life of all. I've been a drinker all my life, have always smoked several packs a day, and I have been a playboy my whole life. I have the best way!' "

José chuckled and chuckled.

I believed José's bluff. So much did I want to believe that he had a firm grip on the earth, I didn't see that sickness was overtaking him, even though there were signs. I didn't take Clara's clues or even the evidence in front of me. I ignored José's nonstop cough and his lack of appetite. It was as though José and I had agreed not to verify certain thoughts.

One day, on the way to La Bonita, we saw Cachorro, the *peón*, walking up the road. Once at the estancia, José explained, "Cachorro is out fetching the rams because tomorrow we're going to be veterinarians. We're going to cut off some fellows' horns." Four or five of La Bonita's rams, he said, had sharp horns curled inward in such a way that the beasts' horns cut their own faces. One ram had bled to death recently when his own horn had cut an artery in his face.

Now, when I think of José, I think of those rams. They say a sheep man knows the body of a sheep better than his own body; José took better care of his rams than he did of himself. His chain-smoking and drinking were an act of defiance, a taunt to fate.

That day, as we were leaving, I looked at José's hands. They were speckled with what I took to be sheep blood. The cough that Clara had mentioned never went away.

For the next month or so spring dusted the prickled land, and we were high-spirited. Clusters of peach-yellow flowers sprouted on the thornbushes. Minuscule purple flowers like forget-me-nots sprinkled themselves over the sandy earth among the bits of shell and black and orange pebbles. The ice plant in front of the house bloomed into an opulent purple bank. I experienced a strange but delicious calm.

Buoyant and sausage fat, the whale calves played, nonstop, beside their long-suffering mothers. The whales' grunts and roars cracked me out of sleep to sunny mornings, and the tranquil days that followed were punctuated by the playful smacks of calves' flippers on the surface of the sea.

Groups of several hundred dolphins passed in front of the camp, like an array of soft gray-and-white birds flashing, flying, leaping from the water.

Whenever we saw sea lions off the beach, we would crunch down the pebbles and do crazy dances and yell to them in high, squeaky voices. The sleek-headed, incurably curious lobos would swim over to us, stretch their necks up out of the water to see us better, and then, imitating us, bark and leap and flop their slippery brown bodies in the sea.

Tuxedoed penguins gathered in caucuses on shore and brayed and carried out comically repetitious courtships. They were caricatures of themselves. A pair of oyster catchers flew back and forth along the beach, their beaks garish with scarlet lipstick.

Drawn to the sea and the dunes, Peter and I would take afternoon hikes to the sand bluffs about six kilometers from our house to collect arrowheads, Indian-chipped stones, and miniature rodent jaws that lay buried in the sands. One evening, at eleven P.M., we hurled our bodies into the sea and swam in the phosphorescence. The sparkling forms of millions of microscopic beings fanned out from our arms and legs, like rays of jewels, as we moved through the silky water.

That night the eerie moans of a whale reached into the house on the breeze. The night was black as pitch, and the whale's voice rang, deep and mournful, into the hollow, expanding air.

We visited Clara and José again during December, when they were forced to stay in Puerto Madryn for three weeks while José underwent medical treatments. We didn't even know that the old couple was in town until we drove down their street and saw Clara helping José out of their little adobe house. Even from the car I could see that José's eyes were sad. He turned around as soon as he saw us and said to Clara, just as she was closing the door, "It's Peter." He seemed relieved to go back inside with us.

Clara explained that José had a cold that wouldn't go away and some throat problems. He was getting injections—one a day for six days—and pills. They didn't know what the injections were for, she said. They had to remain in town until at least the coming Wednesday, to see if he felt better and to receive more test results.

We talked about how awful it was waiting for such news. All of us put a good face on things.

José stood by the big table that occupied the major portion of the room and looked down at its varnished surface as Clara spoke. He looked wooden. He was dressed formally. In place of his comfortable baggy pants and rope-soled shoes, and his faded cotton shirt with a fraying collar, he had on a light blue, textured shirt, neat tan polyester pants, and loafers. The pants dropped around his shoes, in the dress-up style of traditional men. For the first time since I had known him, he had on a gold wedding band. Clara had probably told him what to wear.

As Peter and José sat down side by side, Clara bustled me off to the kitchen to put on the kettle. "We've already had four visitors today," she said, as if to explain to me how thrilling it was to be in town.

In the kitchen at the back of the hall-like house, she told me, "I took coffee with someone just before you came. I haven't even been able to leave the house, there have been so many visitors. One can't go out, you see, because there are things to do, and people come by!" Her words were spun with delight.

She then launched into a long list of the visitors who had been coming. Luis had come by for lunch and again for dinner and had stopped by before he took off in his truck for San Antonio. Her neighbor across the street had been coming by often. Clara said, "My neighbor Pipa!" with great relish, as though this were a delicious friend. "And the neighbor on the other side comes often, too," she added.

"So one can't go out, you see. José has been out, but me, no. José goes out to get the paper every day, and he went out this morning to the laundry. He has been out to see Rafael, who is in town, and to Angel's, and to the doctor. He goes out, but I stay here just in case visitors come."

While the men were having their own conversation, Clara leaned close and talked to me in a hoarse whisper, her eyes darting to José. She said he seemed a little better, but they had to stay in town until they talked to the doctor. She said the doctor, the best in town, had told her she could call him any time.

She said she had thought José might want to go to Gaimán the day before, to see his nephews, but he hadn't wanted to do anything. She pointed to a pile of string-wound boxes on the floor. "José's all ready to go back to the campo. He is tired of the pueblo."

As we were getting up to leave, Clara announced with enormous pride in her voice, "On February 9, José and I will have been married thirty-one years."

José's face became all grin and twinkling eyes, and with a shaky hand he drew a finger across his throat.

In mid-January, when we went to see Clara and José again, they were waiting to go to the doctor. José looked sad, watery-eyed, and weak. The throat cancer had progressed in the last month. José was so thin, he looked tiny, and he sat slumped on his chair.

Elena and two-year-old Pablito came by while we were there and sat at the big table with the rest of us, Pablito on her lap.

Clara said that the day before Pablito and Elena had brought over a flan, and Pablito had given it to José. José had eaten it that night and this morning because Pablito had made it for him. But he would eat nothing else, and for no one else.

The only words José said during the visit came when Pablito asked his mother for some bread. José moved his hand weakly, but with unmistakable command, and said to Clara in a barely audible voice, "Bring him some bread."

José rose to go to the doctor and stood at the door as we said good-bye.

"If it gets too bad," I said, "you go to Buenos Aires. Okay?"

"You get better!" Peter said, and José, almost imperceptibly, shook his hand no.

A few days later we heard that José was in the hospital in Trelew.

For the next five days, Peter and I wandered. José's slight form was with us everywhere we walked.

One afternoon we discovered a starving elephant seal pup on a beach not far from camp. In the rain on the gray beach, the small, gray bundle was almost imperceptible. He was the size of a newborn but had the pelt of a two-time molted weaner. The two-and-a-half-foot-long baby was probably a quarter of its rightful weight. Its skin was wrinkled and folded, loose, over its undernourished, empty body.

As if seized by hope, Peter ran back to camp and returned with a bottle of milk. He lay down by the tiny shriveled being, as a mother seal would, and tried to feed it milk from a bottle. The little fellow nudged in closer but didn't take the milk.

When the yellow-pink streak of dusk defined the boundary between the gray earth and the gray sky at the horizon, we were forced to leave the dying pup, alone, on the beach. We plodded home in the rain, not saying anything.

All through the long days, stories and memories of José oscillated through our thoughts, as if the old rancher were the lodestar of our minds.

My mind kept crystallizing the tender fatherliness of the childless man.

When José entered the asado room after the lamb marking was complete, he did not first greet the women. He spied the only young children in the dank chamber—a one-year-old girl and a three-year-old boy—and went over and tousled their hair. He took Sabrina on his lap, stroked her cheek, and commented on the cake all over her face.

Clara told a story about one of José's nephews who had fallen into the sheep dip as a little boy. José had fished him out, carried him into the house, and washed him from head to toe.

Clara also mentioned to me once that José's nephew in Gaimán, a man of fifty, often sat on his uncle's lap. At the time she told me this, my entire being was flooded with yearning to do the same.

During these days of limbo—a day for each finger on a hand—everywhere we went, people spoke about José. Their comments were brief and hushed with sadness.

José's nearest neighbor, silver-haired Rafael with whom José had exchanged work for twenty years, was close to weeping in his kitchen when we talked about José. His lean, strong frame shuddered as he said, "*Qué hombre*. What a man is this José. A good man. A very good man."

Liliana told me Rafael had said to her that he couldn't go to see José in the hospital because if he did, he would talk. If he talked, that would make José want to talk, and José would not be able to. And that would make Rafael cry.

Even Cachorro, whom we found sitting at La Bonita, listening to the radio for news from the hospital, the man who had competed and differed with José during his entire tenure as *peón* at La Bonita, said, "Don José was different. He was *un señor*, a gentleman."

The windswept campo that was settled by gold-seeking Basques, and that has received the daily devotion of men such as José for decades, is emptying once again. The ups and downs of the wool market, the erratic Argentine economy, and the vagaries of the Patagonian weather have discouraged campo-loving youth, worn out their fathers, and made Península estancias unprofitable. The Península people themselves have changed as well. They have discovered the entertainments of town, acquired a new lust for material possessions, and become convinced that schooling is a gift they must provide their children. These forces, like a powerful collection of magnets, have drawn the descendents of the Península settlers away from the sere yellow-brown land on which they were bred.

The old campo families are dying away. The great, barren length of Patagonia is being left to herself once again.

The wind keened over the campo during these last days of José's life. When I wasn't visiting one of José's friends, I walked the beach, and I walked the campo that José had walked, and Clara and José's Patagonia wrapped herself around me.

In front of me, as I walked, I kept seeing Clara's and José's faces—faces like maps carved with the rough, rutted tracks of a new frontier. The faces were neither grim nor falsely bright, neither depressed nor prideful. They were serene and fateful and accepting.

As I roamed the broad back of the campo, the tawny land spread like a dried animal skin, Patagonia's harsh winds and raw surfaces rippled and hummed inside me. As José was taking himself away from me, I was coming to terms with his land.

In Patagonia, the harsh mortal fact—the beginning of time, the endless cycle of death and life—is laid bare. The land is a giant whale carcass, slumped above the sea. It is a skeleton laid open. The bones show through the earth as wind and water carve away meat and dirt.

In this land of thorns and bones and endless, barren vistas, I was subject to regular bouts of despair. With time I realized that to live in Patagonia with any semblance of contentment there were only certain options. A person had to have been born there and known nothing else; a person had to pare down his expectations; or a person had to have children. To me, a childless foreign woman, Patagonia offered two difficult choices. I could venture out into the open and be beaten by the wind, or I could shut myself in, as in a cave. When I did venture out, it was like eating a withered Patagonian apple. It looked pitiful, but when I bit into it, it was sweet and juicy.

Clara and José's Patagonia doesn't have a pastoral, comforting beauty, but one unvarnished, slender, and true. There is freedom in the bareness. Patagonia is a wild and harborless ocean unless a person can fashion a mooring. If one is patient enough, he or she can find a core of calm in the maelstrom of wind and blankness. Yellow straw flowers shoot from the jabbing bushes. The towering cloud banks diffuse into wisps and airy threads. At dusk the bare earth lights up luminously, like light on bleached bone. Life in Patagonia, where bones of the dead reach out of the soil, is a perpetual choice of rebirth.

As I picked my way over Patagonia's vast and unsigned terrain, I often lost track. At those pinpoints in the void, I learned to gather the sharks' teeth, sheep femurs, and guanaco dung that were scattered around me and fashion a little shrine, a cairn. Then I would set out again.

Through the campesinos of Península Valdés, through Clara and José, and under the dome of the Patagonian sky, I have come to a new understanding of pioneering, independence, vulnerability, and solitude.

Sitting with the Patagonians was a tonic. Listening to the Patagonians' unselfconscious stories about their lives, stories free of any North American posturing, I felt bolstered. During these conversations, I felt sheaves of defense drop from my body. By the end of the talks, in which the Patagonians revealed their difficult times as well as their satisfactions, and a honed ability to chuckle at their own failures and hard luck, I was a sliver of bare, exposed bone. I felt elated. I felt as clean and spare as if I had had a dip in a cold sea. The sense of one's frailties as being natural is the Patagonians' gift to others.

Clara and José gave me a different answer to the question of how to live than I had expected—one my own self-sufficiency-obsessed culture could not give me. In their company I could see that rather than going alone the key to living in any wilderness was to join with others. The old Patagonians showed me, simply be being who they were, that open vulnerability *is* the definition of dignity.

We were possessed by the desire to find the dead whale we had spied early in our stay. We made our way to the spot marked on the map.

The skull was like a monument, high up on the beach. Thornbushes were sprouting little straw flowers all around it. Peter ran his hand along the lobed and tunneled surfaces of the eight-foot-wide braincase, and he squatted to allow his hand to complete its journey down the twelve-foot mandible of the lower jaw. At its greatest part, this bone was fifteen inches thick. The colossal whale head had been bleached white, scrubbed by the sea, and cleaned of flesh. It shone in the cool, midmorning air.

The rest of the bones of the whale were spread for kilometers along the coast.

Starting that week, and over the month or so before we left Patagonia, we were obsessed with the whale's trail. Peter and I made it our purpose to find as many of the bones as we could. The sea had tossed them like toothpicks and set them in a long, ever-moving, mysterious grave. With friends, we discovered fourteen slender, arched ribs, twenty vertebrae, and the one remaining mandible scattered sixty kilometers along the beach. One day, trudging ten kilometers along the outer coast, we even encountered the humerus. This strange, vestigial arm bone is a dinosaur of a bone, a dense round globe set on a stout pedestal. We gathered the bones, took them home on our sagging truck, and arranged them in order—consulting anatomy books—on our front porch.

I was at the Goikoas' when I learned of José's death. The women blew their noses and mopped their eyes as they spoke, and the children stood by, their dark eyes deep as wells.

Later, at La Entrada, Rafael and Liliana said Clara would be all right; she would stay in the house in town, near Teresa and Angel. "It will be okay at first. There will be a lot to do," they said. "It is later that it will be hard. Now she's *solita, solita.*"

I stopped to see Cachorro at La Bonita on my way back to camp. Cachorro said that when José had come back to the campo a few weeks before to send off the year's wool, he had made the *peón* drive him all over the estancia. "José had tears in his eyes as we drove. He knew it would be the last time."

Then Cachorro said, "I don't know what to do about José's dog. She's wandering and wandering, looking for him." When I got back to camp, I walked down the beach. There was a deep calm over the sea. The stillness fit, tailor sewn, inside the ring of the cliffs and spread and flowed and filled the air with a ringing tranquillity that was deepened by the murmur and lapping of the ebbing tide.

The last time we saw José during our first stay in Patagonia, it was on such a silky afternoon. He was down on the beach, bent over, looking for octopus, with his pants rolled up to his seventy-year-old knees. I had watched him until he vanished in the graying light.

Now, as I climbed the cliffs from the beach, light was peaching the rough, vacant land behind camp and spreading raspberry juice over the thornbushes.

It was dusk on the campo.

ACKNOWLEDGMENTS

〜〜〜〜〜〜〜〜〜〜〜〜〜〜〜〜

The humanity of the people of southern Argentina is incomparable. I must thank, first and foremost, the people of Península Valdés and Puerto Madryn who shared their lives with me. The bottomless cups of tea, the endless supplies of crackers and mutton, and the bountiful generosity and patience with which the Patagonians met my questions and nourished me on cold, lonely, dusty days are gifts for which I am deeply grateful. The Patagonians have given me more than I gave to them. I am humble before that fact.

All the historical facts and life stories in this book are drawn from the Península Valdés region. I have changed only the names of the people and of the estancias on which they live.

This could not be the story of everyone who lives on Península Valdés. I was unable to portray many of the lives that touched mine while I was on the Península, but while they have not been featured specifically, they have contributed, in an indispensable way, to my understanding and to the overall picture.

I want to give special thanks to the Ferrero, Echave, Machinea, Bezunartea, García, Delpueche, BenGoa, Jorojuria, Mariezcurena, Olazabal, LaQuirique, Larreburu, San Martín, Sanz, Soos, and Asunción families, and to Pedro Contrera, Aldo Peralta, "Poroto," and Nancucheo.

Emilio Ferro, Joffre Perez-Machi, and others at La Adela provided useful information about life on the Península. Juan Carlos and Diana Lopez were giving friends and interpreters during the first stay on the Península. Alicia and Raúl Fozzari at Torino in Pirámides were friendly and welcoming whenever we showed up.

The Payne family introduced us to the Península and to the Ferreros, gifts I will treasure always. The New York Zoological Society supported the first visit to Península Valdés. Chris and Janie Clark and Bernd and Mel Würsig were guides all through our Patagonian journeys.

Patricia, Graham, Edward, and Sabrina Harris helped in countless ways during my second stay in Argentina. The MacKenzie family supplied fortifying asados and friendship in Trelew and are now doing so in the United States.

Rolando Costa-Picazo of the Fulbright office in Buenos Aires and Teresa Ortíz-Basualdo offered support on journeys through Buenos Aires.

Perspectives offered by Robert LeVine, Sara Lawrence Light-foot, and Byron Good were very helpful during an earlier incarnation of this book, and without Max Katz's timely letters to me in Patagonia, this work would have been much more difficult.

I am deeply grateful for the encouragement and wisdom of my friends. In particular, I want to thank Jim and Mary Bird, Nancy Blum, Renée Burgard, Carol Cogliani, Juliette Fournot, Pamela Hendricks, Suzanne Kirschner, Rosemary Link, Megan Morrissey, Meg Ojala, Fiona Reid, Ron Rooney, Farnaz Seyal, and Maura Sullivan.

Special thanks go to my friend Jon Luoma, who hand-carried the outline for this book to his editor, and to William Strachan, who received it and edited the book it became with care.

Progress on this book was greatly enhanced by the support of a Harvard Sinclair Kennedy Fellowship, a Tinker Summer Travel Grant, a Radcliffe Grant for Graduate Women, and a

National Academy of Education Spencer Fellowship, which afforded me the opportunity to complete this book at the University of Minnesota.

I would also like to acknowledge the help I received from the following books:

Emilio Ferro. *La Patagonia Como La Conocí.* Buenos Aires: Ediciones Marymar, 1977.

David Rock. *Argentina 1516–1982: From Spanish Colonization to the Falklands War.* Berkeley, Calif.: University of California Press, 1985.

Carl C. Taylor. *Rural Life in Argentina.* Baton Rouge, La.: Louisiana State University Press, 1948.

Turismo por Chubut. Oficina de Turismo, Provincia del Chubut, Rawson, Chubut, 1982.

Zampini, V. *Chubut: breve historia de una provincia argentina.* Gaimán, Chubut: El Regional, 1979.

To my parents, who gave a thousand kinds of help at every stage of this journey, I cannot say "thank you" enough. My brother, Andy, was a good companion on visits to us in the field.

It is certain that without the help of my husband, Peter Thomas, I could never have written this book. For his deep-laid belief in me, and the innumerable ways in which he aided me—by changing flat tires, by baking cookies, by acting as scribe on rides home from estancias at dusk, by sharing his insights, by kicking me out the door—my thanks run over.

Finally, I thank Maud for her patience and her readiness to dance whenever I was available.